SERENDIPITY

Serendipity

**Musings on the Precedence of
Numbers and Names used by
Lodges and Chapters
of
The United Grand Lodge of England
and
The Supreme Grand Chapter of England
together with a description of
some of the Badges, Banners
and Mottoes they use**

**(with brief comments on our
Sister Constitutions of
Ireland and Scotland)**

Harry Mendoza

Further titles by Harry Mendoza

The Ensigns of the Twelve Tribes of Israel

First published in England in 1995.

Published jointly by *Lewis Masonic*, Addlestone, Surrey
and *Q.C. Correspondence Circle Sales Ltd*, London.

Lewis Masonic is the publishing imprint of *Ian Allan Regalia Ltd*
who are members of the Ian Allan Group, Coombelands House,
Coombelands Lane, Addlestone, Surrey.

ISBN 085318 204 3

British Library Cataloguing in Publication Data
A Catalogue record for this book is available from the British
Library.

Printed in Great Britain by Latimer Trend & Company Ltd, Plymouth

CONTENTS

EXTENDED CONTENTS

EXTENDED CONTENTS

LIST OF ILLUSTRATIONS

(Coloured illustrations appear between pages 112–113 and depict Lodge or Chapter banner designs)

TELEPHONE 071-831 9811 Ext 239
(FAX 071-831 6021)

THE GRAND CHARITY

OF FREEMASONS UNDER THE UNITED GRAND LODGE OF ENGLAND

60 GREAT QUEEN STREET
LONDON WC2B 5AZ

13 May 1994

FOREWORD

Bro Harry Mendoza has chosen an apt title. SERENDIPITY accurately reflects what the reader will feel - the experience of making happy discoveries by accident - as he dips into this book.

The book deals with the identity of Lodges and Chapters, with comments on their names and numbers (or lack of numbers), their badges and their banners, and on the United Grand Lodge and Supreme Grand Chapter of England and the Grand Lodges and Grand Chapters of Ireland and Scotland. Some of the comments are truly serendipitous, and the book is a compendium of unexpected treasures.

It will be used as a reference book and for simple pleasure, gratifying the spirit of natural "curtiosity" about the less obvious aspects of Freemasonry, which the Grand Master believes should be encouraged among Freemasons and others.

Bro Mendoza has kindly promised to assign all the royalties from the sale of this book to the Grand Charity. The Council is and all members will be grateful to him for this generosity.

Secretary,
Grand Charity

INTRODUCTION

The original intention of this book was to deal with the identification of lodges through their banners. It soon became apparent that in very many cases the emblem shown on the banner was the same as the badge used by the lodge, whether the badge be printed on the summons or incorporated in the jewel of a founder or past master of the lodge.

It was also realized that the badge very often had an association with the name or title of the lodge, though at times this was not always obvious. Indeed, on occasions the reason for the choice of the badge has been impossible to ascertain – the founders having long since died and no record regarding the choice having been kept.

Many lodges have the same name and one has to look at the lodge number to ensure correct identification. Looking at numbers raised many queries, not least amongst which were some apparent quirks with regard to precedence.

It was noticed too that some badges showed a motto; most of these were in Latin, but there were a few in French, Welsh and at least one in Hebrew! Some had an obvious connection with the name of the person or organization after whom the lodge was named; others were more baffling.

So what started as a possible book on lodge banners became a book dealing with all these items, something much wider than had originally been intended and which led to the making of happy and unexpected discoveries; hence the title of the book – SERENDIPITY.

Nearly every lodge in the world – and there are thousands! – has a number and a name. Examples of those that do not can be found in the Grand Lodges of Massachusetts and Cuba; in both these cases the lodge has a name but no number. And both the United Grand Lodge of England and the Grand Lodge of Ireland have a lodge with a name but no number.

Many of the lodges will have a badge, and some, particularly in America, will have their own individual banner. It is, of course, impossible to deal with each lodge; indeed it would be a Herculean task to deal with every lodge under the jurisdiction of the United Grand Lodge of England.

In the main, the information given herein will be confined to the lodges and chapters of the English Constitution, though a brief reference will also be made to our sister Constitutions in Ireland and Scotland. Other masonic Orders will not be dealt with.

Much of the information concerning lodge numbers has been taken from that masterpiece *Masonic Records 1717–1894* by W. Bro. John Lane, PAGDC, the absolute copyright of which, according to the author, 'has been freely offered to and accepted by the Grand Lodge'. I wish to place on record my thanks to both the Board of General Purposes and the Committee of General Purposes for permission to quote from this and other records. I express my thanks also, to the many brethren who have been kind enough to help me in obtaining information; and I owe a particular debt of gratitude to W. Bro. Graham Redman, PJGD, Assistant Grand Secretary, for his kindness in reading the typescript, the many helpful suggestions he made, and in particular, his invaluable help in the translation of the Latin.

Harry Mendoza

PART 1:

LODGE NUMBERS

Before the formation of the premier Grand Lodge

THERE are various references to masonic lodges in England before the formation of the premier Grand Lodge in 1717. Examples are as follows.

(i) The evidence in Ashmole's diary:

1646

Oct, 16, $4^{H}30$ P.M. I was made a Free-Mason at Warrington in Lancashire wth Coll: Henry Mainwaring of Karincham in Cheshire. The Names of those that were then of the Lodge, Mr Rich: Penkett Warden, Mr James Collier, Mr Rich: Sanchey, Henry Littler, John Ellam, Rich: Ellam, & Hugh Brewer.

(ii) The evidence of Randle Holme in his *Academie of Armory*:

I cannot but Honor the Fellowship of the Masons because of its antiquity; and the more, as being a member of that society called Free-Masons; . . . [there is evidence to record that Randle Holme was a member of a lodge meeting at Chester].

(iii) A roll of parchment, endorsed '1712 to 1730' which gives details of a number of admissions into Freemasonry; two examples are given here. (*AQC* 13, pp. 11–12):

March the 19th, 1712

At a private Lodge held at the house of James Boreham situate in Stonegate in the City of York. Mr. Thomas Shipton Mr. Caleb Greenbury, Mr. J^no^ Norrison Mr. J^no^ Russell, J^no^ Whitehead and Francis Norrison were all of them severally sworne and admitted into the honourable Society and fraternity of free-Masons.

Geo, Bowes, Esqr Dep. President

J^no^ Wilcock also admitted at the same Lodge	Tho Shipton	Caleb Greenbury
	J^no^ Norrison	John Russell
	Fran, Norrison	John Whitehead
		John Wilcock.

December the 18th 1713

At a private Lodge held then at the house of Mr James Boreham Scittuate in Stonegate in the City of York Mr Tho: Hardwick Mr Godfrey Giles and Mr Tho: Challener was admitted and Sworne into the Honoble Society and Company of ffree Masons before the Worshipful Sr Walter Hawxworth Kn^t^ and Barr^t^ President.

Tho: Hardwick
Godfrey Giles
his
Thomas **T** Challener
marke

(iv) An endorsement on one of the Old Charges, the Scarborough Manuscript, which reads:

M[emoran]dum Thatt att A private Lodge held at Scarborough in the County of York the tenth day of July 1705 before William Thompson Esqr P^r^sident of the said Lodge & severall others brethren ffree Masons the severall psons whose names are herevnto Subscribed were then admitted into the said ffraternity.

In each of the cases mentioned above the reference is to a lodge meeting at a particular place; there is no mention of either a lodge number or name.

The premier Grand Lodge, 1717–1727.

The earliest record of the formation of the premier Grand Lodge is as follows; it comes from Anderson's second edition of *Constitutions*, published in 1738, twenty-one years after the actual event.

> ... after the Rebellion was over A.D. 1716, the few *Lodges* at *London* finding themselves neglected by Sir *Christopher Wren*, thought fit to cement under a *Grand* Master at the Center of Union and Harmony, viz, the *Lodges* that met,
>
> 1. At the *Goose* and *Gridiron* Ale-House in *St Paul's Church-Yard*.
> 2. At the *Crown* Ale-house in *Parker's-Lane* near *Drury-Lane*.
> 3. At the *Apple-Tree* Tavern in *Charles-street*, Covent-Garden.
> 4. At the *Rummer* and *Grapes* Tavern in *Channel-Row, Westminster*.
>
> They and some old Brothers met at the said *Apple-Tree*, and having put into the Chair the *oldest Master* Mason (now the *Master* of a *Lodge*) they constituted themselves a GRAND LODGE pro Tempore in *Due form*, and forthwith revived the Quarterly *Communication* of the *Officers* of Lodges (call'd the Grand Lodge) resolv'd to hold the *Annual* ASSEMBLY *and Feast*, and then to chuse a GRAND MASTER from among themselves, till they should have the Honour of a *Noble Brother* at their Head.

Before commenting on this quotation, there are two points that should be clarified. The first is the phrase 'the Rebellion was over A.D. 1716' at the start of the quotation; this refers to the Jacobite rebellion which started in Scotland and ended in the defeat of the rebels at Preston in 1715. The second point is the phrase 'revived the Quarterly Communication'. The use of this wording implies that Quarterly Communications, or possibly 'an Annual Assembly and Feast' had previously taken place; there is no evidence to support this.

It will be noted that the lodges mentioned are identified by their meeting-places; there is no lodge name, but the lodges are numbered 1 to 4. However, lodge numbering was not in use in 1717 when the premier Grand Lodge was formed; the numbers were added by Anderson in 1738, some years after Grand Lodge had first settled the order of precedence for lodges.

The earliest Minute of Grand Lodge is dated 25 November 1723. It includes 'A list of the Regular Constituted Lodges together with the names of the Masters Wardens and Members of Each Lodge.' A copy of the list is given in Appendix A.

All but the last two named in the list appear in the first Engraved List of Lodges which was published in 1723. Two more Engraved Lists appeared in 1725. Neither the lodges listed in Grand Lodge Minutes nor in the Engraved Lists printed in 1723 and 1725 showed a number against any lodge.

During the 1720s and 1730s, Grand Lodge was very concerned about the clandestine making of masons. Quite apart from the question of masonic irregularity, they were afraid of the risk of claims being made by such irregular masons on the newly-established Charity Fund. For these reasons Grand Lodge thought it necessary that every regular lodge should be aware of all the other regular lodges. This is evidenced by the following quotations from Anderson's *Constitutions*, (1723 edition).

> Old Regulations. III. The *Master* of each particular *Lodge*, or one of the *Wardens*, or some other Brother by his Order, shall keep a Book containing their *By-Laws*, the Names of their Members, with a List of all the *Lodges* in Town, and the usual Times and Places of their forming, and all their Transactions that are proper to be written.

The second (1738) edition of the Constitutions shows the Old Regulation III (with slightly different wording but essentially the same meaning) and alongside;

> New Regulations. III. In the Mastership of DALKEITH, a List of *all* the *Lodges* was engraven by Brother *John Pyne* in a very small Volume; which is usually reprinted on the Commencement of every *New Grand Master*, and dispersed among the Brethren.

The reference to 'the Mastership of Dalkeith' refers to the period June 1723 to June 1724 when the Earl of Dalkeith was Grand Master. He had previously been Master of the lodge held at the Rummer and Grapes Tavern.

Precedence.

A Grand Lodge Minute dated 27 December 1727 reads:

> That it shall be referr'd to the succeeding Grand Master, Deputy Grand Master and Grand Wardens, to inquire into the Precedency of the several Lodges, and to make Report thereof at the next Quarterly Communication in order that the same may be finally settled, and entered accordingly.

Shortly afterwards, on 17 April 1728, the Minutes record:

> Then most of the Lodges present delivered the Dates of the time of their being Constituted into Lodges in order to have Precedency in the printed Book.

At the following Meeting 'The Grand Master directed the List of regular Lodges to be called over which being done, these following answered to their Names'. There follows a list of twenty-eight consecutively numbered Lodges. After the Minutes had been read, we find:

> Pursuant to an Article in the aforesaid Minutes (requiring all the regular Lodges to give in the exact time when they were severally Constituted) some of the Members delivered the Acco[t] as required, and such as had not complyed with the aforesaid Order were directed to do it before the next Quarterly Communication.

This seemed to have stimulated further action, for in the Minutes of 26 November 1728, we have:

> The Masters and Wardens of the several Lodges underwritten who being called, according to their Seniority, answered to their Names.

There follows a list of thirty consecutively numbered lodges, though the order of the lodges in this list is slightly different from the list printed in the previous Minutes. Further, there were still some lodges that had not yet given the date of their Constitution to Grand Lodge.

The revised Engraved List appeared in 1729; it was headed *A List of Regular Lodges according to their Seniority & Constitution*: each lodge is given a consecutive number. A copy of the list is shown in Appendix B.

These lists are the only occasions in the early Minutes of Grand Lodge when a number is placed against the name of the lodge, presumably to imply precedence. The lists, however, were not accurate.

Anderson's 1738 *Constitutions* also relates the sad story (referred to below) of one of the four original lodges that met in 1717 'to cement under a Grand Master'; they became known as 'time immemorial lodges' because they were in existence before the formation of the premier Grand Lodge.

A List of Lodges in and about London and Westminster', records:

> 10. Queen's Head in Knaves Acre. This was one of the four lodges ... whose Constitution is immemorial; but after they removed to the Queen's Head upon some difference, the members that met came under a New Constitution, tho' they wanted it not, and is therefore placed at this number. [ie No. 10].

It appears that on 27 February 1723 the Lodge accepted a warrant, although it was a time immemorial lodge and did not need one. The consequence of this was that when the lodges were numbered in 1729 according to their dates, the lodge was given the number 11 instead of 3, to which it would have been entitled had the warrant not been accepted. Anderson quoted No. 10, as his list showed only the existing lodges in London and Westminster; at that time one lodge had gone out of existence. The lodge always contended that it was a time immemorial lodge. In 1966 a petition was presented to the Grand Master, and subsequently Grand Lodge resolved that the lodge be allowed to surrender the warrant that had been issued and to resume its time immemorial status. (This lodge is now No. 12 and is known as the Lodge of Fortitude and Old Cumberland. It is unusual in that it does not accept joining members.)

Erasures.

Problems arose when lodges ceased to exist or, in the case of some London lodges, did not attend Quarterly Communications. Erasures on this score were quite frequent and legislation was needed to deal with the matter. On 24 February 1725 a Grand Lodge Minute states:

> That if any lodge for the future, within the Bills of Mortality, shall not regularly meet for the space of one year, such lodge shall be erased out of the Book of Lodges, and in case they should afterwards be desirous of meeting again as a lodge, they shall lose their former rank, and submit themselves to a new Constitution.

This did not always happen though; some lodges were reinstated with their old number and no loss of precedence.

Bro. Michael Spurr referred as follows to 'the Bills of Mortality' (*AQC* 102, p. 197):

> When the premier Grand Lodge was founded it restricted its activities to those parts of London that fell within the area known as 'The Bills of Mortality' which was, at that time, roughly a ten-mile radius from Charing Cross.
>
> 'The Bills of Mortality' was the term used for the weekly lists drawn up by the parish clerks, listing the number of deaths that had occurred within each parish during the preceding week and entered under certain specific headings of a general nature, rather than true medical descriptions of the cause of death.

Some Provincial Grand Masters who had warranted lodges, delayed giving the relevant information to Grand Lodge. There were also lodges who were late in sending in their registration fees. For these reasons, the lodges concerned were not on the 1729 List, although they should have been. Furthermore, when they *were* included, they lost the precedence to which they were rightly entitled.

In 1740 Grand Lodge took the opportunity of rectifying some of the errors that were in the Lists previously issued. They had a general 'close-up' of numbers, using those that had become available because of erasures. Similar changes took place in 1755; 1770; 1780; 1781 and 1792, the changes in the latter years, having been agreed by Grand Lodge, were made known generally in the next following Grand Lodge Proceedings. Errors still occurred, though, in the early Lists; it was not until 1770 that the Lists could be described as being accurate.

As a result of these 'close-ups' many lodges had a variety of numbers. An example is the present Castle Lodge of Harmony; it bore numbers as follows.

In 1729 – number 38. In 1740 – number 34. In 1755 – number 22.
In 1770 – number 21. In 1780 – number 19. In 1792 – number 18.

(It changed again in 1814 to 29; in 1832 to 27 and finally in 1863 to 26.)

The Stewards' Lodge.

An unusual incident occurred in 1792; it concerned the Stewards' Lodge which had been formed in 1735, bearing the number 117. As a result of the closing-up just referred to, the lodge was re-numbered

115 in 1740; 70 in 1755; 60 in 1770 and 47 in 1780.

However, on 18 April 1782 it was 'placed at the Head of the List by order of the Grand Lodge', without a number.

One might well ask why; the answer is found in the history of the lodge. From its very beginnings it seems to have been decided by Grand Lodge that all Grand Officers were to be chosen from amongst those who had served the Office of Steward in Grand Lodge. Bro. Colin Dyer, the author of the authoritative book *Grand Stewards and their Lodge*, tells us;

> From the 1740s it had been the custom to treat the Master of the Stewards' Lodge as the senior Master present when it came to filling an Office in Grand Lodge . . . although there might be Masters of other lodges with lower numbers present.

This gave the Stewards' Lodge a special status. But as might be expected, there were objections, mostly from the Lodge of Antiquity, one of the time immemorial lodges which formed the premier Grand Lodge. It happened that in the 1770s their Master, William Preston (after whom the Prestonian Lecture is named), whilst visiting a lodge, took great exception to another visitor, a member of the Grand Stewards' Lodge, being given preference over him; but his protests were of no avail.

A similar situation may have occurred elsewhere, but whether it did or not, the latest *Constitutions*, which had been issued in 1774, seem to have made the position quite clear. Under the heading 'Grand Lodge', we have Article III which deals with who should preside in Grand Lodge in the absence of the Grand Master or his substitute; it finishes:

> . . . and if no former grand officer be found, then the master of the stewards' lodge; or in his absence, the master of the senior lodge present.

A few years later, on 16 November 1791, the Minutes of the Lodge of Antiquity record:

> Bro. Preston moved, seconded by Bro. Wickens, that a Protest against the Regulation of the Grand Lodge respecting the Precedency of the Master of the Stewards' Lodge over Masters of Lodges of a prior Date, be entered on the Minute Book of this Lodge, Because it appears to be an unwarrantable stretch of Power to give a Junior Lodge a Preference to many Senior Lodges, and because it deprives the Master of this Lodge in Particular of the honour of precedency of Rank to which its Antiquity gives so just a title, for it should never be forgotten that this Lodge flourished long before the Grand Lodge was known and which indeed it called into existence. The Motion was carried unanimously.

Grand Lodge, which had only recently reinstated Preston after he had been expelled from the Society, must have taken a dim view of this. It decided to make the position formal. Five months after the Antiquity Motion just quoted, we have the Grand Lodge Resolution placing the Stewards' Lodge at the head of the List of Lodges.

The Grand Lodge of the Antients.

The first List of Lodges of the Grand Lodge of the Antients is found in what is known as *Morgan's Register*. It is headed 'List of Lodges' and shows the date the lodge was warranted, its number and where and when it met. The first entry is Number 2, the date warranted being 17 July 1751. The last entry is Number 16, the date warranted being 11 December 1752. Like the lists of the premier Grand Lodge, there are no lodge names.

The second list shows similar detail for a total of thirty-seven lodges, again starting with Number 2. The date appearing in the heading of this List is Anno Lap, 5752, corresponding to 1752, 'Lap' is an abbreviation for *Lapidariorum*, thus giving us 'in the year of the Stonecutters' and, by definition, 'of Freemasonry'. This is an early use of the letters A.L. having a meaning other than the one we give them today, Anno Lucis. (For other examples, see the author's Inaugural Address to Quatuor Coronati Lodge 13 November 1980 – *AQC* 94, pp. 1–5.)

The third List is dated 24 June 1755. It purports to show a total of sixty-four lodges, but about one third of them have nothing against the numbers, and much of the information for the other lodges is missing.

The reason for starting the Lists with Number 2 is because the Grand Secretary, Laurence Dermott, was saving Number 1 until the Grand Lodge had a noble Grand Master. This occurred in 1756 with the election of the Earl of Blessington. He was installed by proxy and never visited Grand Lodge. One of the warrants he signed was that for Number 1, The Grand Master's Lodge; it was dated 13 August 1759. However, it is argued that Lodge Number 1 *was* in existence as early as 1756. To quote from *Quatuor Coronatorum Antigrapha*, Vol. 11, page ix;

> ... arrangements had been made in 1752 that any Warrants granted previous to the installation of a Grand Master should be subsequently confirmed by the Grand Master's signature after his appointment, and though Robert Turner was Grand Master from 1754 and was followed by Edward Vaughan, it is suggested that Dermott held over the Warrant of his favoured No. 1 until it could be signed by a noble Grand Master. The United Grand Lodge has now acknowledged the seniority of the Grand Master's Lodge as dating from 2nd September, 1756 ...

Other Lists of Lodges were published in later years, but according to Lane (*Masonic Records 1717–1894* page 11) '... it is impossible to pronounce them correct'. Suffice it to say that at the Union of the two Grand Lodges in 1813, there were just over 500 lodges on the Roll of the Grand Lodge of the Antients. (At the same date, the number of lodges on the Roll of the premier Grand Lodge was just over 1000.)

The Antients had a similar problem to the premier Grand Lodge with respect to erasure of lodges, but only once did they follow the practice of 'closing-up' adopted by the latter. They were far more astute; their method of dealing with the numbers borne by erased lodges was to re-issue the warrant, with the number unchanged, to an existing lodge or to a new lodge in return for a payment to the Charity fund. Early examples are;

> Lodge No. 37 (warrant dated 19 August 1754) purchased warrant of Lodge No. 6 for £1.1.0., October 1754; (now No. 11 and known as Enoch Lodge).
>
> Lodge No. 5 (warrant dated 17 July, 1751) purchased by Laurence Dermott, Grand Secretary, Antients, for £5.5.0. in 1769 for a new Lodge constituted 17 May, 1769: (now No. 9 and known as Albion Lodge).

As late as 2 April 1813 we find the warrant of Lodge No. 15 being granted to Lodge No. 131 in lieu of the warrant they returned (now No. 24 and known as Newcastle upon Tyne Lodge).

This practice of selling warrants is referred to in an Antient Grand Lodge Minute dated 5 September 1792.

> Grand Master or Deputy Grand Master to grant such Warrants as are vacant to such Lodges as apply for the same, giving preference of choice to the senior Lodges respectively, £5.5s.0d. to be the established fee to the fund of Charity for taking out or renewing a Senior Warrant.

Precedence.

There were occasions when, for one reason or another, a lodge decided to unite with another for the purpose of getting a lower number and therefore a higher precedence. This might be done by the mutual agreement of the lodges concerned, but as the following quotation shows, there were occasions when more dubious methods were employed; the lodges concerned owed allegiance to the premier Grand Lodge.

> Thomas Dunckerley and his friends were not content with the rapid rise of the lodge [Somerset House]; they wanted a number in the list higher than 279. So in 1767 they made an illegal purchase of No. 3 Lodge and gave it the name of the Lodge of Friendship; (it still has the same name, but is now No. 6). The story, as read in the minutes of the Committee of Charity and the minutes of the lodge, is disgraceful. (No. 4, *The Royal Somerset House and Inverness Lodge*, p. 23, A.W. Oxford, London, Bernard Quarritch, 1928.)

The Union of the two Grand Lodges.

In December 1813 the two rival Grand Lodges joined forces, giving rise to our present-day United Grand Lodge. Obviously the Union necessitated some action regarding the numbers being used by the various lodges, as each of the two Grand Lodges had its own lodge enumeration.

The procedure to be adopted in dealing with this matter was laid down in the Articles of Union which had been agreed and accepted by both Grand Lodges. The gist of the wording in the relevant Article (No. VIII), was that the first two lodges under each Grand Lodge had to draw a lot to decide which was to take priority in the new list, the successful lodge to be numbered 1 and the other No. 2. Other lodges were then to follow alternately.

The wording of the Article is '... the first two lodges under each Grand Lodge', not 'the first two *numbered* lodges under each Grand Lodge'. One could read this as meaning that it was The Grand Stewards' Lodge, not the Lodge of Antiquity, which should have taken part in the draw, the former having been placed at the head of the list of lodges under the premier Grand Lodge, albeit without a number. But this was not the way it happened, possibly because it was argued that the Grand Stewards' Lodge, being assured of its place at the head of the list, had no interest in the outcome of the draw.

The two lodges which drew the lot were the Lodge of Antiquity for the premier Grand Lodge, and The Grand Master's Lodge for the Grand Lodge of the Antients. The Grand Stewards' Lodge was still to remain at the head of the new United Grand Lodge List, again, without a number. This was confirmed in the 1815 *Book of Constitutions*; Rule 11 under the heading 'Of Grand Stewards' reads:

> The grand stewards' lodge shall not have a number, but shall be registered in the books of grand lodge, and placed in the printed lists at the head of all other lodges and rank accordingly, and shall be represented in the grand lodge by its master, wardens and past master.

In the event the draw gave priority to No. 1 of the Grand Lodge of the Antients, the Grand Master's Lodge; it became No. 1 on the new United Grand Lodge List, and the Lodge of Antiquity (No. 1 on the premier Grand Lodge List) became No. 2.

As the other lodges were to follow alternately, it meant, in effect, that lodges that had owed allegiance to the Grand Lodge of the Antients were to bear odd numbers, whilst lodges that had adhered to the premier Grand Lodge were to bear even numbers; but it did not work out that way. This was because of the gaps in both lists where lodges had either been erased or had otherwise ceased to function and whose number had not been reallocated. Where the numbers were vacant on one list but filled in the other, the latter were allotted the next number in the new list until both lodges had the same number on their respective Grand Lodge list. For example;

No. 10 on the Antients' list became No. 19 on the new list (still No. 19 and known as Royal Athelstan Lodge).

No. 10 on the premier Grand Lodge list became No. 20 on the new list (still No. 20 and known as Royal Kent Lodge of Antiquity).

No. 11 on the Antients' list was vacant, so

No. 11 on the premier Grand Lodge list became No. 21 on the new list (now extinct).

No. 12 on the Antients' list was also vacant, so

No. 12 on the premier Grand Lodge list became No. 22 on the new list (now No. 21 and known as Lodge of Emulation).

No. 13 on the Antients' list became No. 23 on the new list (now No. 22 and known as Neptune Lodge).

No. 13 on the premier Grand Lodge list became No. 24 on the new list (now extinct).

Similar action took place where the vacancy occurred in the premier Grand Lodge list.

Occasionally a lodge was given a wrong number. For example No. 40 (Grand Lodge of the Antients) should have been No. 60; it was given No. 77. No. 65 (1792 enumeration, premier Grand Lodge) should have been No. 88; it was given No. 78. And No. 71 (Grand Lodge of the Antients) should have been No. 95; it was given No. 106; all three are now extinct. The reasons for these discrepancies are not known.

As might have been expected, this arrangement, though accepted, did not please everybody. In particular it did not please some of the members of the time immemorial Lodge of Antiquity. It will be recalled that about twenty years earlier the master of that lodge, William Preston, had objected to The Stewards' Lodge being given precedence over his lodge. However, Preston was not present at the meetings during which objections were raised following the re-numbering of Lodges at the Union; objections which culminated in an Address being sent to the Grand Master, the Duke of Sussex. Some unpleasantness followed, but in due course, all settled down.

Post Union.

At the time of the Union there were just over 1000 lodges on the roll of the premier Grand Lodge and about half that number on the roll of the Grand Lodge of the Antients. In the re-numbering process, only 648 lodges were carried forward, the remainder having ceased to exist.

Between 1813 and 1832, 227 new lodges were warranted, but many others had been removed from the Roll for failing to make returns; another closing-up exercise then took place. The last lodge to be warranted before that took place was No 865, the date being 16 April 1832. On re-numbering, it became No. 594; it is now Commercial Lodge No. 411.

Over the next thirty years, taking us up to 1862, another 706 new lodges were warranted, but only 940 were still in active existence. This resulted in yet another closing-up exercise, but this was to be for the last time. The last lodge to be consecrated before that took place was No. 1276, the date being 8 July 1863. Following the new enumeration, it became No. 974 and is known as Pentalpha Lodge.

Lodges warranted since 1863 have been given the next consecutive number on the list, wherever the lodge is situated. The numbers borne by lodges that cease to exist remain as they were on the Register; they are not re-allocated. Details of all such erasures can be found in *Masonic Year Book Historical Supplement* and the *Supplement* thereto, published by the United Grand Lodge of England.

The *Masonic Year Book 1992–93* shows there were 8637 active lodges on the Register of the United Grand Lodge of England, the last number being 9485.

The Table on pages 25–7 shows the first 100 lodges still extant in 1863 when the last close-up of numbers took place. It gives the date of Constitution, the original number of the lodge and every change of number following each close-up.

The Constitutions.

There is no reference to precedence of lodges in Anderson's first *Constitutions* (1723). The second edition, printed in 1738, shows what Anderson calls the Old and New Regulations, side by side, The 'New Regulations' are (quoting Bro. Lewis Edwards, *AQC* 46, p. 397);

... little more than a jumble of resolutions of Grand Lodge (sometimes appositely quoted in extension, qualification, or amendment of the Old, and sometimes not), footnotes and pious hopes, ... dictated by the typographical necessity of placing some attempt at a New Regulation in the right-hand column opposite to one of the 'Old'.

The entry for New Regulation III includes;

On *27 Dec. 1727*. The *Precedency* of *Lodges* is grounded on the Seniority of their *Constitution*.

This wording remained virtually unchanged for years. In the first *Book of Constitutions* issued after the Union of the two Grand Lodges, the words 'as recorded in the books of the Grand Lodge' were added; and that is how it is today.

Until the 1884 *Book of Constitutions* there was no reference to the lodge having to bear a number; that was implied. The completely revised 1884 edition, however, was more specific. Not only did it repeat the Rule regarding precedence of lodges, it also introduced a new Rule saying that every lodge must have a name or title, as well as a number.

We know that all extant lodges, apart from the Grand Stewards' Lodge, had a number before the 1884 *Constitutions* were published. Indeed, as already indicated, the earlier *Constitutions* implied this.

The age of the Lodge.

Precedence on the books of Grand Lodge does not necessarily reflect the age of the lodge. It will be apparent that, as a result of the method of allocating numbers at the Union of the two Grand Lodges in 1813, many lodges which have a low number, and therefore a higher precedence, are not as old as others with a higher number and lower precedence. To illustrate this a list has been prepared showing forty-four lodges constituted before Lodge No. 3, which was constituted in 1754, but which bear a higher number and therefore lower precedence. The list is given in Appendix C.

The age of a lodge is determined by the date of its Constitution (or nowadays its Consecration), not the date shown on the Warrant, which is usually earlier; there are some old lodges, especially abroad, which met for a short time by dispensation before receiving a warrant. The precedence of the lodge is determined by its number as shown in the books of Grand Lodge.

Some early lodges were granted Centenary Warrants erroneously; the date on the warrants in the eighteenth and early ninetenth century being considered the date of the Constitution of the lodge. These were usually lodges that had purchased the warrant of a lodge which no longer existed. However, under the rules currently applied, their Bi-centenary Warrants will be given only when they can prove 200 years of uninterrupted existence of *their* lodge.

There have been a few occasions where the grant for a Bi-centenary Warrant was refused because the lodge had been unable to satisfy the authorities of its continued existence. One particular case where this happened concerned St George's and Corner Stone Lodge, No. 5. However, the decision was later overturned because sufficient evidence *was* produced.

This particular lodge is almost unique in that there were two lodges, one of which was formerly on the roll of the premier Grand Lodge, and the other formerly on the roll of the Grand Lodge of the Antients; they were united after the Union of the two Grand Lodges. Brief details are as follows.

The date of warrant or constitution shown in Lane's *Masonic Records* for Corner Stone Lodge is 26 February 1730 and the number given as No. 63 on the roll of the premier Grand Lodge. After various changes it became No. 40 at the revised enumeration following the Union; the number was changed to 32 at the next change in 1832.

The date of warrant or constitution in the same book for St George's Lodge is 2 February 1756; it was then No. 55 on the roll of the Grand Lodge of the Antients. On 6 June 1759 this lodge purchased the warrant of lodge No. 3 and henceforth used the lower number, becoming No. 5 on the register of United Grand Lodge; no further changes in number were made.

These two lodges united on 6 December 1843, adopting the name St George's and Corner Stone; the lodge remained No. 5.

According to the author of the history of the lodge, W.Bro. Christopher L. Gotch, PJGD, Corner Stone Lodge applied for a Bi-centenary Warrant just prior to 1930, but was unable to satisfy the authorities that it had an uninterrupted existence; the grant was refused. Whilst the lodge was preparing to apply again for a Bi-centenary Warrant (hoping to satisfy the authorities that St George's Lodge had had an uninterrupted existence since 1756), sufficient evidence was found to prove the authorities were wrong in refusing the application previously made in respect of Corner Stone Lodge. The Bi-centenary Warrant was then granted, the period of existence dating from 1730; it was presented to the lodge by the Grand Master, the Earl of Scarbrough, in May 1952.

The 'serendipity' shown as the title of this book is illustrated by this story which came to the attention of the author when it was found that the 1956 edition of the *Masonic Year Book* showed the date of warrant or constitution for St George's and Corner Stone Lodge, No. 5 as 1730, with an obelisk or 'dagger' (†) against the date, indicating the lodge was formerly on the roll of the Grand Lodge of the Antients – formed some twenty years after the date of constitution! The 'dagger' was removed in the next edition.

St. Luke's Lodge, No. 225 is another example of a lodge formerly on the Atholl or Antient Grand Lodge Roll and a lodge on the premier Grand Lodge Roll, uniting after the Union of the two Grand Lodges. The relevant detail is recited in the Bi-Centenary Warrant granted to the lodge in 1985; the wording is as follows:

WHEREAS it appears by the Records of the Grand Lodge that on the 25th day of September 1785 a Warrant of Constitution was granted to certain Brethren therein named, authorising and empowering them and their regular Successors to hold a Lodge of Free and Accepted Masons at the Green Man on the Quay. Ipswich in the County of Suffolk which Lodge was named the Lodge of Perpetual Friendship and numbered 479 on the Register of the Premier Grand Lodge AND WHEREAS on the closing up of numbers on the Register of the Premier Grand Lodge in the year 1792 the said Lodge became No. 359 AND WHEREAS it appears by the Records of the Grand Lodge that on the 20th day of October 1804 a Warrant of Constitution was granted to certain Brethren therein named, authorising and empowering them and their regular successors to hold a Lodge of Free and Accepted Masons in the Westminster Militia stationed at Colchester in the County of Essex which Lodge was named the St Luke's Lodge and then numbered 309 on the Register of the Atholl Grand Lodge AND WHEREAS in consequence of the Union of the Premier Grand Lodge with the Atholl Grand Lodge on the 27th day of December 1813 the said Lodges became respectively No. 480 and No. 393 on the Register of the United Grand Lodge of England AND WHEREAS on the 14th day of June 1820 the said Lodges united to form a single Lodge retaining and meeting under the sanction of the Warrant of the said St Luke's Lodge then numbered 393 AND WHEREAS in consequence of the subsequent alterations made in the numbers of Lodges in the years 1832 and 1863 the said Lodge became and now stands on the Register as No. 225 meeting at the Freemasons' Hall, Soane Street, Ipswich in the Province of Suffolk under the title or denomination of the

ST, LUKE'S LODGE

AND WHEREAS satisfactory proof has been produced of the uninterrupted existence of the said Lodge for 200 years dating from the 23rd day of September 1785 AND WHEREAS the Brethren comprising the said Lodge desire to be permitted to wear a commemoration bar on the ribbon of the Centenary Jewel authorised by a Warrant dated the 8th day of January 1904 and have prayed our sanction for that purpose

NOW KNOW YE THAT We having taken the Petition into our consideration have acceded to their request and in virtue of Our Prerogative DO HEREBY GIVE AND GRANT to all and each of the subscribing members of the said Lodge being Master Masons permission to wear a Bi-Centenary Bar on the ribbon of the Centenary Jewel illustated herein.

GIVEN at LONDON this 23rd day of September, A.L. 5985, A.D. 1985

BY COMMAND of the MOST WORSHIPFUL GRAND MASTER

HIS ROYAL HIGHNESS THE DUKE OF KENT, *KG*, &c. &c. &c, &c.

M.B.S. Higham, (Signed) G.S.

Local precedence.

The 1815 *Book of Constitutions* made a further reference to numbers. It concerns lodges removed from one Province to another. In such cases, the lodge retained its number and precedence according to the Register, but its precedence in the province to which it had moved was to be determined by the date of registration in the books of the Provincial Grand Lodge.

This is still the position today. Examples are

5731 (Hereditary Lodge, consecrated 1938) moved from London to West Kent on 1 January 1973 where it ranks after 8299;

2399 (Ordnance Lodge, consecrated 1891) moved from London to West Kent on 1 January 1974 where it ranks after 8565.

13 (Union Waterloo Lodge, consecrated 1761) moved from London to West Kent on 29 April 1982 where it ranks after 9022.

The only practical effect this is likely to have is the right of lodges to be represented in the procession of the Provincial Grand Master on special occasions, an honour usually reserved for the most senior lodges in the Province. The number in the procession depends on the Provincial Grand Master, except at his Installation when the masters of the seven most senior lodges form his escort; his own mother lodge is usually deemed for this purpose to be one of the seven most senior.

The information regarding local precedency is not always shown in the Year Book printed by the Province.

A similar principle to 'local precedence' affords the reason why the current *Masonic Year Book* includes the following under the list of lodges;

PART 1: LODGE NUMBERS

No.	*Name of lodge*	*Meeting Place*	*Constituted*
5556	Thornton	Northiam, Sussex	1935
5557	Eureka	Rio de Janeiro	1891
5558	Duke of Clarence	Sąo Paulo	1893
5559	Morro Velho	Belo Horizonte	1899
5560	Lodge of Unity	Sąo Paulo	1902
5561	St George	Sąo Paulo	1904
5562	Lodge of Wanderers	Santos	1907
5563	Lodge of Friendship	Rio de Janeiro	1922
5564	Centenary	Sąo Paulo	1922
5565	Campos Salles	Sąo Paulo	1923
5566	Royal Edward	Rio de Janeiro	1932

It will be noted that lodge No. 5556 was constituted in 1935; the others were constituted before that date yet have a higher number and, as a result, lower precedence. The reason for this is that they were constituted under another masonic jurisdiction before 1935 but during that year they transferred their allegiance to England following an amicable agreement under the Treaty of Fraternal Alliance, 1935, between the Grand Orient of Portugal and the United Grand Lodge of England; they now come under the District Grand Lodge of South America, Northern Division.

The original reference to this matter of the precedence of lodges in the Provinces is found in the 1815 *Book of Constitutions* in a Section headed

Of COUNTRY LODGES *in* DISTRICTS.

FOR WHICH A PROVINCIAL GRAND MASTER IS APPOINTED

A Country Lodge was any Lodge at a greater distance of ten miles from London which came under the immediate superintendance [*sic*] of a Provincial Grand Master. The reference to Country Lodges was dropped in the 1884 *Book of Constitutions*, from which date the terms Provincial or District Grand Lodges are used.

The use of roman numerals.

In all official documents and entries in the *Masonic Year Book* and in most other documents, the number of the lodge is printed in arabic numerals. There are a few lodges that prefer to use roman numerals, although there is not always consistency. In some cases, after the adoption of the use of roman numerals, the same lodge has used arabic figures on various papers such as menu cards, lists of members etc.

Examples of lodges using roman numerals are;

No. IV; Royal Somerset House and Inverness Lodge.
No. VIII; British Lodge
No. IX; Albion Lodge
No. XI; Enoch Lodge
No. XXIII; Globe Lodge
No. CXXXIV; Caledonian Lodge.
No. $\bar{\text{V}}$MDCXI; Rutupaie Lodge. The roman numerals are shown in addition to the usual arabic numerals; they appear in a scroll beneath the lodge badge. Note the use of the vinculum – the line above the V; this indicates a multiple of 1000, the total number being reckoned as follows:

$\bar{\text{V}}$ = 5000; M = 1000; D = 500; C = 100; XI = 11; Total, 6611.

The reason for the use of roman numerals was probably to give the impression that the lodge was older than it actually was.

Current list of lodges up to No. 100.

A list of current lodges up to number 100, showing all the numbers they have borne, is given in Appendix D.

PART 2:

NAMES

The use of a name to identify a band of men with a common interest was prevalent amongst the many clubs that sprang up in England, especially in London, during the eighteenth century. During the first fifty years we find, for example, names like the Hanoverian; the Society of Bachelors; Scribelus; the Kit Kat; the Mourning Bush; the Board and the Coterie. In the next fifty years we have, amongst others, the Dilettante; the Thespian; the Sons of the Thames; the Ivy; the Literary; the Royal Society; the Naviomagians; the Robin Hood; Boodles and the Travellers'.

Names taken from meeting places

It is not until the mid-1700s that some of the early masonic lodges started to adopt the name of the inn or tavern at which they met. Examples of such lodges that are still on the Register of the United Grand Lodge of England are given below, the order being the year in which the lodge was first named. In some cases the present name is quite different from that originally adopted; this is often due to the fact that the lodge has united with one or more lodges.

First named	*Name of inn or tavern*	*Name taken by lodge*	*Present number and name of lodge*
1742	King's Arms	King's Arms	28 Old King's Arms
1767	Horn	Old Horn	4 Royal Somerset House & Inverness
1768	Globe	Globe	23 Globe
1769	Mourning Bush	Mourning Bush	21 Lodge of Emulation
1770	Dundee Arms	Dundee Arms	18 Old Dundee
1770	Castle	Castle	26 Castle Lodge of Harmony
1771	St Alban's	St Alban's	29 St Alban's
1813	Strong Man	Strong Man	45 Strong Man

Other lodges adopted a name that had some connection with the area in which the lodge met or some geographical feature nearby. The examples given below follow a similar pattern to the previous list.

First named	*Locality or feature*	*Name taken by lodge*	*Present number and name of lodge*
1772	London	London	108 London
1779	River Medina	Medina	35 Medina
1814	Glamorganshire	Glamorgan	36 Glamorgan
1814	Newcastle upon Tyne	Newcastle upon Tyne	24 Newcastle upon Tyne

Other names

There were other lodges that adopted names but many of the names taken bore no relation to their meeting place. The following list gives some examples; it shows the year the name was adopted; the name taken by the lodge and the present-day number and name of the lodge. The reason for the change in name in some cases is as stated above.

1758 Old French Lodge, now No. 69 Lodge of Unity.
1761 The West India and American, now No. 2, Lodge of Antiquity.

1767 Lodge of Friendship, now No. 6, bearing same name.
1767 St John the Baptist, now No. 61, Lodge of Probity.
1768 Tyrian Lodge, now No. 10, Westminster and Keystone.
1768 Lodge of Fortitude, now No. 12, Lodge of Fortitude and Old Cumberland.
1768 Ionic, now No. 16, Royal Alpha.
1768 Lodge of Relief with Truth, now No. 59, Royal Naval.
1770 British, now No. 8, bearing same name.
1772 Lodge of Fortitude, now No. 64, bearing same name.
1773 Constitutional, now No. 55, bearing same name.
1773 Corner Stone, now No. 5, St George's and Corner Stone.
1774 Britannic, now No. 33, bearing same name.
1776 Lodge of Industry, now No. 48, bearing same name.
1777 Tuscan, now No. 14, bearing same name.
1778 Lodge of Felicity, now No. 58, bearing same name.
1781 Kentish Lodge of Antiquity, now No. 20, Royal Kent Lodge of Antiquity.
1781 Lodge of Relief, now No. 42, bearing same name.
1789 Lodge of Peace and Harmony, now No. 60, bearing same name.

The adoption of a name

The adoption of a lodge name was voluntary, even after the Union of the two Grand Lodges. The 1815 *Book of Constitutions*, under the heading '*Of* PRIVATE LODGES' has:

> 10. Any lodge which may not be distinguished by a name or title, being desirous of taking one, must, for that purpose, procure the approbation of the Grand Master or Provincial Grand Master, and the name must be registered with the Grand Secretary. No lodge shall be permitted to alter its name without like approbation.

The Rule is repeated in the 1841 edition, but by this time a form of application was needed for all new lodges. This form included the words ... 'we are desirous of forming a lodge to be named ...'. This would imply that all new lodges formed from 1841 were required to have a name, but not those formed before that date. The probability is that most had already adopted a name. However to make the position quite clear, the revised 1884 edition of the *Book of Constitutions* has:

> Every Lodge must be distinguished by a name or title, and no Lodge shall be permitted to make any alteration to its name or title without the approval of the Grand Master, and in the Provinces or Districts, also that of the Provincial or District Grand Master. Any such alteration must be immediately communicated to the Grand Secretary for registration.

Amalgamation of lodges

When for one reason or another two lodges unite, they have to decide on the name by which they would like the united lodge to be known. Often the name of one of the lodges is used, the other name being discarded. Sometimes a new name is adopted, more often than not being a combination of the names of the uniting lodges. Examples of changes of name following the uniting of lodges are evident from the information given in previous lists; brief details of some of these changes are given below.

Royal Somerset House and Inverness Lodge No. 4

Old Horn Lodge No. 4 (T.I.) was united with Somerset House Lodge No. 219 in 1774. The name Old Horn was discarded, but the lodge kept its number and its Time Immemorial status. In 1828 the lodge united with Royal Inverness Lodge No. 628 (Const. 1813); the number and Time Immemorial status was kept but the name changed to Royal Somerset House and Inverness Lodge.

St George's and Corner Stone Lodge No. 5

St George's Lodge No. 5 (Const. 1756) was united in 1843 with Corner Stone Lodge No. 37 (Const. 1730). The name St George's and Corner Stone was adopted and the number remained 5.

Lodge of Fortitude and Old Cumberland No. 12

Lodge of Fortitude No. 12 (T.I., but Const. 1723) united in 1818 with Old Cumberland Lodge No. 119 (Const. 1753); the number was retained and the name changed to Lodge of Fortitude and Old Cumberland.

Royal Alpha Lodge No. 16

In 1800 Ionic Lodge No. 8 (Const. 1722) united with Lodge of Prudence and Peter No. 69. (Ionic was originally Lodge of Prudence No. 69 (Const. 1740); Prudence united in 1793 with St Peter's Lodge No. 327 (Const. 1776), its name being changed to United Lodge of Ionic and Prudence). In 1823 the lodge was united with Alpha Lodge No. 76 (Const. 1730). (This lodge had previously been named Well Disposed Lodge.) A year later (1824) another amalgamation took place, this time with Royal Lodge No. 210 (Const. 1764) and from that date the name Royal Alpha was adopted.

Classification of names.

A glance at the list of lodges in the *Masonic Year Book*, reflected to a limited degree in the lists in the following pages, indicate what might be termed a 'fashion' in the choice of names adopted for lodges. In the early years they were related to the place in which the lodge held its meeting, often an inn; later names reflecting the virtues characteristic of a good freemason came to be used: Amity; Benevolence; Concord; Fellowship; Good . . ., and Loyalty are good examples.

Events such as those connected with the Royal family came to be used; Jubilee and Silver Jubilee are obvious examples. Similarly the appointment of a well-known dignitary gave rise to a number of lodges using his name; a good example here is Zetland following the appointment of the first Earl of Zetland as Deputy Grand Master; many lodges were named after him and, later, the second Earl followed by the first, second and third Marquesses of Zetland as they took up their masonic appointments.

Another feature which resulted in similar names being used was the formation of new lodges in a particular sphere of activity or occupation. Examples are Old (School) lodges; University lodges; Hospital Lodges; Borough Council Lodges and Installed Masters Lodges.

By and large, the names of lodges can be classified under specific headings, whether or not they adopted the name before or after 1813. Some examples are given below; the list is not meant to be exhaustive, many other headings could have been given.

In the main the lists have been classified on a 'family' basis, where the names of the lodges have a common feature with the description at the head of the list. For example, lodges bearing the name of a saint have been listed under the heading 'SAINTS'; those bearing the name of royalty or a peer of the realm have been listed under the heading 'ROYALTY AND PEERS OF THE REALM', etc.

The classification of lodges in other lists is by virtue of a linkage between the name at the head of the list and the lodge listed; the headings have been chosen somewhat arbitrarily. The lists are in alphabetical order.

ARCHITECTURAL TERMS
ASTRONOMY
BIBLICAL ASSOCIATIONS
BOROUGH COUNCILS
CLASSICAL NAMES
EMPIRE, DOMINIONS AND FOREIGN COUNTRIES
H.M. FORCES
'JEWISH'
LATIN PHRASES
LITERARY
LIVERY COMPANIES AND GUILDS
MASONIC EMBLEMS
MEETING PLACES
MUSICAL
NATURE (BIRDS, PLANTS, TREES ETC.)
PERSONAGES – MASONIC AND NON-MASONIC
PLACE NAMES, INCLUDING SAXON AND ROMAN CONNECTIONS
PROFESSIONAL AND OCCUPATIONAL
- Accountants
- Architects and surveyors
- Aviation
- Bakers
- Banks
- Civil Servants
- Ecclesiastical
- Engineering
- Industrial
- Insurance
- Legal
- Medical
- Pottery
- Printing and Publishing
- Public Services and Works
- Railways

Secretaries
Trade and Commerce
Undertakers
RECREATIONAL
RESEARCH AND MASONIC EDUCATION
RIVERS
ROYALTY AND PEERS OF THE REALM
SAINTS
SCHOOLS AND UNIVERSITIES
SCOUT AND YOUTH MOVEMENTS
SOCIETIES AND INSTITUTIONS
TEMPERANCE LODGES
THEATRICAL
THEOLOGICAL
VIRTUES

In some cases the lodge name can be classified under more than one heading, as the following examples show.
In Arduis Fidelis; could be in the Latin Phrases list or H.M. Forces list because the lodge, formed for members of the Royal Army Medical Corps, adopted that name, it being their motto.
St Cecilia; saints or music (St Cecilia is the patroness of music and musicians).
Neptune; could be included in the Meeting Places list (the name of an inn); classical name list (Neptune was the god of the sea, the chief of the water deities) or the list headed Astronomy, as one of the planets.
Marquis of Granby; peer of the realm or name of inn.

It is not suggested that lodges with the same name took the name from the same source. For example, Neptune Lodge No. 22 took its name from one of its meeting places, the Neptune Inn in Neptune Street. Other 'Neptune' lodges (Nos. 1264; 2908; 5150 and 8465) would probably have a different reason for choosing the name.

All the lodges shown in the lists which follow come under the jurisdiction of the United Grand Lodge of England; they are listed in numerical order, reading across the page, where appropriate.

ARCHITECTURAL TERMS

No.	NAME	Const	*Remarks*
14	TUSCAN	1722	One of the five classical orders of architecture
81	DORIC	1812	One of the five classical orders of architecture
227	IONIC	1810	One of the five classical orders of architecture
363	KEYSTONE	1820	Middle stone in an arch or an architectural vault
1208	CORINTHIAN	1867	One of the five classical orders of architecture
2038	PORTCULLIS	1884	Gate built to rise and fall in vertical grooves
2200	PANTILES	1887	Tiles of curved S-shaped section
2222	DORMER	1887	Window placed vertically in sloping plane of roof
4076	COMPOSITE	1920	One of the five classical orders of architecture
4719	TRACERY	1925	Intersecting network in upper part of window or used decoratively in blank arches
4742	ABACUS	1925	Flat slab on top of a capital
4901	ENTABLATURE	1927	In classical architecture the whole of the horizontal members above a column, that is the architrave, frieze and the cornice
4941	CORNER-STONE	1927	A stone forming the quoin or salient angle of a wall
4944	CLOISTERS	1927	Enclosed places; a covered walk or arcade connected with a building
5154	ASHLAR	1929	Masonry of large blocks wrought to even faces and square edges
5284	COLUMN	1931	A cylindrical body erected vertically as a support for some part of a building
5507	CAMPANILE	1934	Isolated bell tower
6481	QUOIN STONE	1947	Dressed stone at angle of building
7027	PORCHWAY	1950	Entrance of a building
7220	COLONNADE	1952	Range of columns
7874	CATENARIAN	1962	A form of arch

PART 2: NAMES

No.	Name	Const	Remarks
8065	Architrave	1965	Lowest part of the three main parts of the entablature
8487	Cope-Stone	1972	A stone used in the covering of a vault.

ASTRONOMY

No.	Name	Const	Remarks
1275	Star	1869	A celestial body seen as a point of light
1719	Evening Star	1877	Name occasionally given to the planet Venus
2615	Zodiac	1896	Belt of heavens outside which sun and moon and major planets do not pass; divided into twelve areas each named after a constellation
2918	Southern Cross	1902	Four bright stars roughly in the shape of a cross, seen within the Southern hemisphere
3113	Aquarius	1905	The Water-carrier; a constellation and the eleventh sign of the zodiac
3927	North Star	1919	The pole star; in the constellation known as Ursa Minor
3981	Taurus	1919	The Bull; a constellation including Pleiades and Hyades; the second sign of the zodiac
4045	Saturnian	1920	'Saturnian' relates to the major planet Saturn; the name may have been adopted because the lodge meets on Saturdays, i.e. Saturn's day
4581	Mercury	1923	The planet nearest the sun; the smallest planet of the solar system after Pluto
5086	Aries	1928	The Ram; a constellation and the first sign of the zodiac
5142	Libra	1929	The Scales; a constellation and the seventh sign of the zodiac
5395	Constellation	1932	Fixed stars seeming to form a group
5768	Aurora	1939	Luminous electrical radiation from northern or southern magnetic pole (Aurora is also the name of the Greek goddess of the dawn).
6040	Sun	1943	Heavenly body around which earth travels, receiving light and warmth
6485	Uranus	1947	The seventh of the major planets: farthest from the earth, except Neptune; discovered in 1781 by Sir William Herschel
7342	Jupiter	1954	The largest of the planets
8142	Planet	1966	Heavenly body revolving round the sun
8756	Orion	1976	A conspicuous constellation containing many bright stars; so called after a giant hunter of Boeotia, changed after his death into a constellation
9190	Comet	1986	Heavenly body with apparently starlike nucleus and tail of light describing ellipse about the sun
9258	Sirius	1987	Known as the dog-star, a brilliant white star in the constellation Canis Major, the brightest star in the skies

BIBLICAL ASSOCIATIONS

No.	Name	Const	Remarks
11	Enoch	1754	Son of Jared and father of Methuselah; he 'walked with God' (*Gen.* 5; 22)
34	Mount Moriah	1754	The hill on which Solomon's Temple was built (2 *Chron.* 3; 1)
49	Gihon	1810	The second of the rivers that flowed out of Eden (*Gen.* 2; 13); also a place near Jerusalem where Solomon was annointed and proclaimed king (1 *Kings* 1; 35)

No.	NAME	Const	*Remarks*
73	MOUNT LEBANON	1760	Area from which cedar trees were sent to Solomon to build the Temple (1 *Kings* 5; 6)
121	MOUNT SINAI	1813	Mountain on which Moses was given Commandments by God (*Lev.*, 23)
188	JOPPA	1789	A major sea-port north-west of Jerusalem (the modern Jaffa) (2 *Chron.* 2; 16)
197	JERUSALEM	1771	The city in which Solomon's Temple was built
201	JORDAN	1810	The great river of the Holy Land
385	MOUNT OLIVE	1826	Mountain overlooking Jerusalem on the east
1668	SAMSON	1877	A Danite judge of Israel renowned for his strength (*Judges*)
1798	ZION	1878	The south-west hill of Jerusalem, the older and higher part of the city; often called the city of David
2416	HIRAM	1891	A king of Tyre who lived on friendly terms with kings David and Solomon; he supplied cedar trees for the building of the temple
3271	ANTIOCH	1907	City in which Paul and Barnabas preached and in which Christianity first flourished (*Acts of the Apostles*)
4136	MORNING STAR	1920	Reference to *Rev.* 22; 16 'I am . . . the bright and morning star.'
5595	GOLIATH	1935	Renowned champion of the Philistines; slain by the boy David (1 *Sam.*, 17 and 23)
5719	KING DAVID	1938	King of Judah, father of Solomon (*Sam., Kings and Chron.*)
7076	REVELATION	1951	Last book of New Testament, commonly called the Apocalypse; appears to present the prophetic history of the Church until the end of the world
9209	GENESIS	1986	First book of the Old Testament.

BOROUGH COUNCILS

No.	NAME	Const	*No.*	NAME	Const
2332	BOROUGH OF GREENWICH	1889	2861	BOROUGH OF ISLINGTON	1901
2884	BOROUGH OF STEPNEY	1901	2896	BOROUGH OF BETHNAL GREEN	1902
2944	BOROUGH OF HACKNEY	1902	2979	WANDSWORTH BOROUGH COUNCIL	1903
3064	BOROUGH OF SHOREDITCH	1904	3303	BOROUGH OF CAMBERWELL	1908
3316	BOROUGH OF ST PANCRAS	1908	3901	BOROUGH OF FINSBURY	1918
4368	BOROUGH OF ACTON	1921	6089	BOROUGH OF FINCHLEY	1945
6610	BOROUGH OF WOOLWICH	1948	8627	BOROUGH OF NEWHAM	1974

CLASSICAL NAMES

No.	NAME	Const	*Remarks*
22	NEPTUNE	1757	Roman name for chief of water deities
173	PHOENIX	1785	Mythical bird; consumes itself by fire every five hundred years and rises again from its ashes
301	APOLLO	1794	A great divinity of the Greeks; son of Zeus
373	SOCRATES	1823	Celebrated Athenian philosopher
546	ETRUSCAN	1847	Native of Tuscany
710	PLEIADES	1857	The daughters of Atlas; pursued by Boeotia but escaped when turned into doves and placed among the stars

No.	NAME	Const	*Remarks*
1920	EURYDICE	1881	Wife of Orpheus; died following serpent's bite and went to Hades; won back by the charms of the lyre of Orpheus and permitted to return to earth provided Orpheus did not look around to see her; in later versions of the myth he did look back, and saw her retreat into the infernal regions
1942	MINERVA	1881	Identified by the Romans with the Greek goddess of wisdom, Athena
2205	PEGASUS	1887	Winged horse which sprang from the body of Medusa when her head was struck off by Perseus. Pegasus was caught and trained by Bellerophon with the aid of Athena. Mounted on Pegasus, Bellerophon overcame the Chimera but when he attempted to fly to heaven, Pegasus threw him. Pegasus, however, continued his flight to heaven, where he dwelt among the stars
2243	ARGONAUTS	1888	The sailors of the Argo who, led by Jason, won the golden fleece
2410	ÆSCULAPIUS	1891	Latinized form of Asclepius, the Greek god of healing and medical art
2879	CERES	1901	Identified by the Romans with the Greek divinity Demeter, protectress of agriculture and all the fruits of the earth; daughter of Cronus and Rhea, sister of Zeus and mother of Persephone
3155	HORUS	1906	Son of Osiris and Isis, the Egyptian god of the sun
3226	PHILAMMON	1907	A mythical poet and musician, said to have been the son of Apollo
3843	DAEDALUS	1917	A mythical personage under whose name (which signifies 'cunning craftsman') the Greek writers personified the earliest development of the arts of sculpture and architecture
3933	HYPERION	1919	A Titan, son of Uranus (Heaven) and Ge (Earth), and father of Helios (the sun), Selene (the moon) and Eos (the dawn)
4047	AURORA	1920	The goddess of dawn; at the close of every night she rose from the couch of her spouse Tithonus, and in a chariot drawn by swift horses ascended to heaven to announce the coming light of the sun
4262	MERCURIUS	1921	Otherwise Mercury, the Roman divinity of commerce and gain, identified by the Romans with the Greek Hermes
4739	GOLDEN FLEECE	1925	Fleece of gold guarded at Colchis by a sleepless dragon until won by Jason
4805	HERCULES	1925	The most celebrated of all the heroes of antiquity. According to Homer he was the son of Zeus by Alcmene, the wife of Amphitryon, of Thebes in Boeotia. He was ordered to serve Eurystheus for a time during which he had twelve labours to perform, as follows: To slay the Nemean lion; to conquer the hydra-headed Lernaean monster; to capture the Arcadian stag or hind of Ceryneia; to destroy the Erymanthian boar; to clean in one day the stables of Augeas; to destroy the Stymphalian birds; to capture the Cretan bull; to capture the mares of the Thracian Diomedes; to sieze the girdle of Hippolyta, the queen of the Amazons; to capture the oxen of Geryones in Erythya; to fetch the golden apples of the Hesperides and to bring Cerebus from the lower world; all were carried out successfully. Hercules was killed by a shirt or tunic poisoned with the blood of the centaur Nessus, whom he had previously slain
4966	PANDORA	1927	Called Pandora, or All-gifted, because each of the gods had given her some power by which she was to work the ruin of man. She brought with her from heaven a box containing every human ill, upon opening which they all escaped and spread over the earth. Hope alone remaining
4977	PROMETHEUS	1927	A great benefactor of men; he stole fire from heaven in a hollow tube, and taught mortals all useful arts. Zeus punished him for the theft of fire by chaining him to a rock and sending an eagle to devour his liver by day, which grew again each night. He was eventually released by Hercules

No.	NAME	Const	*Remarks*
5349	ATHENE	1932	A great divinity of Greece; as her father, Zeus, was the most powerful, and her mother, Metis, the wisest among the gods so Athena was a combination of the two, a goddess in whom power and wisdom were harmoniously blended. According to another version of the myth, she was born without mother, springing fully armed from the head of Zeus
5418	ZEUS	1933	Identified with Jupiter by the Romans; the greatest of the Olympian gods. According to the Homeric account he dwelt on Mount Olympus, which was believed to penetrate with its lofty summit into heaven itself
5532	HERMES	1935	Called Mercurius by the Romans; see Lodge No. 4262
5780	OSIRIS	1939	A great Egyptian divinity, husband of Isis; was once king of Egypt who reclaimed his subjects from a barbarous life by teaching them agriculture and enacting wise laws
6355	THEMIS	1946	Daughter of Uranus and Ge; mother of Zeus
7342	JUPITER	1954	Identified by Romans with Greek god Zeus; see Lodge No. 5418
7454	TERPSICHORE	1956	One of the nine Muses; she presided over the choral song and dancing
7781	ISIS	1961	One of the chief Egyptian divinities, wife of Osiris and mother of Horus. She was originally the goddess of the earth, and afterwards of the moon
9283	ORPHEUS	1988	A mythical personage, regarded by the Greeks as the most celebrated of the poets who lived before the time of Homer. Presented with the lyre by Apollo, and instructed by the Muses in its use, he enchanted with its music not only the wild beasts, but the trees and rocks upon Olympus. See Lodge No. 1920 for his wife Eurydyce

EMPIRE, DOMINIONS AND FOREIGN COUNTRIES

Many lodges bear names that have an association with the old British Empire, the Dominions or foreign countries. The members of these lodges may have served or lived for some time in the country or area with which the name of their lodge is associated.

The names of such lodges immediately conjure up in the minds of some brethren a feeling of nostalgia, particularly for those who have, or have had, a happy association with the place concerned.

Most of these lodges act as a 'host' to brethren from overseas who, when visiting London, want to attend an English Lodge. If the brother concerned makes known to the Enquiry Office at Freemasons' Hall, London, the area from which he comes, he may well be invited to attend a meeting of the lodge having a strong association with that particular part of the world. In addition to the ever-ready welcome to a visitor, he will know that he is amongst brethren who are familiar with his home territory.

Examples of some of these lodges, showing the country with which they are associated, are:

No.	NAME	Const.	Associated with
238	PILGRIM	1779	Germany; lodge works in German
534	POLISH NATIONAL	1846	Poland
2060	LA FRANCE	1884	France; lodge works in French
2108	EMPIRE	1885	Colonies
2191	ANGLO-AMERICAN	1886	America
2319	SCOTS	1889	Scotland
2397	COLUMBIA	1891	America
2687	LODGE ITALIA	1897	Italy; lodge works in Italian
2796	LODGE L'ENTENTE CORDIALE	1899	France
2867	LONDON WELSH	1901	Wales
2895	LODGE OF ERIN	1902	Ireland
2972	ULSTER	1903	Ulster
3175	ANGLO-COLONIAL	1906	Colonial
3368	AMERICA	1909	America

No.	NAME	Const.	Associated with
3444	STAR OF INDIA	1910	India
3527	CANADA	1911	Canada
3556	ROYAL COLONIAL INSTITUTE	1911	Colonial
3623	ANGLO-SOUTH AMERICAN	1912	Brazil
3861	MOTHERLAND	1918	Colonial
3868	UNITED EMPIRE	1918	Colonial
4030	OVER SEAS	1919	Colonial
4664	CARMARTHENSHIRE	1924	Wales
4728	DEWI SANT	1925	Wales
4826	CARIBBEAN	1926	British Guiana, West Indies and British Honduras
4886	ANGLO-OVERSEAS	1926	Colonial
4894	HELVETICA	1926	Switzerland, where the Addresses on Installation nights are given in German, French or Italian
5175	NEW ZEALAND	1930	New Zealand
5213	LODGE MALAYA	1930	Malaya
5340	CITY OF CALIPHS	1932	Iraq
5485	LONDON WEST AFRICA	1934	West Africa
5625	LODGE OF REUNION AND FELLOWSHIP	1936	France
5862	ANGLO-DUTCH	1942	Netherlands
6742	SOUTH AFRICA	1948	South Africa
6783	MELITA	1948	Malta
8595	KYPROS	1974	Cyprus
9284	NKOKONJERU	1988	Nigeria

H.M. FORCES

In his *Masonic Records 1717–1894* Lane records a handful of naval lodges that in the early days of Freemasonry met aboard H.M. ships and over 200 military lodges. Of the latter, over half the number were in the Infantry, the remainder being split between the Cavalry, the Artillery, the Royal Marines, the Militia and the Volunteer Forces. Very few of these military lodges are still active.

As a generalization these lodges were identified by a number and, for the naval lodges, the name of the ship on which the lodge meetings were held; for the military lodges, the regiment or corps to which the lodge members belonged.

The list below shows a selection of present-day lodges catering for H.M. Forces; the name of the lodge indicates the particular unit from which the lodge got its original members. Some of these lodges will now accept candidates from other sources.

No.	NAME	Const	No.	NAME	Const
822	VICTORIA RIFLES	1860	858	SOUTH MIDDLESEX	1861
1593	ROYAL NAVAL COLLEGE AND UNITED SERVICE	1875	1962	LONDON RIFLE BRIDGE	1882
2310	LONDON SCOTTISH RIFLES'	1889	2312	LONDON IRISH RIFLES'	1889
2362	BLOOMSBURY RIFLES'	1890	2484	SECOND MIDDLESEX ARTILLERY	1893
2578	NATIONAL ARTILLERY	1895	2599	ROYAL ENGINEERS	1896
2612	NAVY	1896	2614	HOUSEHOLD BRIGADE	1896
2621	MILITARY	1896	2738	ARMY AND NAVY	1898
2807	PADDINGTON RIFLES	1900	2942	THIRD MIDDLESEX ARTILLERY	1902
3013	MIDDLESEX IMPERIAL YEOMANRY	1904	3192	HERTFORDSHIRE IMPERIAL YEOMANRY	1906

No.	NAME	Const	*No.*	NAME	Const
3386	KING'S COLONIALS	1909	3624	KENSINGTON BATTALION	1912
3757	CITY OF LONDON NATIONAL GUARD	1915	3790	ROYAL NAVAL ANTI-AIRCRAFT	1917
3817	UNITED ARTS RIFLES	1917	3824	IMPERIAL CADET	1917
3923	ROYAL NAVAL VOLUNTEER RESERVE	1919	4323	CONNAUGHT ARMY AND NAVY	1921
5606	CITY OF LONDON RIFLES	1936	7335	ROYAL AIR FORCE	1954

Other names may not be readily identifiable as coming within this category; some are shown below with an occasional explanatory note.

No.	NAME	Unit of H.M. Forces	Const
497	SOCIAL FRIENDSHIP	Royal Irish Fusiliers	1844
569	FITZROY	Honourable Artillery Company	1844
1718	CENTURION	Territorial Officers	1849
1789	UBIQUE	Royal Artillery (Regulars) Everywhere; motto of Royal Artillery	1877
2555	ENGLAND'S CENTRE	Military personnel at Weedon, Northants, said to be the heart of England	1895
2736	NIL SINE LABORE	Royal Army Service Corps Nothing without labour; motto of Royal Corps of Transport	1898
2740	COMRADES	Non-commissioned officers, Guards Regiments	1899
2851	ROSEMARY	Artists' Rifles	1901
3133	ROYAL CROWN	Regulars, Army, Navy and Air Force	1905
3432	IN ARDUIS FIDELIS	Royal Army Medical Corps Faithful in misfortune; motto of Royal Army Medical Corps	1910
3806	MAGUNCOR	Machine Gun Corps Name derived from the telegraphic address; MA[chine] GUN COR[ps].	1917
3808	AD ASTRA	Inspection Department, R.A.F.	1917
3970	GASTVRIJHEID	Naval Brigade interned in Holland 1914–18	1919
4665	AMICI	Royal Army Medical Corps	1924
5637	PEGASUS	Royal Air Force Name associated with flight and the legend of Pegasus, the winged horse of Greek mythology	1936
8003	SUA TELA TONANTI	Royal Army Ordnance Corps Thundering forth his weapons; motto of Royal Army Ordnance Corps	1964
8295	ST ELIGIUS	Royal Electrical & Mechanical Engineers	1969
8925	CERTA CITO	Royal Signals Swift and Sure; motto of Royal Signals	1979

'JEWISH' LODGES

Reference is sometimes made to 'Jewish' lodges; this is a misnomer. What is meant is a lodge in which most, if not all, of the members are of the Jewish faith. This does not mean that non-Jewish brethren are unable to join; that would be quite wrong and not allowed by Grand Lodge. The reason for such lodges is to cater for the needs of the more orthodox members of the Jewish fraternity. Their meetings are so arranged as to avoid Friday evenings,

Saturdays and various Holy Days, and the meals served at their after-proceedings comply with their dietary laws. The names of such lodges are quite varied, as the following list shows.

No.	NAME	Const	*Remarks*
188	LODGE OF JOPPA	1789	
205	LODGE OF ISRAEL	1793	
1017	MONTEFIORE	1864	Named after the Jewish philanthropist, Sir Moses Montefiore,
1668	SAMSON	1877	
2265	BARNATO	1888	Named to commemorate the Barnato diamond mine, Kimberley, South Africa. Lodge formed for freemasons returning to London from mining prospecting in South Africa
5250	CAMPERDOWN	1931	Name taken from Camperdown House, Headquarters of the Jewish Lads' Brigade

LATIN PHRASES

Note: The English translation has been taken from *Elvin's Mottoes Revised* (Heraldry Today); *Registered Badges* (Maj. J.F. Edwards, *MBE FRHist Soc*,); *Debrett's Peerage*, or has kindly been given by the secretary of the appropriate lodge or by W.Bro, Graham Redman, PJGD, Assistant Grand Secretary.

No.	NAME	English translation	*Const*
3015	SEMPER PARATUS	Ever ready	1804
3040	SEMPER VIGILANS	Ever watchful	1904
3091	LODGE SEMPER EADEM	Ever the same	1905
3299	SEMPER FIDELIS	Ever faithful	1907
3409	FACTA NON VERBA	Deeds not words	1909
3562	HONOR DEO	Honour be to God	1911
3609	PER MARE PER TERRAM	By sea and land	1912
3856	LUX IN TENEBRIS	Light in darkness	1918
3908	PAX-HUMANA	Peace among men	1918
3916	PAX MAGNA	Great Peace	1919
3951	IN DEO FIDEMUS	In God shall we trust	1919
4587	FESTINA LENTE	Hasten slowly	1924
4658	FILIA UNITATIS	Daughter of unity	1924
4821	LAUS DEO	Praise be to God	1925
5024	LAPIS MAGNES	Lodestone (or magnet) [Literally magnetic rock]	1928
5151	DOMUS DEI	House of God	1929
5352	AMOR LABORIS	Love of labour	1932
5517	NISI DOMINUS	Except the Lord	1934
5527	VIA PONTIS	Way of the bridge	1935
5622	SEMPER SURSUM	Always upwards	1936
5641	MAGNUM OPUS	Great work	1936
6144	FIAT LUX	Let there be light	1945
6200	PAX-VERA	True peace	1945
6613	MAGNUM BONUM	Great good	1948
6751	ABSIT INVIDIA	Let envy be absent	1948
7483	MELIORA SEQUAMUR	Let us follow better things	1956
7521	IN VERITATE	In truth	1957
7682	SUMMA PETENS	Seeking the heights	1959
7747	ANCORA RUBRA	Red anchor	1960
8003	SUA TELA TONANTI	Thundering forth his weapons	1964
8228	VIA LUCIS	The way of light	1968
8473	VIA MEDIA	The middle way	1972

SERENDIPITY

No.	NAME	English translation	*Const*
8602	PER CAELUM	Through the sky	1974
8744	FONS VITAE	Fount of life	1976
8848	FIDELES AMICI	Faithful friends	1978
9083	CUSTODES PACIS	Guardians of peace	1983
9113	SALVUS SECURUS	Safe and Secure	1983
9264	REGIS AURIGAE	Charioteers of the king	1987
9429	PORTA SAPIENTIAE	Gateway of Wisdom	1991
9430	CUSTODES COPIAE LODGE OF PROVINCIAL GRAND STEWARDS	Guardians of Plenty	1991

LITERARY ORIGIN

No.	NAME	Const	*Remarks*
25	ROBERT BURNS	1810	1759–95, Scotland's national poet
99	SHAKESPEAR	1757	(William) 1564–1616, England's greatest dramatist and poet
1060	MARMION	1865	Title of book published in 1808 by the Scottish novelist Sir Walter Scott, 1771–1832
1144	MILTON	1867	(John) 1608–74, English Puritan poet
1540	CHAUCER	1875	(Geoffrey) 1340?–1400, Famous English poet
1578	MERLIN	1875	In the Arthurian legends, a magician and bard who aided and supported King Arthur and made the Round Table
1750	COLERIDGE	1878	(Samuel Taylor) 1772–1834, English romantic poet
2363	MINNEHAHA	1890	Wife of Hiawatha, the principal character in Longfellow's *The Song of Hiawatha*, published in 1855
2415	TRISTRAM	1891	The hero of various stories based on Arthurian legends; examples are *Tristram and Isolde* (Sir Thomas Malory, d. 1471); *Tristram and Iseult* (Matthew Arnold, 1822–88 and *Tristram of Lyonesse* (Algernon Charles Swinburne, 1837–1909.
2466	CHEERYBLES	1893	The brothers Ned and Charles, characters in Charles Dickens' novel *Nicholas Nickleby* published monthly, 1837.
2467	PICKWICK	1893	Character in Charles Dickens's novel *Pickwick Papers*
2757	CHARLES DICKENS	1899	1812–70, Popular English novelist.
2959	EXCALIBUR	1903	Sword given to King Arthur by the Lady of the Lake. Arthurian legend
3707	DANTE	1913	(Alighieri) 1265–1321 Italian poet
4014	BYRON	1919	(Lord) 1788–1824. English romantic poet
4947	TENNYSON	1927	(Alfred, Lord) 1809–92. English poet. Poet Laureate from 1850
5518	JOHN EVELYN	1934	1620–76. Writer; remembered principally for his *Diary* first published in 1818
5642	ANDREW MARVELL	1936	1621–78. English poet and writer of Parliamentary sympathies
5973	JOHN BUNYAN	1944	1628–88, English Nonconformist preacher; writer of pious poems; remembered principally for his *Pilgrim's Progress* written whilst in Bedford Gaol
6650	SOUTHEY	1948	(Robert) 1774–1843. English poet, essayist and historian
7647	AVALON	1959	In the Arthurian legends, one of the Celtic 'Isles of the Blest' to which Arthur is carried after his death
8330	SAMUEL PEPYS	1979	1633–1703. English diarist, secretary of Admiralty 1673–9 and 1684–8.
8589	BARNABY RUDGE	1974	Novel published by Charles Dickens in 1841

LIVERY COMPANIES AND GUILDS

The great majority of Liveries engage in charitable and educational activities; many take an interest in the industry from which they sprang, or in a modern successor industry; they offer prizes, research fellowships and scholarships in appropriate educational establishments. The wealthier Companies have founded and financed university departments or built complete colleges. Many combined to set up the City and Guilds of London Institute. A very wide range of charities is afforded powerful help, each Company making its own choice.

Some of these Companies have set up their own masonic lodges, details of which are now given. The date of the constitution of the lodge is shown after its name; this is followed by the name of the Livery Company and (in parenthesis) its order of precedence according to the City authorities;; then follows the year showing the year the first Charter was granted, together with other remarks where appropriate.

No.	NAME	Const	*Remarks*
2693	PELLIPAR	1897	Skinners'. (7 and 6) 1327. The Company controlled the English fur trade; following a dispute in 1484 regarding precedence, it was decreed that the Merchant Taylors company was to be sixth and the Skinners seventh, the places to change each subsequent year. This is probably the origin of the phrase 'at sixes and sevens'. The lodge name is derived from a Latin word meaning 'skin' or 'hide'.
2730	CUTLERS'	1898	Cutlers'. (18) 1416. An original craft early in the thirteenth century; they were responsible for the making of swords and surgical instruments.
3743	ST CATHERINE'S	1914	Turner's. (51) 1604. Received Ordinances in 1478; responsible for controlling those who made platters, cups, ale measures, furniture and machine tools. Lodge named after patron saint of turners.
3839	FELTMAKERS	1917	Feltmakers'. (63) 1667. Company incorporated in 1604; formed to protect trade from foreign hatters and the like.
3981	TAURUS	1919	Butchers'. (24) 1605. General Ordinances issued much earlier; company had control of killing and selling of meat, including right to slaughter cattle in the City of London. Name of lodge taken from Latin word for bull, the animal which provides much meat for the butcher's trade.
4041	CORIUM	1919	Leathersellers'. (15) 1444. Received Ordinances for dyeing leather in 1372; responsible for regulating craft of tanners. Name of lodge derived from a Latin word meaning skin or hide of an animal.
4256	PAYNTERS STAINERS	1921	Painters Stainers'. (28) 1581 Fraternity of Stainers, or painters on cloth, dates from 1268; that of Painters on wood from 1283; two bodies joined in 1502. Lodge uses old spelling of name.
4343	NEEDLEMAKERS	1921	Needlemakers'. (65) 1656. Charter signed by Oliver Cromwell. Company disappeared in 1870, but revived four years later.
4821	LAUS DEO	1925	Bakers'. (19) 1486. Control over the craft was exercised by Assize of Bread until the end of the eighteenth century; although the monopoly of the white and brown bakers was protected, their output was subject to strong scrutiny. In 1252 they were forbidden to put the cross or *Agnus Dei* on bread though today the cross is regularly shown on hot cross buns. The name of the lodge comes from the first two words of the motto used by the Worshipful Company of Bakers ('Praise God for all'), the founders preferring Latin rather than English.
5107	LODGE OF ST JULIAN	1929	Innholders'. (32) 1515. Formed for trade protection. The company's plate includes a collection of Julian spoons from 1539. The lodge takes its name from the patron saint of innkeepers.
5639	BASKETMAKERS	1936	Basketmakers'. (52) 1937. Constituted a Court of Aldermen in 1569 and granted a livery in 1825. Regulates and controls basketmaking in the City of London

No.	NAME	Const	*Remarks*
5646	PAVIORS	1936	Paviors'. (56) 1672. Formed to protect trade from infiltration of foreigners; responsible for removing scavenging pigs in the City of London.
6123	LODGE OF LOVE AND FRIENDSHIP	1945	Gold and Silver Wyredrawers'. (74) 1623. Warrant withdrawn but re-incorporated by 1693 Charter. Trade connected with the drawing of fine gold-coated silver thread for use in brocades and later in uniforms.
6305	FARRIERS	1946	Farriers'. (55) 1674. 'Preserving of horses by preventing their destruction by bad shoeing' and 'Increasing the number of skilful and expert farriers.'
6876	POULTERS	1949	Poulters'. (34) (? 1504). Charter from 1665. Controlled the sale of rabbits, pigeons, game, poultry and swans in the City of London.
7175	BLACKSMITHS	1952	Blacksmiths'. (40) 1571. Existed in 1494; were official tooth-drawers.
7390	PLAISTERERS	1955	Plaisterers'. (46) Incorporated 1501.
8602	PER CAELUM	1974	Air Pilots & Navigators Guilds'. (81) 1956 Responsible for the issue of certificates of competence to flyers.
8731	LODGE OF PAUL'S WHARF.	1976	Carmen. (77) Fraternity formed 1516; formed to give Carmen a monopoly of plying for hire in the City in return for moving the royal household whenever required, thus deterring the king from helping himself.
8830	TERGERE	1978	Environmental Cleaners'. (97) 1986 The name comes from the Latin word meaning 'to clean'.

MASONIC EMBLEMS

No.	NAME	Const	*No.*	NAME	Const
872	LEWIS	1861	1178	PERFECT ASHLAR	1867
1336	SQUARE AND COMPASS	1870	4923	THREE PILLARS	1927
5066	LODGE OF THREE LIGHTS	1928	6617	STONE SQUARER	1948
6618	SQUARE AND LEVEL	1948	9030	SQUARE	1982

MEETING PLACES

As already mentioned many early lodges met in inns and taverns and lodges quite often adopted the name of the meeting place as the name of the lodge; some examples have been shown in the list on page 11. Very few lodges are now named in this fashion.

MUSICAL

No.	NAME	Comment	Const
1636	ST CECILIA	Regarded as patron saint of music since sixth century; tradition speaks of her singing to God 'in her heart' while instruments were making music at her wedding.	1863

No.	Name	Comment	Const
1929	Mozart	(Wolfgang Amadeus) 1756–91. Composer of many works, including the music for such operas as *The Magic Flute*; *Don Giovanni*; *Cosi fan Tutte* and *The Marriage of Figaro*.	1881
2156	Arthur Sullivan	(Sir) 1842–1900. Grand Organist, 1887; wrote orchestral music, songs, anthems, hymn tunes; collaborated with W.S. Gilbert (also a member of the Craft in a Scottish lodge) in writing light operas such as *The Mikado, The Gondoliers, Trial by Jury, The Pirates of Penzance, Princess Ida* and many others.	1886
2182	Sterndale Bennett	(Sir William) 1816–75. Professor of Music Cambridge 1856; Principal, Royal Academy of Music 1866; conductor of the Philharmonic Society of London.	1886
2454	Guildhall School of Music		1892
2661	Mendelssohn	(Felix) 1809–47. Composer of oratorios and concert overtures etc.	1897
2881	Incorporated Society of Musicians	A professional society formed in 1882, fell into desuetude; reconstituted 1928.	1901
3028	Orchestral		1904
3213	City of London St Olave's	St Olave's Musical Association.	1907
3688	Music		1913
4236	Purcell	(Henry) 1658(9)–95. A celebrated 'Master of the science of Musick'; organist; composer of church music, royal odes and theatre music.	1926
5039	Madrigal	A part-song for several voices.	1928
8279	Pro Arte	A well-known orchestra.	1969
9254	Elgar	(Sir Edward). 1857–1934. English composer of oratorios such as the setting of Cardinal Newman's *The Dream of Gerontius* and orchestral music.	1987

NATURE (TREES, BIRDS, PLANTS, ETC.)

No.	Name	Const	*Remarks*
190	Oak	1789	A common forest tree with hard wood; consecrated to the god of thunder because oaks are said to be more likely to be struck by lightning than other trees.
312	Lion	1797	Large member of cat family, noted for its strength; common symbolic beast in religious and secular art, with many attributions; frequently used in heraldry where it is generally known as a leopard.
731	Arboretum	1857	A tree garden (Lodge warrant dated 25 December, 1857!)
1212	Elms	1868	Large trees, especially in England, though many were killed in recent years following invasion of Dutch Elm disease.
1309	Acacia	1870	Genus of shrub or trees found in warm climates; used for centuries as a symbol for immortality and resurrection.
1416	Falcon	1872	Small diurnal bird of prey; can be trained to pursuit of other birds or game.
1441	Ivy	1873	Climbing evergreen shrub; dedicated to Bacchus because it is supposed to prevent drunkenness; in Christian art it is a symbol of everlasting life.

No.	NAME	Const	*Remarks*
1622	ROSE	1876	A beautiful flower, often scented; grown on a prickly bush or shrub; frequently used in art and, in a stylized form, in heraldry; sacred to Venus; associated with many saints, a red rose symbolizing martyrdom and a white rose symbolizing purity. The rose is also a symbol of secrecy and silence.
2545	IRIS	1894	Genus of plants with tubers or bulbs; sword-shaped leaves and lovely flower; very often used in art instead of the lily as the flower of the Virgin; the common iris is called 'sword-lily' in German.
2660	CRANE	1897	Large wading bird with very long legs, neck and bill; in secular allegory it represents Vigilance; in art it stands on one foot, the other is raised holding a stone in its claw. Hall's *Dictionary of Subjects and Symbols in Art* (Murray, 1986) states: According to a legend mentioned by Aristotle in the *Historia Animalium* (9;10) and repeated in mediaeval bestiaries, when the bird fell asleep the stone dropped and immediately re-awakened it, so that it was ever watchful.
2715	ACANTHUS	1898	Genus of herbaceous plants with large deeply-cut hair, shining: used in a conventionalized form as a decorative feature in architecture.
4317	CEDARS OF LEBANON	1921	A species of tree used generically in the bible to denote coniferous trees; its wood is said to have been used in the building of King Solomon's Temple but this is doubtful.
4371	HAZEL	1921	Bush or small tree bearing nuts; twigs used for water-divining; the giving of the fruit of this tree to a bride as she and her husband came out of church after the wedding was an old Devon custom; in France the bridal couple are showered with hazel nuts as they kneel at the altar.
4464	DOLPHIN	1922	A mammal resembling a porpoise but with a longer and more slender snout; the fish that symbolized the faith of the early Christians was represented by a dolphin; it has various classical allusions and in mediaeval art it symbolizes social love.
4789	HERONRY	1925	Place where herons breed; they are of a gregarious nature, up to one hundred pairs have been known at one nesting site; they form tree-top colonies, some of which have a history going back for more than one hundred years.
5023	THISTLE	1928	A prickly composite herbaceous plant usually with a globular purple flower. Heraldic emblem of Scotland; legend says it commemorates a victory over the Danes who, in 1010, were intent on attacking a Scottish castle; they approached at night, shoeless so as to make no noise; having reached the moat they jumped in to swim it; the moat, however, was dry and overgrown with thistles; the piercing yells of the bare-footed Danes roused the garrison; the attack was foiled and the Danes defeated. It has to be said though, that the thistle did not make its appearance as a Royal emblem in Scotland until some four hundred years later!
5192	WALNUT TREE	1930	A tree of eastern origin; its fruit, the walnut, was renowned in mid-Victorian times for its medicinal properties and was used for all sorts of ailments. The wood of the tree is highly prized for the making of fine quality furniture.
5320	ACORN	1931	The fruit of the oak tree, hidden by squirrels in the summer to ensure a supply of food for the winter.

No.	NAME	Const	Remarks
5911	LOTUS	1943	Plant represented in ancient Greek legend as inducing luxurious dreaminess and distaste for active life; according to legend the prophet Mahomet said that a lote-tree stands in the seventh heaven, on the right-hand of the throne of God.
6047	MIMOSA LODGE OF BLACKPOOL	1945	Mimosa is a plant bearing clusters of small flowers and leaves which curl up when touched.
6164	ALBATROSS	1945	Very long-winged oceanic bird found chiefly in the Southern hemisphere. Sailors say it is fatal to shoot an albatross; the poem *The Rime of the Ancient Mariner* by Samuel Taylor Coleridge was based on this superstition.
6421	ROSEMARY	1947	Evergreen fragrant shrub; leaves used in perfumery. Taken as a token of remembrance.
8749	CHERRY TREE	1976	The cherry, the fruit of this tree, is called the fruit of Paradise; it is given as a reward for virtuousness and it symbolizes heaven. In religious paintings a cherry may be seen in the hand of the infant Christ.
8914	CYGNET	1979	A young swan, sometimes associated with Cycnus, king of Colonae in the Troad, who was killed by Achilles; on attempting to despoil him of his arms, the body of Cycnus was turned into a swan.
9035	FORGET-ME-NOT	1982	Also called scorpion-grass, the name popularly applied the small annual or perennial herbs forming the genus *Myosotis* of the family Boraginaceae from the Greek word mys, a mouse, and otis, an ear, on account of the shape of the leaves. (See note under the Section headed Badges; Lodge No. 9035 for the derivation of the name.)
9289	ALDER TREE	1988	A tree of the birch family; it grows by lakes and streams and in marshy ground.

PERSONAGES

Another popular idea is to name the lodge after a particular person, whether or not he was a freemason. The following lists show a few such lodges; many more could have been added. The first list is headed 'PERSONAGES' and the second 'PERSONAGES (MASONIC)'. This is not meant to imply that those named in the first list were not freemasons; the distinction is rather that those named in the second list were well-known and active freemasons. The person named may be well-known nationally or just locally.

There is a modern convention that the Grand Master will not approve the idea of naming a lodge after a person unless he be of eminence. In practice a lodge will not nowadays be named after any brother below the rank of Provincial or District Grand Master.

No.	NAME	Const	Remarks
523	JOHN OF GAUNT	1840	Duke of Lancaster, 1340–99; soldier.
548	WELLINGTON	1847	(Duke of) 1769–1852; British general and statesman.
586	LODGE ELIAS DE DERHAM	1850	Canon and architect of the Great Hall at Winchester Castle.
700	NELSON	1857	(Viscount) 1758–1805; British admiral and hero killed at the Battle of Trafalgar.
706	FLORENCE NIGHTINGALE	1185	1820–1910; founder of modern nursing profession.
1017	MONTEFIORE	1864	(Sir Moses); philanthropist and centenarian.
1278	BURDETT-COUTTS	1869	(Sir Francis) 1770–1844; politician.
1500	WALPOLE	1874	(Sir Robert) 1676–1745; English statesman; first Prime Minister of England.
1602	SIR HUGH MYDDELTON	1876	?1560–1631; pioneer of controlling water supply for towns.

No.	NAME	Const	*Remarks*
1686	PAXTON	1877	(Sir Joseph) 1801–65; English architect and ornamental gardener; best remembered for his glass building for the Great Exhibition of 1851, afterwards known as the Crystal Palace.
1820	SIR THOMAS WHITE	1879	1492–1567; Founder of St John's College, Oxford; took a considerable part in the founding of the Merchant Taylors' school.
2417	BOLINGBROKE	1891	(Viscount) 1678–1751; English statesman and writer on politics and philosophy.
2420	FERDINAND DE ROTHSCHILD	1891	1839–1898; Collector of fine objects *d'art*; built Waddesdon Manor in Buckinghamshire (now owned by National Trust).
2649	SIR FRANCIS DRAKE	1897	?1504–96; English admiral circumnavigated the world in *Golden Hind* in 1577–81.
2837	SIR WALTER RALEIGH	1900	(*c.* 1552–1618); English military and naval commander, explorer and poet.
3104	CANUTE	1905	A Danish king of England 1016–35.
3147	LODGE BOADICEA	1906	Queen of Iceni in East Anglia; she led a revolt against the Romans; her name (which has various spellings and may have been assumed) means 'Victory'; her suicide is probably historically correct; there is no definite evidence of her burial place, one suggestion being under platform ten of King's Cross station, London, on which site she is reputed to have fought her last battle (A.D. 62) and which was at one time being considered named as Boadicea's Cross; it actually bore the name Battle Bridge for a while in supposed reference to this battle.
3352	THOMAS À Becket	1908	1117–70; Archbishop of Canterbury (1162) and Chancellor of England under Henry II; murdered in Canterbury Cathedral; canonized 1172.
3396	HOGARTH	1909	(William) 1699–1764; English painter and engraver of social and political caricature.
3884	CABOT	1918	(John) *c.* 1450–98. Venetian navigator in service of England; discovered Labrador in 1407.
4091	VENERABLE BEDE	1919	673–735; English historian and theologian.
4430	ROGER ASCHAM	1922	1515–1568; author of many learned treatises; a Greek reader at St John's College, Cambridge.
4490	HUGH DE PUDSEY	1922	?1125–1195; Bishop of Durham and Earl of Northumberland.
4605	SIR JOSEPH WILLIAMSON	1924	1633–1701; statesman and diplomatist.
4636	CAPTAIN COOK	1924	(James) 1728–79; English navigator and explorer, especially of the South Pacific islands and Australasia,
4692	ADMIRAL BLAKE	1924	(Robert) 1599–1657; English admiral; fought with distinction against Dutch and Spanish fleets.
4782	SIR JOSHUA REYNOLDS	1925	1723–92; English portrait painter; first President of Royal Academy.
4855	CHRISTOPHER WREN	1926	1622–1723; English architect; designer of St Paul's Cathedral and many London churches.
5025	ORIGEN	1928	*c.* 185–253. One of the most distinguished Christian theologians and scholars of the ancient church; considered by some to be second only to Augustine.
5163	ARCHBISHOP TENISON	1930	1636–1715; benefactor of religious societies, especially the Society for the Propagation of the Gospel.
5186	WILBERFORCE	1930	(William) 1759–1833; English member of Parliament; devoted himself to the abolition of slavery.
5546	JAMES WATT	1935	1736–1819; Scottish inventor of the steam engine.
5593	JOHANN GUTENBERG	1935	*c.* 1398–1448. Printer in Mainz, Germany; inventor of moveable type.

No.	NAME	Const	*Remarks*
6196	BISHOP RIDLEY	1945	(Nicholas) ?1500–1555; protestant cleric; burnt at stake.
6413	RICHARD LINNECAR	1946	1722–1800; dramatist; prominent Freemason.
6469	ATHELSTAN	1947	*c.* 894–939, King of West Saxons 925–39; grandson of Alfred the Great. Referred to in many of the masonic documents known as the 'Old Constitutions'; because of this some consider him to be the Patron of Masonry but this cannot be confirmed. Some masonic historians believe he and his supposed son Edwin have been confused with Edwin King of Northumberland, a patron of the church, who reigned three centuries earlier.
7534	RICHARD WHITTINGTON	1957	(Sir) d. 1423; three times Lord Mayor of London; hero of popular legend of Dick Whittington and his cat.
7577	JOHN DALTON	1957	1766–1844; English chemist who formulated the atomic theory.
8029	THOMAS TELFORD	1965	1757–1834; Scottish civil engineer, designer of numerous roads and bridges and the Caledonian Canal.
8247	CANTELUPE	1968	(Thomas de) ?1218–1282; Chancellor; Bishop of Hereford; canonized.
8328	ROBERT BLOOMFIELD	1970	1766–1823; the 'Suffolk Poet', remembered mainly for his work 'The Farmer's Boy', which gives a good insight into Suffolk country life of the period. The lodge meets at Biggleswade, Bedfordshire, not far from the town of Shefford, where Bloomfield lived in his later years.
8908	ISAMBARD BRUNEL	1979	1806–59; engineer; built bridges, railways, ships, etc.; assisted his father (Sir Marc Isambard 1769–1849) in building a tunnel under the River Thames.
9004	CYMBELINE	1981	English king who reigned from AD 5 to after AD 40.
9024	SIMON DE MONTFORT	1981	1208?–65, Norman-English earl of Leicester; married Eleanor, sister of Henry III of England; led barons in revolt against the king in 1263, and captured him at Lewes, 1264; in 1265 summoned a parliament which included, besides the barons, knights and ecclesiastics, two citizens from every borough in England.
9327	SIR HUMPHREY DAVY	1089	1778–1829; English chemist; inventor of the miner's safety lamp.
9354	IZAAC WALTON	1989	1593–1683; English writer, remembered for his *Compleat Angler* (1653) and 'Lives' of several contemporary writers.
9482	VERMUYDEN	1991	Dutch engineer who drained the Isle of Axholme.

PERSONAGES (MASONIC)

No.	NAME	Const	*Remarks*
360	POMFRET	1819	Prov. GM Northants, & Hunts. 1798–1830
375	LAMBTON	1824	Prov. GM Durham 1787–97
631	METHUEN	1854	Prov. GM Wiltshire 1853–91
661	FAWCETT	1856	Prov. GM Durham 1847–80
766	WILLIAM PRESTON	1858	Masonic writer and lecturer; originator Prestonian Lectureship
929	WAVENEY	1862	Prov. GM Suffolk 1860–86
950	HESKETH	1863	Prov. GM W. Lancs. 1865–1872
1036	BOWYER	1864	Prov. GM Oxford 1854–71
1325	STANLEY	1870	Prov. GM W. Lancs. 1910–19
1479	HALSEY	1874	Prov. GM Herts, 1873–1923

No.	NAME	Const	*Remarks*
1503	SIR FRANCIS BURDETT	1874	Prov. GM Middlesex 1869–92
1634	STARKIE	1876	Prov. GM E. Lancs. 1870–99
1679	HENRY MUGGERIDGE	1877	Preceptor, Stability Lodge of Instruction, 1851–85
1910	SHADWELL CLERKE	1881	Grand Secretary 1880-91
2045	WHARTON	1884	Grand Master 1722–3
2048	HENRY LEVANDER	1884	Prov. Grand Secretary, Middlesex 1877
2257	POWELL	1888	[W.A.F.] Prov. GM Bristol 1889–1906
2421	CARRINGTON	1891	Prov. GM Bucks. 1890–5
2683	ADDINGTON	1897	Prov. GM Bucks. 1895–1909
2955	BEACH	1903	Prov. GM Hants. & IOW 1869–1901
3188	BURDON	1906	Prov. GM Northumberland 1906–8
3469	ARTHUR STANLEY	1910	Prov. GM W. Lancs. 1910–19
3878	DUNCKERLEY	1918	Prov. GM Hampshire 1777 & other Provinces
3964	DR OLIVER	1919	Masonic writer; Deputy Prov. GM Lincs.
4225	ANTHONY SAYER	1920	First Grand Master
4238	INGLEFIELD	1921	Prov. GM Bucks. 1916–29
5035	FRANCIS DAVIES	1928	Dep. Grand Master 1935–47 (General Sir Francis; *KCB, KCMG, KCVO, VL*
5083	ALFRED ROBBINS	1928	President Board of General Purposes 1913–31
5374	COLVIN	1932	Prov. GM Essex 1929–36
6133	ALEXANDER BURNETT BROWN	1945	Prov. GM Middlesex 1937–48
6210	KENYON	1945	Prov. GM N. Wales 1958–90
6622	MARTIN FOLKES	1948	Dep. Grand Master 1724–5
6629	NAYLOR	1948	Prov. GM Sussex 1947–59
7318	CHARLES NICHOLL	1953	Prov. GM Berkshire 1938–50
7731	PHILIP BULL	1960	Prov. GM Middlesex 1950–60
7975	CANON STAFFORD MORRIS	1964	Prov. GM Essex 1952–61
7994	TYNTE	1964	Prov. GM Dorset 1820–60
8009	GILBERT INGLEFIELD	1964	Prov. GM Bedfordshire 1958–78
8849	VERNEY	1978	Prov. GM Bucks. 1970–6
9448	SIBELIUS	1991	(Jean) 1865–1957; Finnish composer of tone-poems, symphonies etc. Grand Organist under Swedish Constitution

PLACE NAMES – ENGLISH

Many lodges adopt the name of the town, city or county in which they meet; others use the name of a nearby area. There are lodges that have adopted the name of a county or town other than the one in which they meet. Some examples are given below; the meeting place, where different from the place indicated by the name of the lodge, is shown after the name.

No.	NAME	Const	*No.*	NAME	Const
24	NEWCASTLE UPON TYNE	1766	36	GLAMORGAN	1808
108	LONDON	1760	143	MIDDLESEX (LONDON)	1775
236	YORK	1777	404	WATFORD	1815
1310	HARROW	1870	1476	BLACKPOOL	1873
1547	LIVERPOOL	1876	1635	CANTERBURY (LONDON)	1876

No.	Name	Const	No.	Name	Const
1767	Kensington	1878	1950	Southgate	1881
2090	Hammersmith	1885	2127	Drury Lane	1885
2163	Jersey	1886	2202	Regent's Park	1887
2396	Bishopsgate	1892	2458	Eton	1892
2554	Manchester	1895	2765	Earl's Court	1899
2766	Putney	1890	2852	Norfolk (London)	1901
2883	Wrekin (London)	1901	2920	East Anglian (London)	1902
2925	Somersetshire (London)	1902	2972	Ulster (London)	1903
3020	Whitehall	1904	3088	West Lancashire (Lon)	1905
3096	Aldwych	1905	3116	Guildhall	1905
3134	Lakeland (London)	1905	3538	Hampshire (London)	1911
4034	Southport	1919	4113	Penarth	1920
4522	Bristol (London)	1923	5001	Tring (Leighton Buzz'd)	1927
5193	Isleworth	1930	5301	Farnworth	1931
6939	Kenilworth	1949	7613	Amersham (Marlow, Bucks)	1958
7872	Ulverston	1962	7876	Islip	1962
8344	Tewkesbury (London)	1970			

Other lodges with place names of interest are;

No.	Name	Const	Note
9458	Gnosall St Lawrence	1991	Gnosall is a village near Stafford; St Lawrence is the patron saint of the parish church.
9459	Selig	1991	Name refers to Selig, Suffolk; it means 'holy', so called because Suffolk has a large number of churches.
9462	Sulgrave	1991	Sulgrave is a village in Northamptonshire; Sulgrave Manor was the home of George Washington's great grandfather. The members of the lodge have a close association with members of Britannia Lodge No. 1166, New York.
9484	Sherborne Conduit	1991	'Conduit' was the name for an area adjacent to Sherborne Abbey used as a washhouse by the monks.

PLACE NAMES – SAXON AND ROMAN NAMES

Some lodges adopted a name that is presumably meant to be the Anglo-Saxon or Roman name of, or associated with, the meeting place of the lodge.
Examples are:

No.	Name	Const	Meaning	*Meeting place*
262	Salopian	1788	Shrewsbury (8th C.)	Shrewsbury
425	Cestrian	1829	Chester	Chester
450	Cornubian	1838	Cornish	Hayle, Cornwall
464	Cambrian	1839	Welsh	Haverford, South Wales
606	Segontium	1852	Caernarvon	South Wales
1542	Legiolium	1875	Castleford,	Castleford, Yorkshire
1611	Eboracum	1876	York	York
2435	Wineslai	1892	Winslow	Winslow, Bucks.
3229	Pengwerne	1907	Shrewsbury (6th C.)	Shrewsbury
3447	Deva	1910	Chester	Chester
3532	Cantabrigia	1911	Cambridge	Cambridge
3953	Cambodunum	1919	Lindley	Lindley, Yorkshire
4048	Cytringan	1920	Kettering	Kettering
4089	Carliol	1920	Carlisle	Carlisle
4251	Lenne	1921	Lynn	King's Lynn

No.	NAME	Const	Meaning	*Meeting place*
4540	HESA	1923	Hayes	Uxbridge, Middlesex
4900	SYENES	1927	Sheen	Twickenham, Middlesex
5777	LINDUM	1939	Lincoln	Lincoln
6104	MEDESHAMSTEDE	1945	Peterborough	Peterborough
6314	FERNEBERGA	1946	Farnborough	Farnborough, Hampshire
6674	CESTREHAM	1948	Chesham	Beaconsfield, Bucks.
6872	MANCUNIUM	1949	Manchester	Manchester
6956	DUROBRIVAE	1950	Rochester	Gillingham, Kent
7069	BRIXISTANE	1951	Brixton	London
7206	HYLLENDUNE	1952	Hillingdon	Uxbridge, Middlesex
7385	GLEVUM	1964	Gloucester	Gloucester
7868	MAEIDES STANA	1962	Maidstone	Maidstone
7923	HEMELHEMSTEDE	1963	Hemel Hempstead	St Alban's, Herts.
8342	MULESLAI	1970	Mundesley	Mundesley, Norfolk
8743	LENTUNE	1977	Lymington	Lymington, Hants.
9363	LUTUDARUM	1989	Chesterfield	Chesterfield, Derbys

SAXON/ROMAN CONNECTIONS

The names of many lodges have a connection with a Saxon or Roman site near their meeting place. Some of these are given below.

No.	NAME OF LODGE	Const	Meeting place	Comment on name
471	SILURIAN	1840	Newport, Mon.	Of a Celtic tribe in N. Wales
2926	TAMESIS	1902	Slough, Bucks.	Old name of River Thames
3935	HANLIENSIAN	1919	Shelton, Stoke-on-Trent	Resident of Hanley, part of Stoke-on-Trent
5724	UXACONA	1938	Wellington.	Uxacona, later Oakengates, the Shropshire gateway to the Wrekin, derives from 'Ochr' or Orchren'. Ochren', meaning the street on the hillside.
5840	SARNIA-RIDUNA	1941	London	Sarnia was the Roman name for Guernsey and Riduna the Roman name for Alderney
6066	ICENI	1945	Chingford.	Roman name for British tribe in East Anglia.
7852	VECTENSIAN	1962	Ryde, Isle of Wight	Vectis was Roman name for the Isle of Wight
8079	CORITANI	1965	Daventry	A near-by Roman site
8091	MAGIOVINIVM	1946	Bletchley.	A near-by Roman encampment
8209	OSTREA	1968	Wivenhoe.	Latin word for oyster for which Colchester is famous
8298	COLNEIS	1969	Felixstowe	One of the 'hundreds' of Suffolk
8580	DINORBEN	1974	Colwyn Bay	A local Roman fort
8808	ALAUNA	1977	Maryport	A local Roman fort
8868	ARICONIUM	1979	Ross on Wye	Name of local site
9423	ANDREDESLEAH	1991	Anglo-Saxon name for the district between the North and South Downs; Redhill (where the lodge meets), was a part of this area. Founders of lodge felt it appropriate to use this name because, before his death, VW Bro, Harold Daniels, *DL* PGSwdB, a highly respected public figure who had held many public offices, had lived in a house he had named Andred Eade	

No	NAME OF LODGE	Const	Meeting place	Comment on name
9435	CATUVELLAUNI	1991		Name of the oldest peace-loving Belgae tribe who came to Britain before the Romans and settled in what is now North-east Hertfordshire

PROFESSIONAL AND OCCUPATIONAL

Many lodges are formed with the idea of restricting membership to a particular trade, profession or occupation; the connection may be apparent in the name of the lodge, either by an association with the relevant calling or by some other means. Some are readily recognizable, such as No. 2795 Commercial Travellers Lodge and 8040 Radio Fraternity Lodge; others, like No. 5157 Structure Lodge and No. 5350 Lodge of Construction, both of which are allied to the building industry, are a little more difficult. Further examples are given below; in some cases the original source of membership and a suggestion indicating the reason for the choice of name is also given. Most of these lodges have been unable to restrict membership in the way they envisaged; they have had to widen it to remain viable.

Accountants

No.	NAME	Const	Remarks
3162	CHARTERED ACCOUNTANTS	1906	
7582	CERTIFIED ACCOUNTANTS	1958	

Architects and Surveyors

No.	NAME	Const	Remarks
2416	HIRAM	1891	Hiram Abif, Prince of Architects
3244	CHARTERED ARCHITECTS	1907	
3269	T SQUARE	1907	A drawing implement used in architecture
3724	MENSURA	1914	Latin for a measuring
7950	PORTICO	1963	An architectural term

Aviation

No.	NAME	Const	Remarks
3895	HENDON AERO	1918	For aircraft manufacturers; Hendon is the site of the aircraft museum.
5596	ARIEL	1935	For pilots and other aircrew. Ariel is the name of Shakespeare's airy spirit in *The Tempest*.
5637	PEGASUS	1936	For those at RAF Halton; Pegasus was the winged horse of Greek mythology.
7210	LODGE OF AVIATION	1952	
7710	COMET	1959	For employees at Heathrow Airport; Comet is the name of an aircraft.

No.	NAME	Const	*Remarks*
7999	HEATHROW	1964	For employees at London's main airport.
8721	LODGE OF CONCORDE	1976	For employees at Heathrow; Concorde is the name of an aircraft.
8867	FLEET AIR ARM	1978	
8924	AIR VECTURA	1979	Vectura is Latin for the act of transporting or carrying; lodge formed by members of United Kingdom Air Cargo Club.

Bakers

No.	NAME	Const	*Remarks*
3165	CEREALIA	1906	Cerealia was name given to a festival in honour of Ceres, a Roman divinity, the protectress of agriculture.
4817	CEREPANIA	1925	Unable to find the source or meaning of this name, though the connection with the baking trade can be readily guessed, the secretary of the lodge thought it was supposed to imply 'an ear of corn', a reference to the second degree tracing board.
6524	AUREA CERES	1947	Golden corn.
7602	LODGE OF MANNA	1958	Manna was small seed found by the Israelites during their wandering in the wilderness; prepared for food by grinding and baking.

Banks

No.	NAME	Const	*Remarks*
2946	HOLDEN	1902	For Midland Bank employees; name comes from the site of one of the bank's branches.
3612	LOTHBURY	1912	For Barclays Bank employees; Lothbury is the site of a Barclays Bank building.
3647	NATIONAL WESTMINSTER	1913	For National Westminster employees.
4155	BLACK HORSE OF LOMBARD STREET	1920	For Lloyds Bank employees; black horse used as symbol by bank. Lombard Street is site of a Lloyd's Bank building.
5252	DOMINICOS	1931	For employees of Barclays Bank Dominion, Colonial and Overseas department.
5618	LODGE OF REUNION	1936	For bank messengers; founders were ex-naval men.

Civil Service

No.	NAME	Const	*Remarks*
3864	BURTON COURT	1918	Burton Court was the home of the old Ministry of Pensions from which the lodge was set up.
5569	CHEQUERED CLOTH	1935	For employees of the Inland Revenue. Name derived from lodge floorcloth and the Exchequer connection of its members. (Exchequer; a department of State managed by the Treasurer; so called with reference to a table covered with a cloth divided into squares on which the accounts revenue were kept by means of counters. *Oxford English Dictionary*.)

No.	NAME	Const	*Remarks*
6501	PEREGRINUS	1947	For employees of the War Office. Name meant to imply 'stranger or foreigner', reflecting the nature of the daily avocations of the lodge members.

Ecclesiastical

No.	NAME	Const	*Remarks*
2741	CATHEDRAL	1899	For those associated with St Paul's cathedral.
3051	SANCTUARY	1904	For ministers of religion.
3789	EPWORTH	1916	For methodists. Epworth was the birthplace of John and Charles Wesley, the originators of Methodism.
7347	LODGE OF CONSTANT TRUST	1954	For members of the Salvation Army.
7516	NEW VENTURE	1957	For members of Wellington College Mission, Welworth.

Engineering

No.	NAME	Const	*Remarks*
2087	ELECTRIC	1885	For electrical engineers
2664	HYGEIA	1897	For sanitary engineers, Hygeia being the mythological goddess of health.
3281	AEDILE	1907	For civil engineers, Aedile being a Roman magistrate who superintended public buildings.
3613	ARCHIMEDEAN	1912	For electrical and mechanical engineers. Archimedes was a Greek mathematician said to have made many mechanical inventions.
3736	KELVIN	1914	For electrical engineers; Kelvin was a physicist and professor of natural philosophy who advanced the science of thermo-dynamics and electricity.
4012	FULCRUM	1910	For mechanical engineers, fulcrum being a point about which a level turns.
4200	RADIANT	1920	For gas and heating engineers, radiant being a point or object from which light and heat radiates.
4798	FARADAY	1928	For electrical engineers, Faraday discovered electric and magneto-electric induction.

Industrial

No.	NAME	Const	*Remarks*
2399	ORDNANCE	1891	For ordnance workers at the Royal Arsenal.
2910	CARBON	1910	Chemical element found in coal; for coal merchants.
3181	VULCAN	1906	Roman god of fire who forged weapons; steelworkers.
3776	INVENTIONS	1916	For patent agents.
3898	ARMAMENT	1918	For armament workers.
4318	ARBOR	1921	Latin for tree; for timber industry.
4926	FERRAMENTA	1927	Tools made with iron; for iron and steel workers.

Insurance

No.	NAME	Const	*Remarks*
3049	LUTINE	1904	For Lloyd's underwriters; the Lutine Bell is rung when a ship is lost.
5125	GOOD FAITH	1929	Good faith is a basic requirement of insurance.
5369	SALUS	1932	Salus is Latin for health and soundness, used as a basis for determining life and health insurance premiums.
6272	FIDENTIA	1946	Fidentia is Latin for confidence, an essential requirement for insurance.
9047	LODGE OF PROTECTION	1982	Protection is the function of insurance.

Legal

No.	NAME	Const	*Remarks*
1610	NORTHERN BAR	1876	
2456	CHANCERY BAR	1892	
2694	JUSTINIAN	1897	Roman emperor who re-organized and consolidated Roman law.
2716	MIDLAND, OXFORD, AND SOUTH EASTERN BAR	1876	
3154	WESTERN CIRCUIT	1905	
4302	TEMPLARS	1921	Barristers clerks in Temple, London.
4938	GRAY'S INN	1927	
6398	JURIST	1946	
8668	JUSTICE AND PEACE	1975	For those connected with the administration of the law in Magistrates' Courts.

Medical

No.	NAME	Const	*Remarks*
2394	GALEN	1891	Greek physician b. 130 d. *c.* 200; founder of experimental physiology; Next to Hippocrates the most celebrated of ancient physicians.
2410	Æsculapius	1891	Latinized form of Asclepius, the Greek god of healing and medical art; he was the surgeon of the Greeks in the Trojan war.
2546	RAHERE	1894	d. 1144; an Augustinian canon; founder of St Bartholomew's Hospital.
2620	CAVENDISH	1896	(Henry) 1731–1810; chemist and physician.
2843	MIDDLESEX HOSPITAL	1901	
2845	ROYAL LONDON HOSPITAL	1901	
2870	CHESELDEN	1901	(William) 1688–1753; surgeon who practised at St Thomas's Hospital, London.
2973	KING'S COLLEGE HOSPITAL	1903	
3233	ORGANON	1907	Organon theory is treatment of disease with animal organs or extracts (Homeopathic Hospital).
3781	CITY OF LONDON RED CROSS	1916	

No.	Name	Const	*Remarks*
4031	Radium	1919	A radio-active metallic element discovered by Piere and Marie Curie.
5292	Westminster Hospital	1931	
7099	Royal Dental Hospital	1951	
7621	Machaon	1958	A warrior and physician son of Asclepius the Greek god of healing and medical art.
7715	John Snow	1960	1813–1858; anaesthetist; lecturer on forensic medicine.
8032	Joseph Lister	1965	1827–1912; English surgeon; founder of antiseptic method of surgery.
8980	Roentgen	1980	(William Konrad von) 1845–1923; German physicist; discoverer of X-rays.

Pottery

No.	Name	Const	*Remarks*
546	Etruscan	1847	Name associated with pottery unearthed in early archeological digs.
2214	Josiah Wedgwood	1887	1730–95; founder of pottery works at Etruria, a village he built for his workmen, near Stoke on Trent, England.
3827	Ceramic	1917	Ceramic; pertaining to pottery
4967	Keramos	1927	Greek for baked clay (origin of ceramic). [This lodge has been renamed Seven Dials.]

Printing and Publishing

No.	Name	Const	*Remarks*
1853	Caxton	1879	Caxton was the first printer in England.
2562	Papyrus	1895	Reed from which paper was made in ancient times.
2817	St Bride	1900	St Bride Street, closely associated Fleet Street to which Wynkyn de Worde brought the printing press.
3765	Ex Libris	1915	Latin for 'Out of the books'; a book-plate for librarians and their staff.
9461	Old Ben	1991	Nickname given to the News Trade's own charity.

Public Services and Works

No.	Name	Const	*Remarks*
1632	Stuart	1876	For policemen.
2563	Justicia	1895	For Chief Inspectors of Police and above, Clerks of the Court, Barristers and Judges.
2593	Hugh Owen	1895	For employees of Board of Asylums; Hugh Owen was a prime mover in the setting-up of such places.
2842	Asylums Board	1901	
3015	Semper Paratus	1904	'Ever ready'; motto of fire brigade; firemen.
3113	Aquarius	1905	Aquarius (one of the signs of the Zodiac) is the Latin for water-carrier; for Water Board employees.

No.	NAME	Const	*Remarks*
4106	MERIDIAN	1920	For Post Office workers.
4948	BUILDERS OF THE SILENT CITIES	1927	For employees of War Graves Commission.
5214	INDUSTRIA	1930	For industrial health employees.
6692	ENDYMION	1948	Beautiful youth with whom Selene (the Moon) became enamoured; for telegraph and cable employees.
8467	POSTHORN	1972	Horn used by postman or guard of mailcoach to announce arrival; for employees of the Post Office.

Railways

No.	NAME	Const	*Remarks*
840	SCIENTIFIC	1860	Formed by two famous locomotive engineers, Sir Daniel Gooch and James McConnell.
1295	GOOCH	1869	(Sir Daniel) 1816–1889; Railway pioneer and inventor; Chief mechanical engineer on Great Western Railway
2622	BEACH	1896	Railway director; for employees of Old London and South Western Railway.
2912	ONWARD AND INVICTA	1902	Names of old locomotives; employees of Old South East and Chatham Railway.
4964	IRON ROAD	1927	Name given to railtrack; for railway employees.
5030	CREWE	1928	Crewe, Cheshire; an important railway junction and locomotive works.
8108	TERMINUS	1966	Railway employees in London.

Secretaries

No.	NAME	Const	*Remarks*
3395	NOSOCOMIA	1909	Hospital Administrators.
3505	LETCHWORTH	1911	Clerks in Grand Secretary's office; Sir Edward Letchworth Grand Secretary 1892–1917.
3791	FRATRES CALAMI	1917	Brothers of the pen (literally reed); members originally limited to lodge secretaries.

Trade and Commerce

No.	NAME	Const	*Remarks*
2469	HORTUS	1893	Latin for garden; for Covent Garden traders.
2837	SIR WALTER RALEIGH	1892	1552–1618; English naval commander and explorer who brought tobacco to England; for tobacco trade.
3019	SHERATON	1904	(Thomas) 1751–1806; English furniture designer; for employees in furniture trade.
3037	ROSTRUM	1904	Auctioneer's platform; for auctioneers.
3408	RENAISSANCE	1909	Revival of art; for interior decorators.

No.	Name	Const	Remarks
3443	Billingsgate	1910	Fishmarket, London; for fishmongers.
3774	First Artificer	1916	Tubal Cain first artificer in metals; for watch-makers.
4262	Mercurius	1921	Roman divinity for commerce; for drapers.
5453	Malleus	1933	Latin for hammer; for auctioneers.
7351	Camellia Thea	1954	Botanical name for tea plant; for tea trade.
7746	Lodge of Illumination	1960	For employees in electric lighting trade.

Undertakers

No.	Name	Const	Remarks
3436	Acacia	1910	'A sprig of acacia at the head of the grave'; Acacia wood is burned on Buddhist altars.
8260	Cupressus	1968	Latin name for cypress tree, an emblem of death, the immortal soul and woe. In British folklore, before a funeral procession set out, sprigs of rosemary or evergreen such as cypress, would be given to the mourners.

RECREATIONAL

The lodges listed under this heading are some of those whose members share a particular recreational interest. In most cases the interest is obvious from the name of the lodge; there are one or two, though, where this is not so. In such cases a suitable note has been added.

No.	Name	Const	Comment
3032	Philanthic	1904	Greek for 'friends of the garden'; for amateur gardeners.
3062	Neleus	1904	Boating, formed by members of the Neleus Club. Neleus was one of the two sons of Poseidon and Tyro.
3094	Foxhunters	1905	Foxhunting.
3347	Brixton Ramblers	1908	Cycling.
4674	Athlon	1924	Athletics.
5983	Lodge of the Open Road	1944	Cycling.
6547	Windmill	1947	Golf.
7343	Remigium	1954	Latin for oar; rowing.
7454	Terpsichore	1956	Dancing; Terpsichore was one of the nine muses; she presided over the choral song and dancing.
7557	Piscator	1957	Fishing; name is Latin for a fisherman.
7592	Haste Hill	1958	Golf; name of public golf course.
7820	Phaethon	1961	Motoring. A phaeton was the name of a light four-wheeled open carriage. Phaethon was the son of Helios and Clymene, famous for his driving of the sun-chariot.
7913	Waterways	1963	Yachting and sailing.
8040	Radio Fraternity	1965	Radio amateurs.

No.	Name	Const	*Comment*
8585	Clavis	1974	Bellringers. The name the founders had in mind originally was Bell-ringers Lodge, but this was not acceptable because it used the name of an existing publication; the founders then decided on Clavis, after the title of a well-known book on bellringing, *Clavis Campanologia.* A better choice might have been Campanologists Lodge.
8614	Fairway	1974	Golfing.
8628	Thames Mariner	1974	Yachting.
9347	Flyfishers'	1989	Flyfishers.
9354	Izaak Walton	1989	Fishermen.

RESEARCH AND MASONIC EDUCATION

There are only a few lodges devoted to masonic research, but practically every Province has a Lodge of Installed Masters; some have more than one. These lodges do not initiate, or normally pass and raise brethren (even though empowered by their warrants to do so); their meetings are generally given over to a paper being read, a demonstration or a question and answer session; in short, to masonic education. The names are as shown in the *Masonic Year Book*; the Province is given where it is not evident from the name of the lodge; in all other cases the lodge meets in London.

No.	Name	Const.
2076	Quatuor Coronati	1884
2429	Lodge of Research (Leicestershire)	1892
2494	Humber Installed Masters	1893
2706	Foster Gough (Staffordshire)	1898
2712	Jubilee Masters	1898
3250	Hendre (South Wales E.D.)	1907
3256	Essex Masters	1907
3420	Middlesex Masters	1909
3422	Northamptonshire and Huntingdonshire Lodge of Installed Masters	1909
3477	Northumbrian Masters	1910
3595	Notts Installed Masters	1912
3667	Kensington (S. Wales W.D.)	1913
3672	Sussex Masters	1913
3687	Dean Leigh Masters (Hereford)	1913
3746	Somerset Masters	1915
3905	Norfolk Installed Masters'	1918
3913	Suffolk Installed Masters	1918
3931	East Kent Masters	1919
4538	Warwickshire Installed Masters	1923
5502	Manchester Lodge of Masonic Research	1934
5778	West Kent Masters'	1939
5888	East Surrey Masters	1943
5905	North Surrey Masters	1943
5965	South-West Surrey Masters	1944
6262	Shropshire Installed Masters'	1946
6731	Wiltshire Masters'	1948
6889	Worcestershire Installed Masters'	1949
7248	Wear Lecture (Durham)	1953
7305	Lodge of Benevolence (S. Wales E.D.)	1953
7388	Mid-Surrey Masters	1955
7755	Setantia Lodge of Installed Masters (West Lancs.)	1960

No.	Name	Const.
7770	Oxfordshire Lodge of Installed Masters	1961
7884	Emeritus Lodge of Installed Masters (East Lancs.)	1962
7896	Leicestershire and Rutland Lodge of Installed Masters	1963
7900	Gloucestershire Installed Masters	1963
7918	Leeds and District Lodge of Installed Masters	1963
8087	Harrogate and District Lodge of Installed Masters	1966
8132	Inquirimus Lodge of Installed Masters (Yorks & N.E.)	1966
8312	Loughborough Lodge of Installed Masters	1969
8321	South Surrey Masters	1969
8341	Ashton District Lodge of Installed Masters (E. Lancs.)	1970
8364	Lord Swansea (S. Wales E.D.)	1970
8383	Jersey Lodge of Installed Masters	1971
8449	East Sussex Masters	1972
8517	Middleton Lodge of Installed Masters (E. Lancs.)	1973
8564	Guernsey and Alderney Lodge of Installed Masters	1973
8593	Anderida Lodge of Installed Masters (West Kent)	1974
8615	North Wales Lodge of Installed Masters	1974
8676	Clwyd Lodge of Installed Masters (N. Wales)	1975
8746	High Barnet Masters (Herts)	1976
8766	Hyndburn Lodge of Installed Masters (E. Lancs.)	1977
8772	Maesgwyn Lodge of Installed Masters (N. Wales)	1977
8887	Hafren Lodge of Installed Masters (N. Wales)	1979
8963	West Sussex Masters	1980
8966	Senatores Lodge of Installed Masters (W. Lancs.)	1980
9057	Mersey Valley Lodge of Installed Masters (W. Lancs.)	1982
9111	Pendleside Lodge of Installed Masters (E. Lancs.)	1983
9152	Bournemouth and District Masters	1984
9211	Rochdale District Installed Masters (E. Lancs.)	1986
9240	Middlesex Masters (Southgate)	1987
9243	Dyffryn Clwyd Lodge of Installed Masters (N. Wales)	1987
9292	Middlesex Masters (Uxbridge)	1988
9368	Athenaeum Lodge of Installed Masters (W. Lancs.)	1990

RIVERS

Many lodges have been named after rivers; some examples are given below.

No.	Name	County	Const	No.	Name	County	Const
35	Medina	Hants & IoW.	1761	57	Humber	Yorks. N & E Riding	1775
297	Witham	Lincs.	1793	509	Tees	Durham	1845
599	Cherwell	Oxon.	1852	814	Parrett & Axe	Somerset	1860
884	Derwent	Derbyshire	1861	929	Waveney	Suffolk	1862
977	Fowey	Cornwall	1863	991	Tyne	Northumberland	1863
1576	Dee	Cheshire	1875	1678	Medway	W. Kent	1877
1703	Windrush	Oxon.	1877	1885	Torridge	Devon	1880
1977	Blackwater	Essex	1882	2187	Adur	Sussex	1886
2305	Stour	E. Kent	1889	2641	Dart	Devon	1896
3320	Ithon	S. Wales E.D.	1908	3334	Thet	Norfolk	1908
3375	Misbourne	Bucks.	1909	3569	Avon	Worcs.	1911
3821	Plym	Devon	1917	4239	Tamar	Devon	1921
4242	Isis	Oxon.	1921	4269	Trent	Staffs.	1921

No.	Name	County	Const	No.	Name	County	Const
4414	Kennet	Berkshire	1922	4558	Ribble	W. Lancs.	1923
4564	Calder	E. Lancs.	1923	4724	Lune	W. Lancs.	1925
4950	Granta	Lincs.	1927	5199	Mersey	W. Lancs.	1930
5583	Severn	Worcs.	1935	5764	Thames River	London	1939
6182	Solent	Hants & IoW	1945	6535	Evenlode	Oxon.	1947
6637	Orwell	Suffolk	1948	7018	Teign	Devon	1950
7497	Crouch	Essex	1956	8491	Teme	Worcs.	1972

ROYALTY AND PEERS OF THE REALM

Under the heading Royalty are included names of Kings, Queens, Princes and Royal Dukes. In the list of examples which follows, the Duke of Normandy and the Duke of Lancaster have been shown in the section headed ROYALTY because they are titles held by the sovereign. To illustrate this it is worth recording that 'The Duke of Normandy' is sometimes added to the Loyal Toast when given in some Channel Island lodges; similarly in the Province of West Lancashire 'The Duke of Lancaster' may be added.

There is no lodge which has the title 'Viscount' in its name; there are plenty of 'Lords'; the title holder is usually a baron. Examples are given in the following list; an entry is not meant to imply that the lodge is necessarily named after the named person; the lodge may well have taken the name from an inn or tavern bearing the name.

Kings and Queens

No.	Name	Const	No.	Name	Const
1327	King Harold	1870	1333	Athelstan	1870
1757	King Henry the Eighth	1878	2655	Queen Victoria	1897
2932	Queen Alexandra	1902	2945	King Alfred	1902
3327	Queen Mary's	1908	3306	King Oswald	1908
3514	King George V	1911	3442	King Edward VII	1910
6593	King Arthur [Mythological]	1947	4288	King Egbert	1921
245	Duke of Normandy	1813	1353	Duke of Lancaster	1871

Royal Dukes

No.	Name	Const	No.	Name	Const
1182	Duke of Edinburgh	1867	1529	Duke of Cornwall	1875
1834	Duke of Connaught	1879	2449	Duke of York	1892
3343	Duke of Sussex	1980	5818	Duke of Kent	1939

Princes

No.	Name	Const	No.	Name	Const
128	Prince Edwin's	1763	307	Lodge of Prince Frederick	1809
1218	Prince Alfred	1868	1570	Prince Arthur	1875
1588	Prince Leopold	1875	1648	Prince of Wales'	1876

No.	Name	Const	No.	Name	Const
2109	Prince Edward	1885	2570	Prince Llewellyn	1895
4915	Prince David	1927	7841	Prince Rupert	1962
9120	Prince Michael of Kent	1984			

Dukes

No.	Name	Const	No.	Name	Const
1963	Duke of Albany	1882	2017	Duke of Portland	1883
2345	Duke of Fife	1890	3143	Duke of Richmond	1905
6735	Duke of Devonshire	1948			

Marquesses (Alternative spelling also used)

No.	Name	Const	No.	Name	Const
124	Marquis of Granby	1763	1159	Marquis of Dalhousie	1867
1354	Marquis of Lorne	1871	1379	Marquess of Ripon	1871
3550	Marquis of Titchfield	1911			

Earls

No.	Name	Const	No.	Name	Const
678	Earl Ellesmere	1856	1274	Earl of Durham	1869
1420	Earl Spencer	1872	1520	Earl Shrewsbury	1874
1565	Earl of Chester	1875	1642	Earl of Carnarvon	1876
1922	Earl of Lathom	1881	1984	Earl of Clarendon	1882
2000	Earl of Mornington	1883	2201	Earl of Sussex	1887
2237	Earl of Leicester	1887	2504	Earl of Warwick	1894
2770	Earl of Yarborough	1899	3151	Earl Roberts	1906
3230	Earl Amherst	1907	3279	Earl of Dartmouth	1917
3564	Earl of Derby	1911	3924	Earl of Mount Edgecumbe	1919
4919	Earl of Malmesbury	1927	6081	Earl Leofric	1945
6313	Earl Bathurst	1946	7031	Earl of St Germans	1950
7653	Earl of Courtown	1959			

Barons

No.	Name	Const	No.	Name	Const
1879	Lord Warkworth	1880	2827	Lord Roberts	1900
2891	Lord Stanley	1902	2935	Lord Barnard	1902
3017	Lord Worsley	1904	3074	Lord Armstrong	1904
3200	Lord Desborough	1906	3246	Lord Collingwood	1907
3263	Lord Bolton	1907	3685	Lord Raglan	1913

No.	Name	Const	*No.*	Name	Const
5789	Lord Roborough	1939	5979	Lord Heneage	1944
7889	Lord Leycester	1963			

There are other lodges in this category which use the family or peerage name, but not the peerage rank, Examples are:

708 Carnavon Lodge; named after the fourth Earl of Carnarvon.
865 Dalhousie Lodge; named after the eleventh Earl of Dalhousie.
1194 Villiers Lodge; family name of Earl of Jersey, a founder member of the lodge who later became P.G.M. Oxfordshire (1885–1914).
2163 Jersey Lodge; named after the Earl of Jersey.
8869 Cumton Lodge; a founder was the Marquess of Northampton, whose family name is Compton, the ancient spelling of which is the name of the lodge.

The reason for the choice of the name is usually either because of an historical association or because of a personal connection. Examples are:

1777 Royal Hanover Lodge. The name was chosen to perpetuate the memory of the King of Hanover (who died two months before the consecration of the lodge) and his connection with the British Royal Family. His son, the Duke of Cumberland, approved the choice.
2945 King Alfred Lodge; the founders of the lodge were mainly from the Enfield and Waltham Cross area through which flows the River Lea, a tributary of the River Thames. When the Danes invaded England, contingents sailed up these rivers as far as Waltham Cross, King Alfred ordered the boats to be boarded and the invaders slain.
3500 Earl Strafford Lodge; the founders sought and received permission from the Rt. Hon. the Revd. Francis Edmund Byng, Earl of Strafford, Past Grand Chaplain, to use his title as a name for the lodge; his seat, Wrotham Park, was within the district.

By far the largest number of lodges under this heading are those which include the name Zetland. The first Earl of Zetland held the office of Deputy Grand Master 1821–2, and again 1824–34 when he was promoted to Pro Grand Master in 1834. The second Earl of Zetland was appointed Deputy Grand Master in 1839; he served as Grand Master 1844–70. The names of the lodges are:

No.	Name	Const.
508	Zetland in the East, Singapore, Eastern Archipelago	1845
511	Zetland, London	1844
515	Zetland, Aldershot, Hants. & I.o.W.	1844
525	Zetland, Hong Kong, Hong Kong & Far East	1846
537	Zetland, Birkenhead, Cheshire	1847
561	Zetland, Guisborough, Yorks N. & E. Ridings	1849
603	Zetland, Cleckheaton, Yorks, W. Riding	1852
608	Zetland, Fort Beaufort, South Africa E.D.	1852
852	Zetland, Salford, E. Lancs.	1861
1005	Zetland, Gloucester	1864
1071	Zetland, Saltash, Cornwall	1865
1311	Zetland, Leeds, Yorks W. Riding	1870
1364	Earl of Zetland, London	1871
7665	Zetland and Hong Kong, London	1959
9349	Marquess of Zetland, Yorks, N. & E. Ridings	1989

It is of interest to note that there were two earls and three marquesses in an unbroken run serving as Provincial Grand Master, Yorkshire, N. & E. Ridings from 1817 to 1984, when the present Deputy Grand Master (RW Bro. Iain Bryce *TD, DL*) was appointed; they were:

1817 Lawrence, 1st Earl of Zetland – died 1839;
1839 Thomas, 2nd Earl of Zetland, *KG* – died 1873;
1874 Lawrence John, 1st Marquess of Zetland *KT*, – resigned 1923
1923 Lawrence John, 2nd Marquess of Zetland *KG, GCSI, GCIE*, – resigned 1956
1956 Lawrence Aldred Mervyn 3rd Marquess of Zetland, *TD, DL*, died 1984.

SAINTS

There are over 550 lodges bearing the name of a saint. London has over sixty, the Provinces over 450 and the Districts about 50. The most common names are St John(s), St George(s) and St Andrew(s). The following list gives some examples of the names used.

No.	Name	Const	*No.*	Name	Const
43	St Paul's	1733	63	St Mary's	1757
98	St Martin's	1805	112	Saint George's	1762
142	St Thomas's	1775	144	St Luke's	1765
167	Saint John's	1767	211	St Michael's	1795
222	St Andrew's	1797	393	St David's	1828
442	St Peter's	1836	539	Lodge of St Matthew	1847
588	St Botolph's	1851	597	Lodge of St Cybi	1851
622	Lodge of St Cuthberga	1853	696	Saint Bartholomew	1857
755	Lodge of Saint Tudno	1858	850	St Oswald	1860
857	St Mark's	1861	948	Lodge of St Barnabas	1863
954	St Aubyn	1863	966	St Edward's	1863
972	Saint Augustine	1863	1008	Royal Saint Edmunds	1864
1119	St Bede	1866	1129	Saint Chad's	1866
1222	Saint Kew	1868	1833	St Keyna	1879
1891	St Ambrose	1880	2078	St Lawrence	1884
2311	St Alkmund	1889	2598	St Sampson's	1895
2727	St Audrey	1898	2786	St Albans	1899
2808	St Erkenwald	1900	3460	St Aidan	1910
3691	St Ann's	1913	3743	St Catherine's	1915
4147	St Werburga	1920	4221	St Philip	1920
4453	St Wilfrid	1922	4637	Saint Alfege	1924
4714	St Edmund	1925	4741	Saint Grwst	1925
4755	St Teilo	1925	4778	St Quentin's	1925
4795	St Swithun's	1925	4850	St Modwen's	1926
5295	St Vincent	1931	5383	All Saints	1932
6025	St Euny	1944	6034	Saint Christopher	1944
6078	Lodge of St Illtyd	1945	6261	St Raphael	1946
6321	Lodge of St Cystenin	1946	6376	Lodge of St Simon	1946
6725	St Canna	1948	7973	St Dunstan's	1964
8295	St Eligius	1969	8317	St Pega	1969
8796	St Bega	1977	9046	St Crispin	1982

Many of the saints listed have an association with the place in which the lodge is situated. Examples are;

972 Saint Augustine, Canterbury; missionary bishop, died Canterbury, c.605.

1008 Royal Saint Edmunds, Bury St Edmunds; king and martyr, b.841; enshrined at Bury St Edmunds.

2598 St Sampson's, St Peter Port, Guernsey; abbot-bishop b. South Wales c.490, worked for a while in the Channel Islands.

2727 St Audrey, Ely; St Ethelreda, or Audry, who in c.672 founded a double monastery at Ely over which she presided till her death.

2786 St Albans, St Alban's; martyr, d. at Verulamium (St Alban's) c.287

3460 St Aidan, Northshields, Northumberland; organized a monastery at Lindisfarne, where he is buried.

4755 St Teilo, Llanelli, South Wales; sixth-century bishop, widely venerated in South Wales.

6078 St Illtyd, Neath, South Wales; abbot who had a great monastic school at Llanilltyd Fawn. (Llantwit Major, Glamorgan).

6451 St Edmund, Abingdon; Edmund of Abingdon, bishop c.1170.

7973 St Dunstan's, Glastonbury; bishop b. near Glastonbury c.909

8317 St Pega, Deeping St James, Lincoln; hermitress in Peakirk (= Pega's church), Lincs. c.700

Amongst other reasons why saints' names were adopted by lodges are;

a) because they were patron saints of trades associated with building, for example:

St Thomas; apostle, and patron saint of builders.
St Eligius; artisan bishop, patron saint of smiths, farriers and all kinds of metal workers
The Four Crowned Martyrs (Quatuor Coronati) patron saints of the mason's craft.

b) because their names have a long association with Freemasonry. For example St John the Baptist and St John the Evangelist. The two St John's days, 24 June and 27 December, were regular meeting dates of the early Grand Lodges; from the early part of the seventeenth century freemasons not attached to a specific lodge were known as St John's masons.

c) because of the locality of the lodge meeting. For example St Pancras Lodge No. 2271 met near St Pancras, London. St Paul's Lodge No. 194, when they were first named met in Ludgate Hill, London, which adjoins St Paul's Cathedral.
St Clement Danes Lodge No. 1351 who used to meet in St Clement Danes, London.
St Leonards Lodge No. 1842 who meet at St Leonards, Sussex.
St Asaph Lodge No. 8034 who meet at St Asaph, N. Wales.

d) because of an association with the feast day of the saint whose name has been chosen. An example is Saint George Lodge, No. 6185; quoting from *Masonic Lodges of Middlesex. Their Origins and Names* (Province of Middlesex, ud.)
(Two) founders . . . broke off for luncheon in the City after a morning session to decide the Lodge's name had been fruitless. Passing the Mansion House they noticed a street streamer announcing a war-time charity appeal with the words 'Saint George'. As it was St George's Day also, further discussion was unnecessary.

SCHOOLS AND UNIVERSITIES

There are over 150 lodges that come within this classification; most have the name of the appropriate university or school or the name by which the Old Boys are known. Some of these are shown in the list below. It is of interest to record that the first lodge to adopt a distinctive title was University Lodge No. 74; it was constituted in November 1730 and met at the Bear and Harrow, Butcher Row, Temple Bar, London. It is believed that it adopted the name because its members had been educated at Oxford University; the lodge was erased in 1736.

No.	Name	Const	*No.*	Name	Const
1118	Oxford and Cambridge University	1866	2033	University of London	1818
2233	Old Westminsters'	1887	2352	Universities	1890
2700	Old Masonians	1898	2885	Charterhouse Deo Dante Dedi	1901
2951	Culham College	1903	2974	University of Edinburgh	1903
3030	University of Durham	1904	3153	Trinity College Dublin	1906
3223	Old Cheltonian	1907	3280	Carmarthen College	1907
3304	Old Shirburnian	1908	3340	Old Cliftonian	1908
3404	Old Wellingtonian	1909	3533	Old Marlburian	1911
3549	Old Bradfield	1911	3551	Old Rugbeian	1911
3561	Old Epsomian	1911	3578	Woolwich Polytechnic	1912
3662	Old Felstedian	1913	3680	South Western Polytechnic	1913
3725	Old Reptonian	1914	3969	Old Pauline	1919
4104	Old Brightonian	1920	4145	Old Tonbridgian	1920
4197	Kingswood School	1220	4227	Old Uppinghamian	1920
4257	King's College School	1921	4305	Westminster City School	1921
4363	Old Malvernian	1921	4500	Old Etonian	1922
4653	Old Harrovian	1924	4660	Old Lancing	1924
4732	Old Bedfordian	1925	4903	Old Berkhamstedian	1927
4992	Old Crosbeian	1927	5398	Goldsmiths' College	1933
5461	Universities Lodge Cardiff	1934	5481	Old Wrekinian	1934
5499	Old Chelmsfordian	1934	5628	University of Birmingham	1936
5662	Old Dunstonian	1937	5682	Old Oundelian	1937
5683	University of Manchester	1937	5694	Old Northamptonian	1937

No.	NAME	Const	*No.*	NAME	Const
5752	OLD MILLHILLIAN	1938	5974	OLD DUNSTABLIANS	1944
6255	OLD STOPFORDIANS'	1946	6602	OLD WILSONIANS	1947
6734	OLD DUDLEIAN	1948	6766	SHOREDITCH COLLEGE	1948
6797	OLD HELEAN	1948	6963	OLD WORKSOPIAN	1950
6988	QUEEN'S COLLEGE, TAUNTON	1950	7022	SOUTHAMPTON UNIVERSITY	1950
7062	OLD HULMEIANS	1951	7181	OLD PALUDIANS	1952
7193	OLD GOREANS	1952	7311	OLD LOUGHTONIANS	1953
7408	OLD LUTONIANS'	1955	7411	OLD WULFRUNIANS	1955
7412	OLD COLFEIANS	1955	7460	STATIONERS' COMPANY'S SCHOOL	1956
7598	UNIVERSITY OF NOTTINGHAM	1958	7636	OLD MANWOODIAN	1959
7725	OLD BLOXHAMIST	1960	7924	OLD VESEYAN	1963
7933	OLD BLACKBURNIAN	1963	7988	OLD VERULAMIANS	1964
8006	OLD ROFFENSIAN	1964	8033	OLD OAKHAMIAN	1965
8170	ROYAL WOLVERHAMPTON SCHOOL	1967	8285	OLD PORTMUTHIAN	1969
8499	OLD MARLINGTONIAN	1973	9037	WEST BUCKLAND SCHOOL	1982
9270	OLD LERPOOLIAN	1987	9331	UNIVERSITY LODGE OF GUYANA	1989

Other names may not be readily identifiable as university or school lodges; these are shown in the following list with a remark against each entry indicating why the name was chosen.

No.	NAME	Const	*Remarks*
357	APOLLO UNIVERSITY	1786	Oxford; one of Apollo's attributes is the god of youth.
1492	ALMA MATER	1874	Literally 'Bounteous mother'; now applied to universities and schools as 'fostering mother' to their *alumni*. Lodge formed to cater for dons of Oxford and Cambridge universities.
1731	CHOLMELEY	1877	Highgate School. Sir Roger Cholmeley was founder of the school.
1820	SIR THOMAS WHITE	1879	Merchant Taylors School; founder and first headmaster of school.
1997	JOHN CARPENTER	1883	City of London School. John Carpenter was virtual founder of school.
2823	WILLIAM ROGERS	1900	Cowper Street School. Named after William Rogers, founder of school.
2956	ROBERT MITCHELL	1903	Regent St Polytechnic. Named after Robert Mitchell, architect, who lived locally.
3439	JOSEPH LANCASTER	1910	Borough Road and Bangor Training College. Joseph Lancaster was founder of the Lancastrian system of education.
3562	HONOR DEO	1911	Mercers' School. Honour be to God; motto of Mercers' Company.
3951	IN DEO FIDEMUS	1919	Varndean School, Brighton. We shall trust in God; motto of Brighton County Borough Council.
5191	ALDWORTH	1930	Reading Blue Coat School. Takes its name from Aldworth's Hospital, generally known as the Reading Blue Coat School.
6517	VOTUM	1947	Christ's Hospital School. Votum is Latin for a vow; it is also name of school song.
6754	OLD WYCOMBIENSIAN	1948	Royal Grammar School, High Wycombe. Name adopted from Arms of school; 'Schola Regia Wycombriensis'.
7181	OLD PALUDIANS	1952	Slough General School. 'Paludian' comes from 'palus', the Latin word for bog or slough.
8422	ACRE	1971	Royal Free Boys' School, Windsor. Name taken from Bachelors Acre, an area of land traditionally used by the bachelors of Windsor to pursue their sports and used as the school playground for over a century.
9304	AEDES CHRISTI	1988	Christ Church, Oxford. Literally, the house of Christ.

SCOUT AND YOUTH MOVEMENT

Nearly all the lodges that may be listed under this heading belong to an association known as the Kindred Lodges.

No.	Name	Const	*Remarks*
3546	Halcyon	1911	Boys' Club.
4425	Pro Deo et Patria	1922	Church Lads' Brigade. For God and our Country; motto of Church Lads' Brigade.
5250	Camperdown	1931	Jewish Lads' Brigade.
5800	Quest	1939	Scouts Association.
6473	Juventus	1947	Scouts Association.
6999	Pro Juventute	1950	Scouts Association; 'For [the service of] youth'.
8198	Venture	1967	Lodge formed for Venture Scouts.
8236	Pathfinder	1968	Scouts Association; 'The Pathfinder'; a painting by Ernest Carlos depicting Christ guiding a young lad.
8426	Pinewood	1972	Scouts Association; Named after scout training ground in Croydon.
8448	Red Scarf	1972	Scouts Association; the 'Gang-Show' lodge formed by Ralph Reader. The 'Gang-Show' members always wore a red scarf.
8500	Arrowhead	1973	Scouts Association; an arrowhead is the symbol of the Scout movement.
8662	Kudu	1975	Scouts Association; a kudu is an African antelope. The Matabele tribe use a horn from this animal to call their people together. Baden-Powell, the founder of the Scout movement, captured such a horn and used it for the first Scout Jamboree, or training course; similar horns are still used on such occasions.
8927	Sure and Stedfast	1979	Motto of the Boys' Brigade.
8992	Fleur de Lis	1981	Scouts Association; fleur de lys is stylized shape of the emblem (an arrowhead) of the Scout movement.
9454	Indaba	1991	Scouts Association; Indaba is a scouting term for a meeting of leaders.

SOCIETIES AND INSTITUTIONS

No.	Name	Const	*Remarks*
3537	Forum	1911	Society of Public Speakers.
3856	Lux in Tenebris	1918	Light in darkness; Society for Welfare of the Blind.
4000	Red Triangle	1919	Y.M.C.A.
4195	Rotarian	1920	Rotary Club.
4509	Edifice	1922	Institute of Builders.
7255	Pathfinder	1953	Pathfinder Asociation.
7619	Round Table	1958	Round Table Association.
8407	Ajex	1971	Association of Jewish ex-Servicemen.
8687	Prior Walter	1975	Order of St John of Jerusalem.

TEMPERANCE LODGES

Temperance is one of the four cardinal virtues; it is defined in the *Oxford English Dictionary* as 'the practice of restraining oneself in provocation, passion, desire etc.; rational self-restraint'. The word also has an attributed meaning; 'pertaining to, practising, or advocating total abstinence'. This led to the formation of temperance hotels and inns where no intoxicants are provided.

Some freemasons who favoured the temperance movement formed or joined temperance lodges where no intoxicants were provided at the after proceedings of the lodge. With the passage of time some of these lodges relaxed their rules to a greater or lesser degree.

It is not always apparent from the name of the lodge that it forbids alcohol, as the following list shows.

No.	NAME	Const.
2029	LODGE OF KING SOLOMON	1884
3027	KINGSWAY	1904
3096	ALDWYCH	1905
3237	PORTAL	1907
3302	THOMAS PROCTOR BAPTIE	1908
3750	BON ACCORD	1915
3784	STREATHAM HILL	1916
3947	PEACE AND CONCORD	1919
4153	FOREST GATE	1920
4652	ORION	1924

THEATRICAL

No.	NAME	Const	*Remarks*
2127	DRURY LANE	1885	A well-known theatre in London.
2190	SAVAGE CLUB	1886	Many actors amongst Club members.
2771	YORICK	1899	A reference to the skull of the king's jester found by a clown in Shakespeare's *Hamlet*; 'Alas! poor Yorick. I knew him, Horatio.' (Act 5).
2957	GREEN ROOM	1903	Members of Green Room Club have close connection with theatre.
3016	LYRIC	1904	A well-known theatre in London.
3098	CHELSEA	1905	Named to honour Chelsea Palace of Varieties.
3435	PROSCENIUM	1910	Stage space between curtain and orchestra, especially with the enclosing arch.
4246	GARRICK	1921	(David) 1717–79. Actor-manager of Drury Lane, theatre.
4875	TABLEAU	1926	Theatrical term
5177	THALIA	1930	Greek Muse of comedy and idyllic poetry.
5188	CRANBOURN	1930	For employees of Moss Empires and Associated companies; lodge met at Cranbourn Mansions.
5592	VAUDEVILLE	1935	Music Hall variety entertainment.
5670	OTHELLO	1937	Title of, and principal character in, a play by Shakespeare.
6269	ALLIED ARTS	1946	For variety artists.
6527	ALHAMBRA	1947	A well-known theatre in London.

VIRTUES

As might be expected there are very many lodges which chose to be known by a virtue, or in some cases, virtues. The four cardinal and the three theological virtues come readily to mind, but there were very many other characteristics chosen which might well be included under the heading 'Virtues'; some of these are shown in the following list.

The Cardinal Virtues

No.	LODGE	Const	*No.*	LODGE	Const
131	LODGE OF FORTITUDE	1772	147	LODGE OF JUSTICE	1801
169	LODGE OF TEMPERANCE	1784	219	LODGE OF PRUDENCE	1774
6275	LODGE OF FOUR VIRTUES	1946	8270	LODGE OF THE CARDINAL VIRTUES	1968

The Theological Virtues

No.	Lodge	Const	*No.*	Lodge	Const
141	Lodge of Faith	1774	223	Lodge of Charity	1797
302	Lodge of Hope	1794	4102	Faith, Hope and Charity	1920

The General Virtues

No.	Lodge	Const	*No.*	Lodge	Const
58	Lodge of Felicity	1737	89	Lodge of Unanimity	1754
137	Lodge of Amity	1761	149	Lodge of Peace	1820
156	Harmony	1804	160	Lodge of True Friendship	1766
174	Lodge of Sincerity	1768	186	Lodge of Industry	1788
199	Lodge of Peace & Harmony	1801	202	Lodge of Friendship	1771
226	Lodge of Benevolence	1797	230	Lodge of Fidelity	1810
276	Lodge of Good Fellowship	1789	317	Lodge of Affability	1799
321	Lodge of Unity	1806	335	Lodge of Rectitude	1812
343	Lodge of Concord	1814	466	Lodge of Merit	1840
494	Lodge of Virtue and Honor	1844	564	Lodge of Stability	1849
573	Lodge of Perseverance	1850	581	Lodge of Faith	1850
1384	Lodge of Equity	1871	1607	Lodge of Loyalty	1876
1616	Friendship and Harmony	1876	1753	Lodge of Obedience	1878
2535	Fellowship	1894	3589	Fervency	1912
4072	Fraternity	1920	4358	Goodwill	1921
5270	Lodge of Good Counsel	1931	5353	Lodge of Happiness	1932
5830	Friendship and Justice	1940	5954	Diligence	1944
6065	Peace and Concord	1945	6199	Good Samaritan	1945
6372	Lodge of Chivalry	1946	6584	Lodge of Friendship and Service	1947
6628	Lodge of Good Endeavour	1948	6821	Lodge of Mercy	1949
7029	Lodge of Good Intent	1950	7366	Lodge of High Endeavour	1954
7428	Lodge of Dedication	1955	7656	Lodge of Noble Endeavour	1959
8106	Lodge of Harmony and Concord	1966	8150	Lodge of Light and Learning	1966
8451	Harmony and Unity	1972	8457	Bond of Friendship	1972
8562	True and Faithful	1973	8646	Lodge of Good Report	1975
8668	Justice and Peace	1975	8802	Lodge of Friendship and Care	1977
8807	Justice and Equity	1977	8890	Lodge of Good Heart	1979

This category was quite popular in the early days of Freemasonry; during the period 1980–90, however, when over 450 lodges were consecrated, there were scarcely half-a-dozen lodges which adopted such a name.

'Family connections'

The name adopted by a newly-formed lodge is chosen by its founders and submitted for approval by the Grand Master. In some cases the name of the new (daughter) lodge will have an association with the name of the sponsoring (mother) lodge. And as the family tree grew one might assume there would be an association between the names of the 'generation' of lodges. This, however, does not happen very often, and certainly not for more than a few 'generations'. Here are some examples.

a) *The 'French' connection.* Jeanne d'Arc Lodge No. 4168 was named after Jeanne d'Arc Lodge No. 5, Grande Loge Nationale Française, with whom the founders had a close association during the 1914–18 war. In 1947 it sponsored Fleur de Lys Lodge No. 6479 and in 1952 Lodge of Lorraine No. 7176, which in turn sponsored (in 1963) Lodge of Orleans, No. 7955, thus maintaining the French connection.

b) *The 'astronomy' connection.* Herschel Lodge No. 1894 was sponsored by Windsor Castle Lodge No. 771 with the help of Etonian Lodge of St John No. 209. The lodge was named after William Herschel (1738–1822), the Astronomer Royal. In 1945 this lodge sponsored Observatory Lodge No. 6094 which in turn sponsored, in 1966, Planet Lodge No. 8142, thereby maintaining the link with astronomy.

Another 'astronomical' connection is found in Neptune Lodge No. 1264 (Neptune being a planet) and the lodge it sponsored Uranus Lodge No. 6485.

c) *The 'local area' connection.* This example deals with lodges bearing the names of towns or villages in one area. It starts with Reading Lodge of Union Lodge 414. Reading is a town in Berkshire. In 1859 this lodge sponsored Windsor Castle Lodge No. 771; Windsor Castle is situated in Windsor, a neighbouring town to Reading; it also sponsored Wycombe Lodge No. 1501. Beaconsfield Lodge No. 2849 is a daughter lodge of Wycombe Lodge and it sponsored Chilterns Lodge No. 4634. (The Chilterns is the name of the local area; it is also the name of the hills surrounding the area.) Their daughter lodge was named Penn and Tyler's Green Lodge No. 5876, both being names of nearby villages. From the latter lodge came Hall Barn Lodge No. 8480, this being the name of the ancestral home, near Beaconsfield, of Lord Burnham, (Prov. GM Bucks, 1976–). Other place name lodges in this 'family' include Marlow Lodge No. 2752; Hughenden Lodge No. 6308; Stokenchurch Lodge No. 7438; Bourne End Lodge No. 7943; Seer Green Lodge No. 9055 and Chenies Lodge, No. 9127.

General comments

Lodge names are derived from many sources. The founders of a lodge are free to choose whatever name they like to submit to the Grand Master for his approval, provided (a) it is not the name of a living person (though in practice names of Provincial Grand Masters and some eminent freemasons are allowed); (b) the appropriate permission has been obtained if the name is of a titled or armigerous person and (c) the name is not already in use by another lodge in the same Province or District, or in London if the new lodge is to meet there, although the latter restriction was not always applied; there are a few duplicated lodge names. Examples are:

Lodge name	*No.*	Constd.	Meeting in
Lodge of Friendship	6	1721	London
	206	1772	London.
St John's	70	1759	The Province of Devon
	1247	1868	The Province of Devon
St John's	221	1797	The Province of East Lancashire
	348	1815	The Province of East Lancashire
St Andrew's	222	1797	London
	231	1776	London

The classification of lodges shown in the foregoing pages are but an example of the various sources from which lodge names are derived; there are many others. However, little purpose would be served in making a comprehensive list, interesting though that might be.

Adopting a name to emphasize a point

The Lodge of Antiquity No. 2 is an interesting example of a name being adopted to emphasize a point; one is tempted to say 'cocking-a-snook' at Grand Lodge. This lodge was one of the four original lodges which, according to Anderson's 1738 *Constitutions*, met in 1717 and 'constituted themselves a GRAND LODGE . . .'. It was shown as the lodge that met 'At the *Goose* and *Gridiron* Ale-House in *St Paul's Church-Yard*'.

According to the author of the history of the lodge (*Records of the Lodge of Antiquity No. 2*, W.H. Rylands, privately printed, 1911) in about 1759 'a number of members were admitted who are described as 'Barbadoes, Bermuda and elsewhere'. This seemed to have prompted a change in the name of the lodge; hitherto it was known as 'the Queen's Arms Lodge', though it had also been known as the Old Lodge of St Paul's; from July 1759 it became known as The West India and American Lodge.

Lane's *Masonic Records, 1717–1894* shows the name of the lodge was changed to the Lodge of Antiquity in 1770; there is nothing in the lodge history to support this. The name was certainly being used in 1776 for the *Records* give a facsimile copy of a printed list of members for that year.

A revision of the by-laws of the lodge took place in 1777; one item reads

That the fifteenth Article remain as it is, the Lodge for the future be call[ed] ye Lodge of Antiquity instead of the West India & American Lodge, as lately called.

The following information is taken from the lodge history; note the words which have been underlined by the author of this book.

[Page 6, describing an entry in a Minute Book] The writing is fairly modern in character, clerk-like and could not have been written earlier than the year 1768. Old Lodge of St Paul *or the Lodge of Antiquity.*

[Page 34] Original No. 1, *the old Lodge of St. Paul's* . . .

[Page 370] . . . in the year 1693, . . . At which time the *Lodge of ANTIQUITY, or (as it was then called) the OLD LODGE OF ST. PAUL* . . .

[Page 371] . . . The OLD LODGE OF ST PAUL, or *as it is now emphatically styled. THE LODGE OF ANTIQUITY* . . .

[Page 377] . . . & Members of the R^t W, *Lodge of Antiquity No. 1 formerly called the Old Lodge of St. Pauls.*

The extracts from pages 370–1 and 377 come from documents dealing with events resulting in the expulsion of William Preston by Grand Lodge. These events took place between late 1777 and early 1779. Preston had committed what Grand Lodge considered a gross error of judgement. When called to task, he refused to accept that Grand Lodge had the power to enforce laws it had made following its formation in 1717 on *his* lodge, the Lodge of Antiquity, which at that date (1717) had already been in existence for some years; he contended his lodge had an inherent right to act in the way it did.

It was just before these events that the Lodge of Antiquity adopted its present name, a name not hitherto adopted by any lodge. In the light of the information just given, it could well be that the reason the name was adopted, and its reiteration in the documents quoted, was to support Preston's argument by stressing the antiquity of the lodge. Grand Lodge, however, was not impressed; it still expelled Preston, though, happily, he was later reinstated.

PART 3:

BADGES.

Introduction.

IN the *Oxford English Dictionary* the word 'badge' is defined as 'a distinctive device, emblem or mark; a distinguishing sign'. For the purpose of this book the term may be defined as the device which forms the decorative part of the Founders' or Past Masters' Jewels; the device or motif appearing on the lodge summons.

The device depicted on a badge may serve various functions; it may be symbolic; indicate ownership; be purely decorative or serve as a rallying point. The device on a lodge badge usually has some bearing on the name of the lodge; its purpose is to enhance the identity of the lodge.

Many of the badges used by lodges may be described as canting or allusive; that is to say the badge is a graphic or pictorial pun on the name of the lodge, or the badge refers to an incident connected with the person or place from whom the name is taken. Some examples of heraldic allusive or canting arms are as follows.

The arms of William Speed depict three swifts, fast-flying birds of the swallow family;
dolphins, the swiftest 'fish' of ancient naturalists, are shown on the arms of Sir John Fleet;
three eagles are shown on the arms of Robert de Eglesfield, founder of Queen's College, Oxford;
the arms of Oxford show an ox and a ford;
the arms of Cambridge show a bridge and the River Cam;
the Islip arms depict an eye and a slip of a tree;
the Bream shield shows three bream (a fresh-water fish);
the Arms of the Royal College of Physicians show a hand coming out of the clouds feeling the pulse of an arm coming from the left side of the shield; the arms of Thomas Miller bear a windmill, denoting his occupation; the arms of Rochdale show a woolpack encircled by two branches of cotton because of the town's association with cotton and woollen goods, especially flannel:
the arms of Liverpool show a liver-bird (or cormorant) with a branch of laver (or sea-weed) in its beak, and the arms of James Fraser, Bishop of Manchester, bear a fraise or strawberry flower.

The authority for using masonic badges.

The present Rule 241, *Book of Constitutions* (1989 edition) reads;

> No Masonic jewel, medal, device, or emblem shall be worn in the Grand Lodge, or any subordinate Lodge, unless it appertains to, or is consistent with, those degrees which are recognised and acknowledged by the Grand Lodge in the preliminary declaration to these Rules, as part of pure Antient Masonry, and has been approved or allowed by the Grand Master.

Neither the *Constitutions* of the premier Grand Lodge nor those of the Grand Lodge of the Antients had a comparable Rule. The first *Book of Constitutions* issued after the Union of the two Grand Lodges was published in 1815. The relevant wording there was;

> The following masonic clothing and insignia are to be worn by the craft, and no other, on any pretence, be permitted in grand lodge, or in a subordinate lodge.

It then listed details of the jewels and aprons to be worn.

The next *Book of Constitutions* was issued in 1843; this, and all subsequent editions, contained almost word-for-word the present Rule 241 with the exception of the last few important words 'and has been approved or allowed by the Grand Master'; these words first appeared in the 1926 edition.

A 'device or emblem' printed on a lodge summons or shown on a lodge banner is not 'worn in [a] subordinate lodge'. It may be argued therefore, that it is not necessary to have such device or emblem 'approved or allowed by the Grand Master'. In practice, though, the contrary is generally the case.

It has to be said that this was not always so; some lodges that had been using badges before the present procedure was introduced still use them even though they have no authority from the Grand Master.

The Grand Secretary's office has recently revised their 'Notes on Lodge and Chapter badges' which are available from the General Office, Freemasons' Hall, Great Queen Street, London, WC2B 5AZ; the Grand Secretary has kindly given permission for them to be reproduced here.

Notes on Lodge and Chapter Badges

1. The following notes are intended to help Lodges and Chapters in preparing designs for their badges before submitting them to the Grand Secretary or Grand Scribe E (via the Provincial or District Grand Secretary or Scribe E, where appropriate) for the approval of the MW The Grand Master or the ME The First Grand Principal.
2. The principles explained in the notes apply equally to designs – which also require approval – for Founders' Jewels, Past Masters' Jewels and Banners, etc.
3. However, it is not possible to foresee every problem that might arise, and it should therefore be noted that adherence to every point in the notes does not guarantee that the design will be approved.
4. The notes contain a depressing number of negatives, but design is possible. If extreme difficulty is encountered, the Grand Secretary's office (General Department) will almost certainly be able to help further.

LODGE BADGES

Arms or Armorial Bearings, and Badges

5. Lodges are recommended to adopt *Badges* instead of *Arms*. Arms are heraldic devices borne on a shield. A Badge consists of some object or objects combined to form a design without the use of a shield.
6. The grant of Arms, which carries the right to bear them, is a Royal Prerogative. Lodges which wish to design and assume arms must consult the College of Arms.

Arms

7. No part of the Royal Coat of Arms may be assumed by a Lodge without the express consent of the Sovereign, or other Royal Person whose Arms are concerned.
8. No private Lodge is permitted to use the Arms of the United Grand Lodge.
9. No Arms of an individual or Corporation may be adopted without the written consent of such individual or Corporation, and in the case of consent being given the Arms must be used in their entirety. *NB*: Even when such consent is obtained, it may not be appropriate for the Lodge to use Arms which have been designed to represent an individual or public body, and therefore approval may be withheld.
10. No Lodge may adopt as Arms a portion of an existing Coat of Arms, even if permission be given by the holder, since such adoption would amount to the assumption of a new Coat of Arms.
11. Designs may not be approved if they are heraldic in character or attempt to avoid the Laws of Arms by using a corruption of a shield outline.
12. Arms that have become extinct cannot be used.
13. A small shield carried by a knight as part of the design of a badge is permitted, since this is only coincidental to his accoutrements; in most cases the shield is seen in perspective, and thus cannot be regarded as Arms in the ordinary sense.

General

14. Designs for Lodge Badges are sometime submitted with the Petition for a new Lodge, but they cannot be approved until a Warrant has been granted. However, if the matter is urgent, the design may sometimes be approved *subject to the grant of a Warrant*.
15. Symbols foreign to the Craft, for example interlaced triangles (which are Royal Arch) should not occur. Most Craft badges have a (or the) square and compasses incorporated, but these are not essential.

Religious Symbols

16. Symbols associated with one particular religion or religious denomination, for example the Cross, must not be included as a predominant part of the design. If the Lodge is named after a Saint who is depicted in the badge, then a small cross may be carried by the Saint.

Imperial Crown

17. The Imperial Crown is the one shown on Government documents and publications (– for example; British Passports, United Kingdom Driving licences and top right corner on obverse of £5 Sterling bank notes). These vary slightly but are intended to be the same Crown, and will not be approved as part of a badge. A Saxon crown or a nondescript one (such as is shown in Plate 31 of the Royal Arch *Regulations*) may be allowed.

Corn and Acacia

18. A wreath composed or corn and acacia (as shown in the jewels of Grand Officers) is not allowed, since these are symbolic of Grand Rank.

CHAPTER BADGES

19. Rules on Lodge badges apply *mutatis mutandis* to Chapter Badges. Most Chapter badges are based on those of the Lodges to which they are attached, with some Royal Arch allusion in place of the square and compasses – for example interlaced triangles, the triple tau, etc. The Lodge's title must be changed to the Chapter's.

M.B.S. HIGHAM
Grand Secretary and Grand Scribe E
18 November, 1992

These notes, or something like them, have been available for many years. However it seems fairly evident from the following description of selected badges that some lodges are unaware of the Notes – or have chosen to ignore them. As indicated earlier some badges may well have been adopted by lodges long before the notes were available.

Examples of lodge badges

Examples of badges used by lodges are now given. The lodge number and name, in order of precedence, are followed by a general rather than a detailed description of the badge, together (where known) with a reason for the choice of the less obvious items or other interesting information; sometimes however it has not been possible to find the reason for the choice of the badge. The name of the town in which the lodge meets, together, where appropriate, with the Province or District, is also shown. It should be noted that the Province does not always tally with the County in which the town is situated; for example Linslade and Slough are in the masonic Province of Buckinghamshire, but the former is in the County of Bedfordshire, and the latter is in the County of Berkshire.

Reference to concentric circles and the like, many of which show the name and number of the lodge and enclose the badge of the lodge, has generally been omitted; so too has reference to masonic emblems. One or two lodges are mentioned where the badge is nothing more than circles enclosing the square and compasses; this is because the badge used by the chapter differs from that borne by the lodge (see under 'Chapters), and it was thought a comparison may be helpful.

Many lodge badges are composed of, or incorporate the arms of, an individual or corporation. The language of heraldry is not easy to understand, so in describing such badges heraldic terms have generally been avoided; where they have been used a simple explanation has been given.

The use of the terms 'arms' or 'armorial bearings' is intended to indicate what is shown on the shield. The correct term for the total armorial display, that is the shield and the emblems thereon, the colours used, and (where applicable) the crest, supporters, motto and decorative features surrounding the whole, is 'an achievement'.

The Kings of Arms, under the Earl Marshal of England, the Duke of Norfolk, are the only legal authority for the granting of arms in England and Wales; in Scotland it is the Lord Lyon and his officers. They are officers of the Sovereign who is the Fount of Honour, from whom all British heraldic insignia, which are marks of honour, ultimately derive. But a school may 'display commemoratively' the arms of the founder, provided that these arms have themselves been granted by the Kings of Arms to the founder or that he is entitled to them by descent from the grantee or that the arms have been duly and correctly registered in the past; and provided that the school does not claim its founder's arms as its own.

There are certain requirements to be observed regarding the colours and the emblems on the shield, the style of the crest and the use of supporters, all of which come under the control of the officers of the College of Arms. The decorative features, or mantling, are at the discretion of the heraldic painter. Some mottoes, where incorporated in the badge, are given in the following descriptions, though not their meaning; these are given in the next following section.

The cost of printing precludes an illustration of every badge described; those particularly interested in seeing a copy can probably get a copy of the summons showing the badge from the secretary of the relevant lodge. Illustrations of some of the more interesting badges have been reproduced elsewhere in this book.

Some detail regarding the badges has been taken from lodge histories or kindly given by lodge secretaries; other detail has been taken, with permission, from that excellent book *The History of Freemasonry in Berkshire and Buckinghamshire* (L.R. Harborne and R.L.W. White, Abbey Press, Abingdon, 1990).

In some cases the information supplied comes from a description of the lodge banner rather than the lodge badge, but in by far the majority of cases where a lodge has a badge and a banner the detail shown on each is the same, though there are some exceptions. Some further information on this point will be found under the section of this book dealing with banners.

The Grand Stewards'. London.

A cornucopia between the legs of the compasses extended, i.e. the jewel of a Past Grand Steward, but with the words 'Grand Stewards' Lodge on the double oval. A cornucopia is the horn of plenty, containing an endless supply of food and drink; an attribute of hospitality. It was the gift of the Greek god Zeus to Amalthea who nursed him as an infant.

1 Grand Master's. London.

A blazing sun (the central feature of the Grand Master's apron) within a concentric circle bearing the name and number of the lodge, topped by a five-pointed celestial crown.

2 Lodge of Antiquity. London.

Three oval shields, the first bearing the arms of the Grand Lodge of the Antients, the second the arms of Grand Lodge South of the River Trent, the third the arms of the premier Grand Lodge, all three within cherubim supporters, the ark of the covenant and the Hebrew words meaning 'Holiness to the Lord'. The lodge was associated with all three Grand Lodges.

4 Royal Somerset House and Inverness. London.

The Scottish Royal Arms differenced by a label with three points, the outer two bearing the cross of St George, the middle bearing two hearts in pale. The Earl of Inverness was one of the titles borne by the Duke of Sussex, a member of this lodge.

This badge is seen on the obverse side of the lodge jewel, the reverse side of which shows a hunting horn, the badge of the old Horn Lodge (then No. 2 on the roll of the premier Grand Lodge) which united with Somerset House Lodge in 1774; in 1828 the lodge united with Royal Inverness Lodge and took its current name.

The difference between the Scottish Royal Arms and the Royal Arms as used by the Sovereign when in Scotland today should be noted. The former is a red lion rampant within a double tressure (or bordure) of fleur-de-lys. This dates from Alexander III (d. 1286); before then the tressure, said to signify an antient alliance between Scotland and France, was not used.

The Royal Arms used by the Sovereign today when in Scotland are the same as those used in England except that Scotland is given precedence. Scotland occupies the first and third quarters instead of England; there is also a change in the supporters; when used in England the dexter supporter is a crowned lion and the sinister a unicorn; when used in Scotland the dexter becomes a crowned unicorn and the sinister an uncrowned lion. There are other differences too, mainly in the use of the mottoes.

5 St George's and Corner Stone. London.

St George slaying the dragon. St George, a martyr, is the patron saint of the kingdom of England; no particulars of his life have survived. There are various legends about him; the story of his saving a maiden by slaying a dragon comes from the *Golden Legend*, a collection of the lives of saints made by Jacques de Voragine in the thirteenth century.

Other saints are also shown as slaying a dragon, but St. George is often identified by a red cross on a silver field. Examples of dragon-slaying saints are:

St Philip the Apostle destroying a huge snake at Hierapolis, in Phrygia;
St Martha who killed the dragon Tarasque at Aix (la Chapelle);
St Florent killed a dragon which haunted the Loire;
St Cado, St Maudet and St Pauld who did similar feats in Brittany;
St Romain of Rouen destroyed the dragon La Gargouille in the Seine;
St. Michael the Archangel, St Margaret, Pope Sylvester, St Samson (Archbishop of Dol), Donatus (fourth century), St Clement of Metz all killed dragons.

10 Westminster and Keystone. London.

A portcullis from the arms of the City of Westminster, above which is a keystone of an arch bearing the number 10. The portcullis was originally the badge of John Beaufort, son of John of Gaunt, and was subsequently adopted by his descendant Henry VII, first of the Tudor dynasty. Since under the Tudors Westminster became the seat of the Court, a Bishop's See and hence a City, and a Parliamentary Borough, the portcullis was adopted by Westminster in 1601. It is presumed the lodge adopted the device as part of their badge shortly after it had started meeting in Westminster after changing its name from Tyrian in 1792. The lodge records indicate that the old seal of the lodge bore the Masons' arms, a chevron bearing compasses between three castles, a castle as a crest and the name Westminster and Keystone No. 5 shown at the top, together with the motto beneath 'In the Lord is all our Trust', The lodge was number 5 from the 1755 enumeration until the Union in 1813 when it was given No. 10.

14 Tuscan. London.

A pillar of the Tuscan, the first and simplest order of architecture; it bears the number 14.

21 Lodge of Emulation. London.

A bee-hive with bees. In his history of the lodge *The Lodge of Emulation No 21, 1723–1906*. (H. Sadler, London: Warrington & Co./Spencer & Co. 1906) the author wrote:

> I regret to find that the existing records throw no light on the subject of the distinctive emblem adopted by the lodge – the bee-hive. It is a very old masonic symbol and has doubtless been used by the lodge for a long period; signifying Industry, Perseverance and Diligence, it seems to be quite in harmony with the name of the lodge; it may also have a wider application – that of an orderly and well-disciplined community of builders, all working together to the same end.

33 Britannic. London.

Britannia, a woman with shield, helmet and trident. The author of *Two hundred years of Freemansonry; a history of the Britannic Lodge, No. 33, Annis Domini 1730–1930* (Sanderson, Kenning: London, no date) surmises that the name Britannic was adopted in 1774 as a patriotic title during 'a period of patriotic fervour'. The lodge had a close connection with Royalty; HRH Henry Frederick Duke of Cumberland was for a time its 'Perpetual' Master. There is nothing to indicate when the figure of Britannia was adopted as the lodge badge. Britannia was the name given to the island of England and Scotland.

91 Lodge of Regularity. London.

A scythe and an hour-glass within two concentric circles, the innermost bearing the name and number of the lodge, the outer the motto 'Jam ducentos floruit annos'.

114 British Union. Ipswich, Suffolk.

A rose, thistle and shamrock springing from a common stem above a scroll bearing the inscription 'Sic tria juncta virent'. The name was first used in 1777 during a period of intense political awareness. The badge reflects the association with the three countries shown in the Union flag: England, Scotland and Ireland; Wales being a Principality is not shown.

144 St. Luke's. London.

A winged ox, one of the four apocalyptic beasts (*Ezekiel* 1; 5–14 and *Rev.* 4; 6–8.) The ox, the sacrificial beast, is the emblem of St Luke, whose gospel begins with the account of the sacrifice of the priest Zacharias.

185 Lodge of Tranquility. London.

A shield showing quarterly the armorial bearings of the areas in which the lodge at one time met. In the first quarter the Borough of Holborn, a red cross on a silver shield; in the centre of the cross a hind pierced by an arrow; in chief (the top part of the shield) three shells on a black background; in the second the City of London, a red cross on a white background, a sword, point uppermost, in the first quarter; in the third the City of Westminster, a golden portcullis on a blue background in chief, a red and white rose on either side of the arms of Edward the Confessor, a cross flory between five martins; in the fourth the Borough of St. Marylebone, on a black background in the upper dexter corner a gold fleur-de-lys; in the upper sinister corner a gold rose; below in the area formed by a chevron blue and white lines representing waves. The mottoes of the boroughs are not shown, but the lodge has adopted its own motto: 'Tranquillitas heri hodie et in aeternum'. Above the shield as a crest on a chaplet, is a blazing sun.

192 Lion and Lamb. London.

The arms of United Grand Lodge of England. The lodge was named in 1816; the reason for the name as given in a leaflet by Bro. C. MacCall Botley in 1966 states;

To the lodge brethren, the lion was self evident; it is the lion rampant of Scotland, one of the emblems on the banner of the Antient Grand Lodge, which Arms had also been adopted in their entirety by our lodge (and appear on our present banner).
... the lion also appeared on the armorial bearings of the Duke of Kent, whilst the lamb was on those of the Duke of Sussex.
Thus the name 'Lion and Lamb' was adopted by the lodge at the time of the formation of the United Grand Lodge, and it symbolizes the merging of the Antients represented by the 'lion', with the Moderns represented by the 'lamb' of the Duke of Sussex. There is also the Old Testament quotation; 'The lion and the lamb shall lie down together.'

This is a misquotation; the correct wording, from *Isaiah* 11:6 is:

The wolf also shall dwell with the lamb, and the leopard shall lie down with the kid; and the calf and the young lion and the fatling together; and a little child shall lead them.

The Past Master's jewel, adopted in 1886, shows on the ribbon a lion on which is superimposed a lamb.
The lodge discontinued using the arms of the Grand Lodge of the Antients and adopted the arms of the United Grand Lodge of England.

214 Hope and Unity. Hutton, Essex.

An anchor above clasped hands symbolizing unity. (An anchor was an early Christian symbol of hope, from *Heb.* 18–19.) It is a symbol often seen on the first degree tracing board and is dealt with at some length in the fourth section of the First Lecture.

235 Lodge of Nine Muses. London.

A shield flanked by branches of laurel and palm, showing a fountain against a landscape background with a crescent in the top dexter corner; as a crest an arm holding a palm branch. A note on the fly-leaf of the first minute book lists the names of the nine Muses, daughters of Jupiter and Mnemosyne, each of whom presided over a particular art, as follows; Clio, the Muse of history; Euterpe, music, lyric poetry; Thalia, comedy, pastoral poetry; Melpomene, tragedy; Terpsichore, dancing and song; Erato, lyric and love poetry; Polyhymnia, heroic poems; Calliope, epic poetry, and Urania, astronomy. The note also says 'The palm tree, the laurel and all the fountains of Pindus, Helicon, Parnassus, &c. were sacred to the Nile. This has been used as a theme for the Coat of Arms achieved for the lodge.'

259 Prince of Wales's. London.

The badge of the Prince of Wales showing three feathers within a royal coronet, surrounded by concentric circles bearing the motto 'Honi soit qui mal y pense', the whole topped by a royal crown. The lodge was originally intended to consist only of those honoured with appointments under HRH George, Prince of Wales, or men firmly attached to his person and interests.

The badge showing three ostrich feathers generally known as 'the Prince of Wales's feathers' is in fact the badge of the Heir Apparent who, though he may be the eldest son of the Sovereign may not have been created Prince of Wales. There is no succession to this title; at every vacancy it becomes merged in the Crown and is renewed only at the pleasure of the Sovereign. The badge and the motto 'Ich Dien' (I serve) was appropriated by the Black Prince at the Battle of Crécy in 1346, after the slaying of the King of Bohemia.

295 Combermere Lodge of Union. Macclesfield, Cheshire.

The armorial bearings of Viscount Combermere; in first and fourth quarters a chevron between three hanks of white cotton palewise, and in chief pendant from a red ribbon a representation of the medal and clasps presented to the first viscount (Cotton); in the second and third quarters a black lion rampant. The motto, crest and supporters are not shown.

386 Lodge of Unity. Wareham, Dorset.

Standing on a square of chequered tiles on which is inscribed the name Wareham, are two columns, one of the Doric and one of the Corinthian Order, surmounted by globes; these represent the senior and junior wardens. They are conjoined by a square bearing the name of the lodge to give stability, this represents the Master of the lodge. Under the square is the All-Seeing Eye, a reminder of the infinite knowledge of God; at the base of the Eye is a shield bearing the arms of the town of Wareham; this rests on an oblong ashlar showing the lodge number.

414 Reading Lodge of Union. Sindlesham, Berkshire.

The early arms of the borough of Reading within concentric circles bearing the words Radingie S. Communitatis, the whole encompassed by the square and compasses.

567 Lodge of Unity. Warwick, Warwickshire.

Fasces surrounded by a continuous cord tasselled at the ends and which forms four circles, two of which enclose an oak leaf surmounted by the square and compasses, the other two an oak leaf surmounted by a scrip purse. The oak leaves represent the Forest of Arden, the area in which the lodge meets. The whole design is meant to represent unity.

Fasces date back to at least Roman times and were probably of Etruscan origin; they were bundles of rods bound up with an axe in the middle, its blade projecting, an ensign of authority or power. Fasces were born by the lictors (or officers) who attended on certain of the magistrates of ancient Rome the number of lictors varying according to the rank of the magistrate.

574 The Loyal Berkshire Lodge of Hope. Newbury, Berkshire.

An anchor cross, signifying hope. (See comment under Lodge No. 214 above.)

599 Cherwell. Banbury, Oxfordshire.

A representation of an Eleanor Cross (known here as the Banbury Cross) beneath a rising sun. The lodge meets at Banbury; the rising sun is from the arms of the borough. Eleanor crosses were erected at each of the twelve places where the funeral cortege of Eleanor of Castile (d. 1290, wife of Edward I) rested on its journey from Harby, Nottinghamshire to Westminster Abbey, London.

601 St John's. Wellington, Shropshire.

The figure of St John holding a book in his left hand and a pen in his right hand; these are attributes of the saint, being a reference to his writings. The design of this badge should be compared with the design shown on the banner, details of which are given in the appropriate section of this book.

611 Lodge of the Marches. Ludlow, Shropshire.

The arms of the Borough of Ludlow, where the lodge meets; the arms show a lion couchant guardant (that is to say resting with its fore-limbs forward, head up and full faced) between three white roses; the word 'Silurian' is on the dexter side and the word 'Mercian' on the sinister side, these were the names of two old Shropshire Lodges with which Ludlow was closely associated. The name of the lodge is derived from those districts on the border of Wales of which Ludlow is the centre.

637 Portland. Stoke-on-Trent, Staffordshire.

The Portland vase, a Roman vase (*c.* first century AD) of dark blue transparent glass with engraved figure decoration in white opaque glass; acquired in eighteenth century by the Duchess of Portland from Barberini Palace, Rome; now in British Museum.

707 St Mary's. Bridport, Dorset.

St Mary holding the Christ child.

710 Pleiades. Totnes, Devon.

A waning moon surrounded by eight stars. The Pleiades are a close group of small stars in the constellation Taurus; the stars usually number seven, associated with the seven daughters of Atlas, though only six stars are visible to the naked eye. According to Greek mythology the eldest daughter, Electra, was 'the lost Pleiad', and not represented by a star. It is not known why the badge depicts eight stars.

726 Staffordshire Knot. Stafford, Staffordshire.

A Staffordshire Knot, i.e. a half-hitch or overhand knot, part of the arms of Staffordshire; the design is derived from the old-fashioned cursive script of the capital S.

739 Temperance Lodge. Birmingham, Warwickshire.

A two-humped camel with the motto 'Nulla Pallescere Culpa'. Presumably the camel, with its ability to be able to be sustained by the water it stores, is meant to illustrate that no stronger drink is required by man to sustain his life.

754 High Cross. London.

A tall steeple with a cross on top. The motto beneath is 'Dieu pour la tranches qui contre'. [*sic*]

757 Concord. Audenshaw, East Lancashire.

An eastern setting showing a man stroking a lion.

767 Union. St Alban, Hertfordshire.

Clasped hands; the motto beneath is 'Vis una fortior'.

823 Everton. Liverpool, West Lancashire.

The Everton Beacon; this was an ancient fire beacon, a well-known landmark, now destroyed.

840 Scientific Lodge. Wolverton, Buckinghamshire.

A train crossing the old Haversham viaduct. The motto beneath is 'Mind moves the masses'; this emphasizes the connection of the founders of the lodge with railway engineering, two of whom, Sir Daniel Gooch and James McConnell were famous locomotive engineers.

857 St Mark's. London.

A winged lion on top of the upper part of a pillar. The lion, one of the apocalyptic beasts, is attributable to Mark because his gospel begins with the voice crying in the wilderness which the early commentators on the bible took to be an allusion to the lion.

869 Gresham. Cheshunt, Hertfordshire.

A bust of Sir Thomas Gresham (1519–79), a London merchant and founder of the Royal Exchange, London.

871 Royal Oak. London.

An oak tree; on the ground, a man and a ladder. Probably a reference to Charles II hiding in an oak tree at the battle of Worcester. The name of the lodge (which meets in London) is taken from the Royal Oak Tavern, Deptford, its first meeting place.

872 Lewis Lodge. Whitehaven, Cumberland and Westmorland.

A shield, the dexter side showing a chevron bearing the compasses, between three castles, and the sinister side the device known as the lewis as seen on the senior warden's pedestal.

873 Lodge of Industry. Hyderabad, Pakistan.

A bee-hive and bees; beneath, the motto 'Industria et labore'. The bee has always been associated with being industrious as is evidenced by the saying 'as busy as a bee'.

879 Southwark Lodge. London.

The Southwark Cross as shown in the third quarter of the armorial bearings of the Borough of Southwark, namely an annulet ensigned with a cross patee and interlaced with a saltire conjoined in base. This is commemorative of the martyrdom of St George and refers to the church of St George the Martyr in Borough High Street, Southwark. The motto used by the lodge is 'Antiquum obtinens'.

902 Burgoyne. London.

The Tower of London surrounded by the motto 'Peritia potius quam vi'. The lodge was originally known as The Tower Hamlets Engineers Lodge; it was formed by members of the Tower Hamlets Voluntary Engineers. The name was changed to Burgoyne in May 1869, after the then Constable of the Tower, Field Marshal Sir John Burgoyne.

904 Phoenix. Rotherham, Yorkshire, West Riding.

A phoenix, the mythical bird said to consume itself in flames every five hundred years and then arise from its ashes with renewed youth.

917 Cosmopolitan. London.

A globe within the square and compasses. The *Oxford English Dictionary* gives one meaning of 'cosmopolitan' as 'Belonging to all parts of the world'.

938 Grosvenor. Birmingham, Warwickshire.

A wheatsheaf. The lodge was named as a compliment to Lady Leigh, wife of the then Provincial Grand Master of Warwickshire, whose maiden name was Grosvenor. A wheatsheaf appears in the second and third quarters of the Grosvenor arms.

1067 Royal Forest of Dean. Newnham-on-Severn, Gloucestershire.

A Royal Forest of Dean free-miner. The miners of this forest had special customs and privileges which are recorded in fourteenth century documents; these state that the customs had *then* been granted 'time out of mind'.

1076 Capper Lodge. London.

A three-masted sailing ship, symbolizing the close association of the lodge with the sea and shipping. It has not been possible to establish precisely why the lodge adopted the name 'Capper', though there is a strong possibility that the title was chosen in order to commemorate the works of charity performed among the poor of the district by one of the founders, Charles Capper, a ship owner who was probably wealthy.

1124 St Oswald. Oswestry, Shropshire.

Badge adapted from arms of Borough of Oswestry where the lodge meets; it displays a crowned figure of St Oswald seated upon a throne, a sword in his right hand and a branch in his left hand. King Oswald (b. 605) was brought up in Columba's monastery at Iona; he had great power and was said by Bede to have ruled over 'all the peoples and provinces of Britain, which includes four languages, those of the Britons, Picts, Scots and Angles'. He co-operated with Bishop Aidan in building many churches; he was slain in 642 at the battle of Maserfield, said to be seven miles from Shrewsbury. The town of Oswestry is named after King Oswald.

1147 St David's. Manchester, East Lancashire.

The red dragon of Wales with the Welsh motto 'Y ddraig goch ddyry gychwyn'; St David is the patron saint of Wales. Henry VII adopted the device of a red dragon for his standard at Bosworth Field in 1485; it was the device of Cadwalader, 659?–689 (there are different spellings of the name), from whom the Tudors were descended. The dragon is an example of a tribal emblem which has survived as an heraldic device.

1381 Kennington. London.

A wicket used in cricket in front of which are two cricket bats in saltire and two cricket balls. This is a reference to the Oval cricket ground at Kennington, London.

1400 Curwen. Workington.

Cumberland and Westmorland. Arms of Curwen family (fretty, giving the impression of network); on the dexter side, in pale, the Volume of the Sacred Law, the square and the level; on the sinister side, also in pale, the square and compasses, a pentalpha and the plumb-rule. The motto beneath reads; 'Si je n'estoy.'

1402 Jordan. Torquay, Devon.

A representation of the River Jordan.

1404 Saint Vincent. Bristol.

On a field, against a background of sea and rocks, St Vincent holding a palm frond, and a wolf, a raven and a gridiron. St Vincent is associated with Clifton Rocks, Bristol; he was a Spanish deacon, imprisoned in A.D. 304, tortured on the rack then by fire on a gridiron. On his death his body was thrown to the wild beasts, represented by the wolf; a raven defended the body from mutilation. The motto shown is 'Patiendo vincens'. The palm occurs frequently in art as the attribute of the Christian martyr.

1410 Saint Peter and Saint Pauls'. Wolverton, Buckinghamshire.

Crossed keys and a sword. The keys are the emblem of St Peter ('You are Peter, the Rock; and on this rock I will build my church ... I will give you the keys of the Kingdom of heaven', Matt. 16, 18–19); the sword, which representes the sword of the Spirit, ('that which the Spirit gives you', Eph. 6, 17) is the emblem of St Paul; the sword was the instrument of his martyrdom.

1432 Fitz Alan. Oswestry, Shropshire.

A shield showing a lion rampant taken from the Fitzalan arms; a white horse with a slip of oak leaves in its mouth (the Fitzalan crest) is shown above. The Fitzalan family were the Lords of Oswestry in the twelfth century.

1461 Clausentum. Woolston, Hampshire and Isle of Wight.

Within a circle a spread-eagle, the emblem of the Roman empire, standing on a fasces; the All-seeing Eye above, radiated and the name of the lodge below. The lodge was named after the Roman city on the Woolston side of the River Itchen.

1474 Lodge of Israel. Birmingham, Warwickshire.

A banner showing a lion couchant bearing a sceptre, a crown above. (This is often seen on the Judah banner in the Royal Arch); beneath is the word 'Israel' written in Hebrew.

1491 Athenaeum. London.

A bust of Athena, goddess of wisdom. The motto beneath is 'Sapientia summa felicitas'.

1493 Robin Hood. Nottingham, Nottinghamshire.

A representation of a golden meadow on which stands an oak tree (typical of the trees that grow in Sherwood Forest), three stags (animals of the forest and part of the arms of the city of Nottingham), and a wild boar eating acorns, (representing other animals of the Forest); the whole portraying Robin Hood country. The words 'Oriens sylva' meaning 'East wood' are also shown; the lodge meets at Eastwood.

1522 Olicana. Ilkley, Yorkshire, West Riding.

Three Roman pillars beside a river. Olicana was the name of an old Roman town. The pillars are a photographic reproduction of those found in the grounds of Ilkley church.

1532 Bective. Carlisle, Cumberland and Westmorland.

The square and compasses on a semé or scattering of stars, a larger one in the dexter corner and a waxing moon in the sinister corner.

1534 Concord. Radcliffe, East Lancashire.

Beneath an All-seeing Eye, a winged angel bearing a stringed instrument and surrounded by a waxing moon and stars.

1538 St Martin's-le-Grand. London.

A pentalpha on a shield below a sword and crozier (or pastoral staff) in saltire, topped by a bishop's mitre.

1545 Baildon. Baildon, Yorkshire, West Riding.

Two Egyptian columns with a winged circle between. The design was taken from the panelling which decorated the dais in the room in which the lodge used to meet in Baildon.

1575 Clive Lodge. Market Drayton, Shropshire.

A bust of Lord Clive (1725–74), the statesman and general who founded the empire of British India. The Clives, or Clyves, were one of the oldest families in the county of Shropshire.

1583 Corbet. Tywyn, North Wales.

A raven, a bird of the corvus family; taken from the Corbet canting (or punning) arms.

1589 St Dunstan's. London.

St Dunstan holding a crozier and a pair of tongs (his emblem) with which he is said to have tweaked the nose of the devil. The crozier refers to his office as Archbishop of Canterbury; the story of the tongs is given in the following extract from Brewer's *Dictionary of Phase and Fable*.

> Dunstan was painter, jeweller and blacksmith. Being expelled from court, he built a cell, near Glastonbury church, and there worked at his handicrafts. It was in this cell that tradition says the Devil had a gossip with the saint through the lattice window. Dunstan went on talking till his tongs were red hot, when he turned round suddenly and caught his Satanic Majesty by the nose.

1598 Ley Spring. London.

Æagle, the goddess of spring, emptying a pitcher of water into the Ley spring, near what is now Leytonstone. The modern spelling of the nearby river is Lea.

1622 Rose. London.

A red rose.

1625 Tredegar. London.

The armorial bearings of Viscount Tredegar, the first and fourth quarters a black griffin; in the second and third quarters on a gold background a chevron bearing three thistles, between three blue roses; the badge also includes the motto 'Si Deus nobiscum quis contra nos.' The name is pronounced 'Tredeegar'.

1662 Beaconsfield Lodge. London.

The arms of Disraeli, Earl of Beaconsfield, per saltire, that is quarterly diagonally; in the top quarter a tower, triple towered; in the lower quarter a golden eagle displayed, and in the side quarters, a black lion rampant. The motto 'Forti nihil difficile,' is also shown. The castle and the lions show the family connection with Castile. Disraeli had some tutoring from a clergyman at Walthamstow, where the lodge was formed.

1677 Crusaders Lodge. London.

A fully armed crusader mounted upon a caparisoned horse.

1752 Ogmore Lodge. Bridgend, South Wales, Eastern Division.

A steam locomotive with trucks on a brick bridge crossing a river.

1772 Pimlico. London.

The Royal Standard; this badge has been used by the lodge since December 1892. The address of one of the members at that time was given as the Standard Music Hall, Victoria; the site is now occupied by the Victoria Palace.

1816 Victoria Park. London.

A past-master's jewel in the form of a ten-pointed star on which rest concentric circles enclosing a shield bearing the Royal Arms.

1817 St Andrew's. Southend-on-Sea, Essex.

St Andrew standing against a cross in saltire; on the dexter side a field gun; on the sinister side a steamship, yacht and boat. The cross in saltire is the attribute of St Andrew and represents his suffering on a cross of that shape, an idea that seems to have been unknown before the late middle ages.

1894 Herschel Lodge. Slough, Buckinghamshire.

A shield showing in the upper portion the astronomical symbol of Uranus and the escutcheon charged with the Badge of Ulster from Herschel's armorial bearings; below, a representation of the reflecting telescope. Surmounting the shield, an eagle on a demi-terrestrial sphere; the motto beneath is 'Coelis exploratis'. The badge reflects the work of Herschel, the great astronomer who discovered the planet Uranus.

1920 Eurydice. London.

A sun rising out of (?or setting in) water. Eurydice was the bride of Orpheus, son of Apollo, god of the sun.

1962 London Rifle Brigade. London.

Superimposed on rifles in saltire a shield bearing the arms of the City of London; at the top an imperial crown; beneath, the square and compasses.

1967 Beacon Court. Gillingham, East Kent.

A representation of a large building which was known by that name.

1983 Martyn Lodge. Southwold, Suffolk.

Concentric ovals bearing the name and number of the lodge and enclosing the square and compasses.

1984 Earl of Clarendon Lodge. Watford, Hertfordshire.

The original badge of the lodge showed the armorial bearings of the Earl of Clarendon; on a white background, a red cross charged with five gold shells; crest, a white lion rampant; supporters, two black eagles, wings expanded, wearing a ducal crown and a plain white cross on the breast; the motto beneath is 'Fidei coticula crux'.

The lodge history records that in 1946 a 'new crest' was presented to the lodge; it is now used as the lodge badge and can be described as follows; on a spread-eagle, crowned, an orb held in the sinister claw and (what may be) a sceptre held in the dexter claw, a shield showing the cross of St George, with a crescent in the first quarter. The same supporters as in the Clarendon arms plus, over the dexter supporter, the spread-eagle just described appears as a crest, and over the sinister supporter, the crest as shown in the Clarendon arms. A motto is not shown.

1996 Priory Lodge of Acton. London.

A building representing the Priory, previously known as the Acton Priory and later the Berrymead Priory; a tree in the foreground is said by some to be a reminder of the 'finely wooded grounds' in which the Priory stood, by others a reference to the Tree Tavern built by a local architect who played an important part in the affairs of the lodge.

2076 Quatuor Coronati (London).

Concentric ovals bearing the name and number of the lodge; four men are shown within the inner oval. The name of the lodge refers to the four crowned martyrs, the legendary saints of masonry mentioned in the *Regius MS c.* 1390, lines 497–534; this is the earliest-known masonic manuscript. The lines reflect a legend of certain craftsmen put to death in Rome.

There are two legends which indicate that there were two separate groups, one of four soldiers and another of four civilians along with one other person, making a total of nine in all. To reflect this the petition for the lodge was signed by nine brethren, four of whom were soldiers, the other five, civilians. The Feast Day of the Quatuor Coronati is 8 November; this was the date of the Installation Meeting which was given in the first By-Laws of the Lodge.

The badge adopted by the lodge is taken from the Missal presented to Isabella of Castille, Queen of Spain and Sicily, on the occasion of the marriage of the Infante Don Juan to the Archduchess Margaret, daughter of the Emperor Maximillian, in April, 1497. This Queen was the mother of Katharine of Aragon, who became the first wife of King Henry VIII who died in 1536 and is buried in Peterborough Cathedral.

In 1974, following the formation of Quatuor Coronati Correspondence Circle Limited (a company set up to deal with the business aspects of the lodge), another logo was adopted, namely four crowns each pierced by a sword; these are placed in a diamond formation, each being connected with a short line; in the centre is the number of the lodge. The four crowns are meant to represent one of the earlier-mentioned groups of four and the sword piercing each crown, the martyrdom they suffered.

2127 Drury Lane. London.

Concentric circles bearing the name and number of the lodge; an Imperial crown above.

2131 Brownlow. Ellesmere, Shropshire.

The crest of the arms of the third Earl of Brownlow after whom the lodge was named, namely a black lion's head with a collar of silver and blue; the family owned most of the district.

2140 Huguenot Lodge. London.

A lighted candle surrounded by seven stars; beneath, the motto 'Lux lucet in tenebris'. The badge is an adaption of the arms of the Waldenses or Vaudios who formed a communion separate from the Roman Church and lived in three high valleys of Piedmont on the eastern side of the Cottian Alps. The seven stars are meant to represent the seven liberal arts and sciences, namely, grammar, rhetoric, logic, arithmetic, geometry, music and astronomy.

2153 Lodge of Hope. Portsmouth, Hampshire and Isle of Wight.

The figure of Hope holding an anchor. The motto on Past Masters' jewels is 'In te domine speravimus' (In thee, O Lord, have we hoped [put our trust]), but in 1900 the lodge changed its motto to 'In Deo spes nostra' (In God is our hope).

2182 Sterndale Bennett. London.

Trumpets in saltire surmounted by a lute. Sterndale Bennett was a famous composer.

2190 Savage Club Lodge. London.

Within a wreath of corn and a sprig of acacia, a head of a man wearing feathered head-dress, meant to illustrate a savage. The lodge was founded by members of the Savage Club which was principally formed for the association of brethren connected professionally with Literature, Art, Drama, Music and Science. The lodge owes its origin to a suggestion made by King Edward VII when Prince of Wales and MW Grand Master, an Honorary Member of the Club.

2191 Anglo-American Lodge. London.

Two shields, the dexter showing the Royal Arms, the sinister the Stars and Stripes of the United States of America; superimposed above, the square and compasses, and below, a representation of the bald eagle, the emblem of the United States of America. Surrounding the shields, concentric circles between which, on the dexter side, the Royal motto 'Dieu et mon droit' (God and my right) and, on the sinister side the motto of the United States of America 'E pluribus unum' (One out of many); above, an Imperial Crown. Beneath the badge, in saltire, the Union Flag and the Stars and Stripes. The lodge was founded with the view to drawing closer together the bonds of masonic union existing between the two countries.

2195 Military Jubilee Lodge. Dover, East Kent.

Superimposed on Union flags in saltire, a terrestrial globe with a wreath of roses, representing England, on both the dexter and sinister sides; below is a pair of leeks representing Wales; surmounting the Union flags are, on one side a thistle representing Scotland, and on the other side a shamrock representing Ireland. An Imperial crown tops the globe.

2202 Regent's Park Lodge. London.

Within concentric circles bearing the words 'Merit & Ability' an Indian elephant with the square and compasses above. The Indian elephant was adopted as the lodge badge in honour of the first master of the lodge, V.W. Bro,

Dorabjee Pestonjee Cama, Grand Treasurer, the first Parsee to receive Grand Rank. Another reason for its adoption may be because the London Zoo, the headquarters of the Zoological Society, is within the boundaries of Regent's Park.

2226 St David's Lodge. Rhymney, Monmouthshire.

A leek resting upon a harp. A leek is the emblem of Wales; it is worn on St David's Day. It is traditionally said that St David caused the Britons under King Cadwallader to distinguish themselves by a leek in their caps. They conquered the Saxons, and recall their victory by adopting the leek on every anniversary, 1 March. St. David is the patron saint of Wales. A harp is a musical instrument indicating the love of music by the Welsh.

2228 Dene Lodge. Cookham Dean, Berkshire.

A yacht; the lodge used to meet in the upper rooms of a boathouse.

2233 Old Westminsters'. London.

The armorial bearings of Westminster School with the motto 'Dat Deus incrementum'.

2246 Cyclist Lodge. Surbiton, Surrey.

A man riding a 'penny-farthing' bicycle, that is one with a large front wheel, the rear a much smaller wheel.

2271 St Pancras. London.

A figure of St Pancras (or Pancratius), a young Roman martyr, holding a palm (an attribute of a Christian martyr), and a book (a symbol of learning); the connection of a book with the saint is not known.

2302 St Mary's. Nottingham, Nottinghamshire.

A representation of St Mary holding the Christ child.

2430 Runymede Lodge. Slough, Buckinghamshire.

A representation of King John signing the Magna Carta at Runymede. The Magna Carta was the great charter of liberty obtained by the barons of England from King John in 1215.

2435 Wineslai Lodge. Winslow, Buckinghamshire.

Below a saxon crown representing King Offa who is said to have had a camp at Winslow, a gridiron representing the instrument on which St Lawrence was burned (St Lawrence is the name of the parish church of Winslow, originally Wineslai).

2467 Pickwick. London.

Between the square and compasses, the fictional character from *Pickwick Papers*, Samuel Pickwick, standing on a chair. The founders of the lodge were members of the Pickwick Bicycle Club, the oldest bicycle club.

2475 Border. Farnham, Hampshire and Isle of Wight.

Shields showing the armorial bearings of the counties of Berkshire, Hampshire and Surrey, together with a pentalpha on the dexter side and a pentalpha on the sinister side.

2488 Eccentric. London.

An owl in flight holding in its beak a clockface. This is a copy of the clock which used to be in the premises of the Eccentric Club in Ryder Street, London, S.W.1; the figures on the clockface were reversed from left to right and the hands travelled anti-clockwise. The club was founded in 1890 by a theatrical costumier, mainly for those connected with the theatre and music hall. It is said that one of the early members, unwittingly gave the club its name; exasperated by the failure of the committee to choose a name, he exclaimed that they were a 'bunch of eccentrics!' Some of the founder members of the lodge were members of the club and the lodge met at the premises of the club for many years.

2533 Fitzwilliam Lodge. Peterborough, Northamptonshire and Huntingdonshire.

The arms of the Earl of Fitzwilliam, quarterly; the first and fourth quarters lozengy, silver and red; in the second and third quarters a chevron between three leopards' faces, gold; the motto 'Appetitus rationi pareat' is also shown.

2536 Staines Lodge. Staines, Middlesex.

A shield showing on the dexter side a representation of the London Stone with two swans beneath, and on the sinister side the three seaxes associated with the County of Middlesex. The chapter attached to the lodge bears the name London Stone Chapter.

2571 Holmes Lodge. Newcastle upon Tyne, Northumberland.

A shield impaling the arms of Grand Lodge with those of Holmes; the motto beneath being 'Deus mihi adjutor'.

2654 Arter Lodge. King's Heath, Worcestershire.

A shield showing the head and shoulders of Queen Victoria; the lodge was formed during her Jubilee year. The name of the lodge is that of one of its founders; this was before the modern convention of the Grand Master not approving the name of a lodge being that of a living person.

2656 Adam's Peak Lodge. Talawakelle, Sri Lanka.

The local landmark known as Adam's Peak.

2682 Sancta Maria Lodge. London.

Within an oval, the radiated figure of St Mary.

2699 Wandle Lodge. London.

Between two pillars topped with a globe and standing upon a chequered floor, a pentalpha beneath concentric circles bearing the name of the lodge and its number in the centre, the whole encircled (dexter) by an ear of corn, and (sinister) a sprig of acacia.

2700 Old Masonians Lodge. London.

Within a radiated star, concentric circles showing the name and number of the lodge and enclosing the monogram OM; alongside, a representation of the building once used as the Royal Masonic School for Boys, at Bushey, Hertfordshire.

2809 Bee Hive Lodge. London.

A shield impaling the arms of the City of London and three lions in a vertical line, walking head full-faced to the front. A coronet above.

2812 St Martin's. Bletchley, Buckinghamshire.

A man on horseback giving his cloak to a beggar. This represents the charity of St Martin who, whilst serving in Gaul with the Roman army, found a beggar shivering in the winter cold. He cut his cloak in half and shared it with the beggar.

2862 Grant Lodge. Galle, Sri Lanka.

A radiated star on which is superimposed a shield bearing three crowns.

2884 Borough of Stepney. London.

Within concentric circles showing the name and number of the lodge, broken at the top and bottom by a rectangle, four smaller circles each containing a representation of a saint associated with the Borough of Stepney, namely.

St Anne, to whom a church in Limehouse, designed by Nicholas Hawksmoor, is dedicated; the church clock is the highest in London;

St Mary, to whom a church in Bow, built in 1311, is dedicated;

St Dunstan, bishop of London who, in the thirteenth century, rebuilt the only church then in Stepney; it remained the only church for almost another one hundred years, and

St George, to whom a church is dedicated and known as St George-in-the-East; it was built in 1714–26 to the design of Nicholas Hawksmoor; it has a massive tower, 160 feet high; the saint is shown slaying a dragon. The rectangle at the top contains a representation of the Tower of London; the rectangle at the bottom shows Tower Bridge, both of which are within the county boundaries.

In a vertical line between the circles are illustrations of a clipper ship, symbolizing the borough's sea-faring associations; a facade representing the entrance to the northern end of the tunnel which starts in the borough and runs under the River Thames to Rotherhithe, and Wapping Dock gate. There is also an illustration of St Katharine's Dock, serving as a reminder that the docks were very active in the borough.

2885 Charterhouse Deo Dante Dedi. London.

The armorial bearings used by Charterhouse School bearing the words 'Deo dante dedi' beneath the shield and below that the words Ædes Carthunianæ. The lodge was constituted in 1901 and named Charterhouse Lodge; the words 'Deo dante dedi' were added to the name of the lodge in 1907. The arms are gold, three crescents on a chevron between three red rings; the arms are those of Thomas Sutton, the founder of the school.

2901 King's Navy Lodge. Gillingham, East Kent.

An anchor and crown in pale between, on the dexter side, a flagpole bearing the White ensign above the Union Flag, and on the sinister side, a flagpole bearing four flags as used in the old system of signalling indicating the numbers, from top to bottom, 2; 9; 0; 1, the number of the lodge. (The Navy now uses different pennants from those shown.) The crown and anchor is a punning representation of the King's Navy.

2913 Junior Engineers' Lodge. London.

The figure of Vulcan, the Roman mythological god of fire and metal working; above, a representation of a governor.

The founders of the lodge were professional engineers who belonged to a learned body known as the Vulcanite Society; they worked for a company which built marine engines which at that time would have been steam powered. Steam engines would usually be fitted with a governor to regulate the engine speed within set limits.

2941 Lambeth Borough Council. London.

Two shields within a scrolled frame, one bearing the arms of the Archbishopric of Canterbury (Lambeth Palace is the Archbishop's official residence) and the other the arms of the Duchy of Cornwall (which has extensive land-ownings such as the Oval cricket ground, in the borough); the letters ER between them, these being the cypher of Edward VII the monarch at the time of the constitution of the lodge. The arms of the Archbishopric are on a black background an Achiespicopal Cross surmounted by a pall showing four black crosses each similar in shape to the Victoria Cross but with the lower limb tapering to a point; the arms of the Duchy of Cornwall are black with fifteen gold coins in lines of five, four, three, two and one.

3058 Loyd Lindsay Lodge. Wantage, Berkshire.

A tent of the type used in the Crimean War; above, the motto 'Astra Castra Lumen Numen,' from the arms of the Loyd-Lindsay family (no longer used by the present branch of the family).

3092 Elstree Lodge. Radlett, Hertfordshire.

A stag passant; a stag or hart is often used as a punning reference to the county of Hertfordshire, in which Elstree is situated.

3098 Chelsea Lodge. London.

The arms of the Borough of Chelsea, namely red, within a double cross of gold, a crozier; in the first quarter a winged bull, in the second a lion rampant with its head turned to the rear, in the third a sword, point downwards, between two boar's heads cut off at the neck and in the fourth a stag's head; the motto beneath is 'Nisi Dominus frustra'. The winged bull represents St Luke, patron saint of Chelsea; the lion comes from the arms of Lord Cadogan, Lord of the Manor. The boar's heads and sword and the stag's head are taken respectively from the arms of the Sloanes and the Stanleys. The lodge was named to honour the Chelsea Palace of Varieties.

3131 Heather Lodge. Sindlesham, Berkshire.

The great memorial avenue of Wellingtonia pines on the Wellington College estate; the lodge was sponsored by Wellesley Lodge (Wellesley being the family name of the Duke of Wellington); the lodge took its name from the heather which grew in abundance in that area.

3221 London Dorset Lodge. London.

On the interwoven letters LD (London Dorset) a shield bearing three seaxes and another bearing the arms of the county of Dorset; between them the square and compasses.

3252 King Edward VII Lodge. Gillingham, East Kent.

The monogram ER ensigned by an Imperial crown and enclosing VII.

3261 Randle Holme Lodge. Birkenhead, Cheshire.

The armorial bearings, including the crest, of Randle Holme, a seventeenth century antiquary and genealogist known to have been a freemason in Chester *c*. 1675. The earliest extant evidence of speculative Freemasonry in England is found amongst some notes written by him and his contemporary Elias Ashmole, quoted at the beginning of this book.

3343 Duke of Sussex Lodge. London.

The undifferenced Royal arms, topped by an Imperial crown and 'Dieu et mon droit' beneath. Undifferenced Royal Arms are borne only by the sovereign; sons and daughters have a 'label', a narrow band across the top of the shield, from which are pendent (usually) three branches or 'points'. In the case of the heir apparent, these points are plain; for other sons and daughters of the sovereign one or more of the points bear one or more charges in the form of a plain cross, a rose, a heart or an anchor. For Royalty the colour of the label is silver and the colours of the charges either red or blue. The charges on the points shown on the arms of the Duke of Sussex were two red hearts, one above the other, on the centre point, and a red cross on the other two points. It is not known why the undifferenced arms are used as a badge by the lodge.

3387 Arts and Crafts Lodge. London.

A triple arch standing on a chequered floor within two columns of the doric order supporting an entablature.

3427 Loddon Lodge. Wargrave, Berkshire.

The Loddon lily which grows on the banks of the River Loddon.

3439 Joseph Lancaster. London.

A shield showing a bee; above, the motto 'Floreat apis', a punning reference to the familiar appellation of 'Old Bs', as past students of the Borough Road Training College became known. The lodge was formed by members of London lodges connected with the scholastic profession; it was named after a distinguished educationalist who, early in the nineteenth century, established the first system of really popular education in England.

3526 Pecunia Lodge. Southgate (London).

A stylized shield showing St. Paul's and other London buildings, with the figure of Mercury flying above them. The founders of the lodge were Rate Collectors, members of the Metropolitan Rate Collectors' Association, living and working in London. 'Pecunia' is Latin for 'money', the commodity being collected by the Rate Collectors; Mercury was the servant and messenger of the gods (as well as the god of commerce and of thieves!) whose duties may well have included collecting what was due to them.

3547 Old Fraternity. London.

Bluebells, which like all flowers, are things of beauty and a joy to see. In particular, the bluebell denotes constancy, and is meant to remind members of the lodge to be constant in their devotion to God and their friendship to mankind. The motto 'Ad finem esto fidelis' is shown above.

3684 Berkshire Masters. Sindlesham, Berkshire.

The Berkshire stag alongside a tree.

3700 Commercial Travellers. Newcastle upon Tyne, Northumberland.

A representation of a globe at the foot of which are three mottoes; 'Ubique', 'Per mare per terram' and 'Nulla dies sine linea'; beneath, the armorial bearings of the county of Northumberland.

No. 3743 St Catherine's Lodge. London.

The badge of the lodge is shown in the centre of a decorative panel of roses and foliage above another panel flanked by two columns. The badge itself composed on concentric circles enclosing a portrayal of a crowned St Catherine, seated and leaning against a spiked wheel, holding in her right hand a sword, point downwards; the name and number of the lodge is shown in the upper part of the concentric circles; the lower half shows a wreath of laurels with a shield in the centre on which the arms of the City of London are shown.

The lodge was formed by members of The Worshipful Company of Turners in London and takes its name from their patron saint, Catherine of Alexandria who was formerly venerated as a Christian saint, virgin and martyr. With little convincing evidence about her existence, she was removed from the Roman Catholic Church Calendar in 1969; at one time she was second only to Mary Magdalene in popularity among female saints.

According to the *Golden Legend* she was of Royal birth who was converted to Christianity after becoming queen; in a vision she underwent a mystic marriage with Christ. The Emperor Maxentius desired her and tried to undermine her faith by argument; having failed he sent fifty philosophers to try; they too failed and the emperor had them burnt at the stake. He then devised an instrument consisting of four wheels studded with iron spikes to which St Catherine was bound, ready for torture, but a thunderbolt destroyed it before she was harmed; she was then beheaded. The spiked wheel became her main emblem; another is the sword of execution.

3749 Hale Lodge. Altrincham, Cheshire.

A reproduction of a photograph of the old Tithe Barn in Hale Barns, an area to the east of Hale village. The motto 'A ma puissance' comes from the armorial bearings of the Earl of Stamford, Lord of the Manor, whose seat was at Dunham Hall.

3791 Fratres Calami. London.

Clio, the first of the Muses, the daughter of Jupiter and Mnemosyne, crowned with laurels, holding in one hand a scroll or book; beneath, quill pens in saltire; all within a sprig of acacia and an ear of corn and surrounded by concentric circles bearing the name and number of the lodge. The name Clio signifies honour and reputation; her office was faithfully to record the actions of the brave and illustrious heroes. Fratres Calami Lodge was formed for the purpose of furthering the influence of the masonic pen; the founders were mostly lodge secretaries. The name means 'brothers of the pen', literally 'of the reed' – from which pens were made in classical times.

3900 Helio. London.

A blazing sun; helio is Greek for sun.

3954 Victory Lodge. Newbury, Berkshire.

A 'Winged Victory' figure.

4041 Corium Lodge. London.

A tanned hide, neck uppermost, showing an oak tree upon which rest the square and compasses, surrounded in the corners by the head of a cow, the head of a buffalo, a sheep and a goat; the motto 'Fraternus amor maneto' is shown below. The oak tree is a reference to the main tanning agent of leather; the four animals are a reference to the principal sources of the raw material used by those employed in the leather industry, indicated by the tanned hide.

4106 Meridian. London.

A sundial indicating noon, the meridian.

4158 Sabrina Lodge. Shrewsbury, Shropshire.

A representation of the statue of Sabrina with the motto 'Floreat Salopia' in a scroll above. Sabrina is the nymph of the River Severn in Milton's 'Comus' which was first presented in Ludlow Castle in 1634. Sabrina is Latin for River Severn.

4191 Cookham Manor. Sindlesham, Berkshire.

A rare token halfpenny issued in 1668 by Martha Spot, then the landlady of the King's Arms in Cookham; both sides of the coin are shown beneath the Berkshire stag.

4222 Vespasian Lodge. Woolston, Hampshire and Isle of Wight.

A reproduction of the old Roman silver coin, a denarius, showing the head of the emperor Vespasian, with the motto 'Servabo fidem'.

4280 Harmony Lodge. Carlisle, Cumberland and Westmorland.

A lyre on which is superimposed a sheet of music showing the musical notation used for the phrase 'So mote it be'.

4443 Cheyne Lodge. London.

A design based on the armorial bearings of the Sloane-Stanley family, one of whom was the joint first initiate of the lodge. The arms are: in the first and fourth quarters three eagles' legs on a gold background; in chief (that is at the top of the shield) an indented line above which are three bucks' heads, (Stanley); in the second and third quarters, on a red background, a silver sword, point down, between three boars' heads cut off at the neck; in chief (see above), on a furry background a red lion walking between two black diamonds (Sloane).

4586 Joppa Lodge. Birkenhead, Cheshire.

A man being assisted up the face of a cliff. The idea of a lodge bearing the name Joppa is said to have come from Joppa Mark Lodge No. 11 whose members persuaded St Aidan Lodge to sponsor the new lodge. The name Joppa was considered (wrongly) by some of the founders to have originated from the 9th degree of the Ancient and Accepted Rite Intermediate Degrees which is related to events after the death of Hiram Abiff. The significance may be apparent to members of the Mark degree. The mottoes beneath the badge are 'Je tiens' (I hold) and 'Je tiendras' (I will hold you).

4717 Whitsters' Lodge. Windsor, Berkshire.

A scene from 'The Merry Wives of Windsor' depicting Mistress Ford's kitchen at Windsor where Falstaff was concealed in a basket containing dirty laundry being carried from the house to the Whitsters at Datchet Mead where he was dumped in a muddy ditch (Shakespeare *The Merry Wives of Windsor*, act 3, scene 3.) The motto of the lodge is 'Proxima munditia pietati', meaning Cleanliness is next to Godliness. The lodge was formed by members of the National Federation of Launderers.

4733 Collagen Lodge. London.

Within concentric circles showing the name and number of the lodge a tanned skin, tail uppermost, showing objects illustrative of the process of tanning, namely fleshing knives, a chemist's wash bottle, an acacia tree the bark of which is used in the process of tanning, and curriers' knives used in the dressing and finishing of leather. The name Collagen is a scientific term given to the gelatinous substance of the hide which is capable of being converted to leather, thus differentiating it from the whole skin or hide possessing wool or hair and other matters requiring removal before tanning. The lodge was sponsored by Corium Lodge (see above) 'to promote and foster Freemasonry and good comradeship between past students, masters and professors of the Leathersellers' College'.

4821 Laus Deo Lodge. London.

The badge used is very similar to the armorial bearings of the Worshipful Company of Bakers, the main source of recruitment for the lodge members; a shield showing, on a red background, scales between three golden wheat sheaves; at the top of the shield two anchors on wavy lines representing the sea; between the anchors and issuing from a cloud an arm and hand supporting the scales shown in the main body of the shield; the crest is a wreath of wheat held aloft by two hands; the supporters are bucks with a chaplet of wheat as a collar around the neck.

The wheat sheaves are an obvious reference to the raw material used by bakers; the scales a reminder of the 'Assize of Bread' which governed and strictly controlled the bakers' trade (the 'bakers' dozen', thirteen, was a 'voluntary insurance' against short weight); the anchors are a reference to St Clement, the patron saint of the Livery Company. The supporters are a very good example of canting or punning arms, being bucks with wheat, indicating buckwheat, a cereal plant, very popular in the United States of America when prepared as breakfast cakes; the term seems to have been beech wheat, so called because of its three-cornered seeds like beech-mast.

It is not known why St Clement is the patron saint of bakers; he was a pope who died at the end of the first century and venerated as a martyr; but there is no good evidence that he was one. His death by drowning with an anchor around his neck is legendary. The anchor was probably originally associated with Clement simply as the Christian symbol of hope and steadfastness, the legend being invented later to explain the situation.

There is a St Clement who was a baker; he became a priest and was canonized in 1909. But any suggestion of confusion between the two saints so far as the Bakers' Company is concerned is easily discounted by the fact that they received up-dated armorial bearings from Clarenceaux King of Arms in 1536, the charges including two anchors; there was also a clear reference to St Clement in their original title.

4855 Christopher Wren Lodge. Windsor, Berkshire.

St. Paul's cathedral above the interwoven initials of Christopher Wren, the architect of the cathedral.

5009 Isma Lodge. London.

Four circles; in the first, Mercury, the god of commerce, with his caduceus; in the second, a waxing moon and stars; in the third, the letters ISMA, and in the fourth, a unicorn. The name of the lodge is formed from the initials of the Incorporated Sales Managers' Association (now the Chartered Institute of Marketing). The design is meant to symbolize the attributes of industry, particularly in relation to salesmanship. The Latin quotation beneath the badge is 'Cura communis venditoris venditori'.

5024 Lapis Magnes. London.

The north pole with a stone from which rises a flash to the letter N above. The name of the lodge means 'magnetic stone'; as the majority of the founders had a close association with the General Electric Company they decided that the trademark of that firm, 'Magnet', be used as a basis for the name of the lodge.

5146 Dormer. London.

A dormer window. In considering the name for the new lodge the founders felt that as the dormer is the window that gives light to the Sanctum Sanctorum, so the new lodge would provide opportunities to give the light of Freemasonry to all its members.

5214 Industria Lodge. Slough, Buckinghamshire.

A pentalpha or five-pointed star depicting aspects of industry associated with the Slough Trading Estate with which the founders were associated; the items depicted are two bi-planes, two airships, a lorry and a steam locomotive. In the centre of the star is a sun with radiation tooling spreading therefrom and displaying a complex of factories, chimneys and water towers, all supported by a human figure. The name 'Industria' is also shown.

5368 Old Ellesmerian. Ellesmere, Shropshire.

On a purple background, two celestial crowns and a cross flory (that is each end shaped like a fleur-de-lys), all gold; the lower part of the shield is a chevron, that is like an inverted V coloured gold, on which is a black raven with a gold ring in its beak; a similar raven is shown as the crest. Below is the motto 'Pro patria dimicans'.

The shield, crest and motto are a reference to the saintly King Oswald to whom the school is dedicated and who fought a battle near Oswestry. The crowns refer to his kingship and the heavenly crown gained by him; the cross stands for the cross he raised before his victory against the heathen Penda at Heavenfield and for Oswald's saintly life; the colours purple and gold are royal colours. The raven refers to a legend concerning Oswald's coronation, when the vessel containing the sacramental annointing oil was accidentally broken; a raven miraculously appeared with new oil, bearing in its beak a letter containing the assurance that the oil had been consecrated by St Peter himself. The ring in the raven's beak refers to the story of Oswald's sending the bird to a heathen princess whom he wished to convert and marry.

In Christian art the raven is an emblem of God's providence in allusion to the symbolical ravens which fed Elijah.

5560 Lodge of Unity. Sao Paulo, Brazil, South America, Northern Division.

A beehive with a sprig of acacia on the dexter side and an ear of corn on the sinister side; above, the word 'Prudence'.

5655 Parsifal Lodge. Twickenham, Middlesex.

Within concentric ovals bearing the name and number of the lodge in the top half and the words 'Victor mannae occultae sumet' (see *Rev.* 2: 17) in the lower half, a chalice with a dove above, both radiated. These emblems refer to the Holy Grail, the vessel from which Christ drank when He instituted the Last Supper, which according to secular literature, had been placed in the safe keeping of a band of Christian knights. In Wagner's opera *Parsifal* the hero is a knight of that name, a personification of Christianity, whilst Klingsor, a sorcerer and an enemy of good, is the personification of Paganism; the triumph of Parsifal over Klingsor is the triumph of Christianity over Paganism.

5688 West Croydon Lodge. Croydon, Surrey.

A shield resting upon open compasses; in the first and fourth quarters a caboshed wolf's head; in the second, a lion rampant; in the third, a leopard passant guardant; the motto beneath reads 'Mens sana in corpore sano'.

5719 King David Lodge. London.

The boy David with sling standing on the prostrate body of the giant Goliath.

5739 Bittern Lodge. Woolston, Hampshire and Isle of Wight.

A bittern standing in marsh reeds. In medieval times the area in which the lodge meets was marshland, the home of the bittern, a bird of the heron family.

5840 Sarnia-Riduna. London.

Within concentric circles bearing the name and number of the lodge, a shield showing the armorial bearings of the Island of Guernsey (three leopards en passant guardant) with an escutcheon showing a shield bearing the armorial bearings of the island of Alderney (a lion rampant wearing a crown).

Sarnia was the Roman name for Guernsey and Riduna the Roman name for Alderney. The lodge was formed to provide a masonic home for those Channel Island masons who has left or who were evacuated because they were serving in H.M. forces during the occupation of the Islands by the German forces in the second world war. The founders later agreed the lodge be open to 'those connected or associated in some way with the Channel Islands'.

5841 Civic Lodge. Sunderland, Durham.

A stylized ship on waves surmounted by a mayoral mace. The ship refers to the town of Sunderland, for many years one of the greatest shipbuilding towns; the waves represent the River Wear and the mayoral sceptre the Civic authority.

5847 Sword and Trowel Lodge. Surbiton, Surrey.

Within concentric circles bearing the name and number of the lodge, a sword and trowel in saltire. The name of the lodge referring to emblems mentioned in the Royal Arch, is more usually associated with a Chapter; that attached to this particular lodge was constituted eight years after the lodge was formed.

5986 Maidenhead Lodge. Sindlesham, Berkshire.

The head of a maiden within the square and compasses.

6091 Lodge of Good Companions. London.

Within an oval beneath a horn a harp between two doves in a semi-circle beneath, the motto 'Fidelis et constans'. The horn indicates good cheer and has allusion to the association of the lodge with the Worshipful Company of Horners; the doves may be regarded as an emblem of peace; peace was restored in 1945 after the war, the year the lodge was founded; two doves at rest appear on the badge of the Lodge of Harmony No. 255, the sponsor lodge; the harp, the central feature of the badge, is indicative of harmony; it also appears as the central item of the badge of the sponsoring lodge.

The trade association representing the plastics industry was the British Plastics Federation, a noteworthy feature of which was the friendly feeling existing among members of the Council, even though in many cases they were competitors in business. This prompted some of them to form a masonic lodge within the plastics industry and, in recognition of the friendly spirit, the name Lodge of Good Companions was chosen.

6262 Shropshire Installed Masters'. Shrewsbury, Shropshire.

Within concentric circles bearing the name and number of the lodge the huntsman's bugle horn from the arms of Lord Forester (Provincial Grand Master, Shropshire 1938–77) the first master of the lodge, the pentalpha and the square. The horn indicates the medieval occupation of the family of Lord Forester (Royal Foresters) as Keepers of Wellington Haye; the pentalpha forms part of the jewel of a Provincial Grand Master and the square is the emblem of the master of a lodge. The badge was designed by Bro. Sir Gerald Wollaston, *KCB, KCVO*, PJGW who was at one time Garter King of Arms.

6290 Hampden. Thame, Oxfordshire.

A representation of John Hampden (1594–1643), an English MP famous for his resistance to Charles I's 'ship-money' tax; he was killed in the Civil War.

6326 Hundred of Bray. Wokingham, Berkshire.

The tower of Bray church whose vicar was immortalized in the ballad 'The Vicar of Bray', which tells how the vicar held his position by a conversion of churchmanship according to necessity.

6410 Diaconus. Croydon, Surrey.

A clock-face without numbers but showing twenty-four divisions representing the twenty-four hours of the day; deacons' wands in saltire appear in the lower part of the clock-face; in the upper part is a dove of peace; the lodge was formed in 1946, soon after the finish of the second world war.

6485 Uranus. Liverpool, West Lancashire.

The symbol of the planet Uranus.

6501 Peregrinus. Southgate, London.

A man wandering in the countryside; a pictorial representation of the meaning of the Latin name, namely a foreigner or stranger.

6545 Oriel Lodge. London.

A representation of an oriel window. The lodge is a daughter lodge of Dormer, No. 5146.

6586 Honor per Onus. London.

Laurel leaves circling a hand holding a sceptre topped by a crown, orb and cross with the name of the lodge below.

6605 Otterspool. Woolton, West Lancashire.

An otter on a rock beside a pool.

6608 Cambrensis. Cardiff, South Wales, Eastern Division.

The badge of Wales, a red dragon passant (i.e. represented as walking) with the motto 'More majorum'.

6609 Excelsior. Gosforth, Northumberland.

Within a circle, an arch joining two columns of the doric order, with the letter G on the centre of the arch; a ladder reaching from the floor to just above and behind the letter G; an All-Seeing Eye above; a maul on the dexter side and a skirret on the sinister side. The motto beneath is 'Altus altior'. The whole is a punning reference to the need to aim for higher things, the significance of the name Excelsior.

6613 Magnum Bonum. London.

In concentric circles, an All-Seeing Eye above an open volume of the Sacred Law. The motto shown is 'Vestigia nulla retrorsum'.

6618 Square and Level. London.

A square and level with the motto 'Unitas et fidelitas'.

6648 Old Chigwellian Lodge. London.

The arms used by Chigwell School which was founded by Archbishop Harsnett in the seventeenth century; he signed the Foundation Deed on 13 April 1629 saying that his action was a thanksgiving to God who had brought him from humble beginnings to become Archbishop of York in 1628; the motto beneath reads 'Aut viam inveniam aut faciam'. The arms are those of York Minster, crossed keys below a crown, impaling those of Archbishop Harsnett, on a blue background, two lines across the shield inclining up and down, thereby forming three peaks and showing the heraldic device for ermine, between six crosses crosslet, three, two and one. A cross crosslet is a cross that is 'criss-crossed' at the end of each limb.

6742 South Africa Lodge. London.

Within concentric circles showing the name of the lodge in both English and Afrikaans, the head of a springbok, a species of antelope which abounds in South Africa and used as an emblem of that country; surrounding the circles is a wreath of proteas bearing cone-like flowers, a native plant of South Africa; the motto beneath is Afrikaans: 'Eendrag maak mag'.

6777 Cloister Lodge. Heaton Moor, West Lancashire.

The cloistered walk of a monastic building.

6785 Vega Lodge. London.

A 'falling vulture' and some stars, one of which is irradiated. The founders of the lodge considered it important that the name and badge should emphasize the association they had with the Royal Air Force. Vega is the name of the brightest star in the constellation Lyra situated in the northern hemisphere and is incorporated in the badge to symbolize the part played by the stars in navigating by night, particularly when aircraft were returning to their British bases from the Continent of Europe. The star Vega is depicted in the badge to the bottom right of the 'Plough', although that position may not be astronomically correct! 'Lyra' (see above) is medieval Latin (from Arabic) and is, in rough translation, 'the falling vulture', indicated by the bird in the badge.

6809 Christopher Wren. London.

The facade of Christopher Wren's masterpiece, St Paul's Cathedral; below, 'In omnibus rectum rebus'.

6814 St Nicholas'. Sunderland, Durham.

Within a triangle, two men standing beside St Nicholas who has his left arm outstretched over a wavy sea on which is a small boat bearing three men appealing for help. This is presumably a representation of the story that the fourth century bishop St Nicholas, usually associated with 'Father Christmas', miraculously saved sailors in distress off the Lycian coast.

6815 Poseidon. London.

Between a Doric, an Ionic and a Corinthian pillar on a chequered floorcloth, a whale on the crest of a wave. Poseidon is the name given to the Greek god of the sea, brother of Zeus and Pluto; he is identified by the Romans as Neptune.

6822 Perfect Cube. London.

Two flaming torches in saltire, a perfect cube between the flames; beneath, the motto 'Pacem servitas fidelity' [*sic*].

6850 Lodge of Justice. Liverpool, West Lancashire.

The figure of Justice holding a sword in her right hand and the scales of justice in her left hand; the motto beneath reads 'Truth shall prevail'.

6854 Aarheus. London.

A winged pentalpha with an All-Seeing Eye in the centre, resting on the upper part of a terrestrial globe.

6884 Gunfleet. Frinton-on-Sea, Essex.

Between a Doric pillar topped by a celestial globe and an Ionic pillar topped by a terrestrial globe, a lighthouse arising out of the sea, its lamp shining brightly. The motto; 'Sit lux et lux fuit'.

6901 Crowley Lodge. Dunston-on-Tyne, Durham.

An octagon representing the indented design shown on the border of the lodge carpet. On the top edge are three rosettes representing the three who rule the lodge; at the lower two corners are double circles representing the two fellowcrafts necessary to provide the five who hold the lodge; at the two corners still lower are plain circles to represent the two entered apprentices which, when added to the former five, make a perfect lodge.

The interior of the octagon is divided diagonally into four quarters; that in the 'three-o'clock' position shows a contraction of the arms of the Liddell family, being the badge of the mother lodge Liddell Lodge No. 3816; that in the 'six-o'clock' position shows a leather jerkin worn by the ironmongers (the 'operative masons') employed by Sir Ambrose Crowley (after whom the lodge was named) as a protection from flying anvil sparks; that in the 'nine-o'clock' position shows a beehive, the badge of the grandmother lodge, the Lodge of Industry, No. 48, and that in the 'twelve-o'clock' position the badge of the Masons Craft Guild with the compasses added and placed on the chevron, as used by the premier Grand Lodge, illustrating the allegiance of the lodge.

7064 Mentor Lodge. Derby, Derbyshire.

The Derbyshire rose above an open book which is generally taken to be the Volume of the Sacred Law but in this case is also meant to represent the Emulation book of ritual to which the lodge members should strictly adhere. The motto 'Æmulari ad amussim' is shown between the square and compasses and an interlaced triangle on a scroll beneath. A literal translation of the motto would be 'Emulate by the plumb line'; more freely translated it would infer 'Emulate (imitate zealously) that which is correct' . . . (the Emulation book of ritual above the motto). The name Mentor was chosen to reflect . . . an experienced and trusted counsellor.

7077 Friendship and Fidelity. London.

A representation of Athos, Porthos and Aramis, the fictional characters in Alexandre Dumas's book *The Three Musketeers*, who were renowned for their friendship and fidelity.

7174 Arranwell Lodge. Wantage, Berkshire.

A well-known local fir tree with seven stems.

7197 St Paul's Column Lodge. London.

Against a background of St Paul's Cathedral, a column topped by St Paul holding a cross.

7213 Banks Lodge. Southport, West Lancashire.

The armorial bearings of Lt Col Roger Fleetwood Hesketh; a black shield with three golden wheatsheaves; the township of Banks is a good wheat growing district.

7314 Pattern Lodge. Bromley, West Kent.

A rising sun, a reference to the wording from the Address to the Master, 'that PATTERN of excellence, the Grand Luminary, the sun . . .'.

7326 Faith and Friendship. London.

The Hebrew word for 'faith' above the biblical figures of David and Jonathan, signifying 'friendship'.

7351 Camellia Thea. London.

St Paul's cathedral surmounting a tea bush (camellia thea) and a white rhinoceros, symbolizing the tea-growing area of Assam. The lodge was formed by retired tea planters from Assam in India.

7505 Padworth Lodge. Aldermaston, Berkshire.

A stag's head over a rising sun, fir trees and a stream running through an estate, all within the square and compasses. The stag was the emblem used by the Keyser Estate at Aldermaston, through which runs the stream; fir trees grow in profusion around the area of Tadley where people settled, and the rising sun is the emblem of the Atomic Weapons Research Establishment, the employer of some of the founder members of the lodge.

7684 Towan. Newquay, Cornwall.

Towan beach and a chough at each corner.

7725 Old Bloxhamist. Chipping Norton, Oxfordshire.

The arms attributed to Revd Philip Reginald Egerton, the founder of Bloxham School, on a black background, a chevron between three barbed arrowheads. In a scroll below, the motto 'Justorum semita lux splendens'.

7876 Islip Lodge. Oxford, Oxfordshire.

A portrayal of Edward the Confessor; he is said to have been born and baptized in the town and manor of Islip.

7892 Three Pillars. (Croydon, Surrey).

A Doric, an Ionic and a Corinthian pillar standing on a chequered floorcloth.

7897 Venturer Lodge. Chingford, Essex.

An axe embedded in a log. One of the scout lodges.

7955 Lodge of Orleans. London.

Joan of Arc, the Maid of Orleans, bearing the shield of Orleans, standing in the poppy fields of Lorraine, within a wreath of the lilies of France. The lodge was sponsored by the Lodge of Lorraine, No. 7176, which in turn was sponsored by Jeanne d'Arc Lodge, No. 4168 which had its origins in France.

During the 1914–18 war some freemasons stationed with the British Military Forces in the Rouen area wanted to form a lodge in that city as a meeting place for freemasons passing through on their way to, and from, the front lines. The name of the new lodge was Jeanne d'Arc, a name having historical associations with Rouen and not unknown in British history. The lodge was consecrated on 16 December 1916 under the constitution of the Grand Lodge now known as La Grande Lodge Nationale Française.

In 1920, following their return to England, some members, having no home in a lodge under the United Grand Lodge of England, sought to form a new Lodge under that constitution. They were given permission to do so and decided to use the same name as their mother lodge in France.

8050 Lodge of Contentment. London.

A lamb lying beside a lion. This is presumably a reference to *Isaiah* 11; 6, see note under 192 Lion and Lamb Lodge.

8091 Magiovinivm Lodge. Bletchley, Buckinghamshire.

The head and shoulders of a Roman centurion, reflecting the Roman encampment from which the lodge derives its name.

8100 Old Dunelmian. Durham, Durham.

The badge of Durham School.

8145 Staplehurst Lodge. Cranbrook, East Kent.

An oak tree surrounded by acorns; on the tree, three staples; the badge is meant to be a punning reference to the name, staples and hurst, the latter word indicating a group of trees. The design of the badge was taken from a window of the church at Staplehurst; one of the members of the lodge was the vicar of the church. Surrounding the badge are the Latin words 'Deo Regi et fratribus honor fidelitas benevolentia. (See comments in the next section, Mottoes, under this lodge number.)

8151 Homelea. Woolston, Hampshire and Isle of Wight.

The armorial bearings of the Earls of Hardwicke whose family seat was at Hamble, a town near the meeting place of the lodge. Homelea was the first recorded name of Hamble, the word being derived from the Old English Hamel, meaning hamlet or village.

8198 Venture Lodge. Whitley Bay, Northumberland.

Within the square and compasses, a Venture Scout holding a flagpole with flag; another scout lodge.

8226 Engineers Lodge. Sindlesham, Berkshire.

Epicyclic gearing representing a train of gears all working together; the main gears are the annulus gear (the outer), the planetary gear, and the sun gear in the centre, all working in harmony.

8236 Pathfinder. Sheffield, Yorkshire, West Riding.

In front of a terrestrial globe a three-fingered signpost, one finger pointing towards Truth, another towards Fidelity and the third towards Service; above the globe, the arrowhead scout emblem; below, the words 'This is the way . . . walk ye in it.' The lodge was formed primarily for those with scouting affinities. The reasons given for the choice of name are first, that Baden-Powell, the founder of the scout movement, said: 'Among the Red Indian Scouts the man who was good at finding his way in a strange country was termed "Pathfinder", which was with them a name of great honour, because a scout who cannot find his way is of little use' and secondly in allusion to a well-known painting by Ernest S. Carlos of the young scout with The Master's hand upon his shoulder, entitled The Pathfinder, which was a source of inspiration. The virtues written on the fingers of the signpost have a close association with scouting.

8238 Pillars of Friendship. Sindlesham, Berkshire.

Two pillars standing on a squared pavement; on top of one is the terrestrial globe; on top of the other, the celestial globe showing five stars. Between them, clasped hands and the square and compasses. A cornfield is shown at the outer side of each pillar and water is depicted in the centre.

The terrestrial globe represents the United Kingdom and other parts of the world signifying the United Grand Lodge of England and other recognized constitutions; the five stars on the celestial globe represent the five points of fellowship.

The cornfields represent respectively Britain and the rest of the world; the water represents the sea surrounding Britain; the whole represents Freemasonry Universal. From the solid foundation on which Freemasonry rests, all brothers throughout the world unite in the grand design of being happy and communicating happiness.

8255 Kenelm. Harrow, Middlesex.

Harrow Hill and a flock of sheep; above three seaxes (or scimitars) representing Middlesex (the lodge meets at Harrow); below, the motto 'Alta Petens', Kenelm was the son of the King of Mercia.

8270 Lodge of the Cardinal Virtues. Heston Moor, West Lancashire.

A Carrick Bend, which is a knot used to join two ropes whose extremities are subject to equal pull. The badge is meant to imply that no single virtue should be considered as having more pull or be more important than the others and the exercise of all would give perfect stability.

8279 Pro Arte. London.

An artist's palette and brushes.

8362 Sons of Kendrick. Sindlesham, Berkshire.

On the square and compasses an oval with a chevron; above it, on the dexter side, is the lion rampant from the arms of the local Kendrick family; on the sinister side the arms of the Lydall family; below the chevron, a stag beside an oak tree (the Berkshire County emblem). Alongside the top of the compasses are, on the dexter side, the seal of the grandmother lodge, Grey Friars, No. 1101 depicting a Franciscan monk bearing a skull, the emblem of the order, and on the sinister side, the centre part of the badge of the Reading Lodge of Union, No. 414, the great-grandmother lodge. The mother lodge is Kendrick Lodge, No. 2043; hence the name Sons of Kendrick.

8378 Good Neighbour Lodge. Chislehurst, West Kent.

An acorn and a forget-me-not in saltire. The lodge was formed to provide inexpensive freemasonry for occupants of the Royal Masonic Benevolent Institution homes, so that they were able to qualify as paid-up members to visit other lodges to which they receive many invitations from Friends of the Homes and other brethren. The badge is that used by the Institution, and complements their motto, 'Forget not those in need'; the acorn, with its association of being stored during the summer by the squirrel for nourishment in the winter is intended to symbolize the care and attention given to the residents of the homes during their stay in what is often the latter years of their life.

8414 Lodge of Harmony. Cardiff, South Wales, Eastern Division.

Between two Ionic pillars on a chequered carpet a clarsach (Welsh harp) on which is superimposed the Welsh dragon; the lodge meets in Cardiff, South Wales, Eastern Division.

8421 Vale of Loddon Lodge. Sindlesham, Berkshire.

The River Loddon and the Loddon lily.

8500 Arrowhead Lodge. Wigan, West Lancashire.

Within the square and compasses, the scout badge, which is in the form of an arrowhead; a lodge for scouts.

8503 Edwin Flavell Lodge. Sindlesham, Berkshire.

Within a warrior's shield, a winged Pegasus, the motif of the Airborne Divisions of the Army, and the Royal lions of the County of Berkshire separated by lines to indicate the River Thames which flows through the Province of Berkshire.

RW Bro. Brig. E.W.C. Flavell, *DSO, MC, TD, DL*, Prov. G.M. Berkshire, (1967–85) was a soldier of distinction who won the first of his three Military Crosses at the age of 20 at the Somme in 1918. He was recalled to the colours in 1938, became Brigadier of the 1st Parachute Regiment in 1942, took over the 6th Airborne Division in Normandy and ended the war as Deputy Chief of Staff Allied Airborne Army.

8505 Sandhurst Lodge. Sindlesham, Berkshire.

The facade of Sandhurst Military Academy behind a pictorial representation of the Sandhurst Village Well.

8539 Seven Sisters Lodge. Peaceheven, Sussex.

A view of the chalk cliffs known as the 'Seven sisters', situated between Seaford and Beachy Head.

8549 Berkshire St David's. Sindlesham, Berkshire.

The lodge, the square and compasses on a background of wavy lines representing the River Thames which flows through Berkshire; between the arms of the compasses is an English rose, to indicate that although the members of the lodge have a Welsh connection, the lodge meets in an English County; the whole supported by, on the dexter side the red dragon of Wales and on the sinister side the Berkshire stag, all standing on the green ground of peace. The motto is 'Gwrando edrych tewi' which is the motto on the arms of Grand Lodge translated into Welsh.

8550 St Swithun's. Abingdon, Berkshire.

The figure of St Swithun, to whom the parish church at Kennington is dedicated; many of the lodge founders came from this village. The veneration of St Swithun, or Swithin, appears to date from the removal of his bones from the churchyard into the cathedral at Winchester, a century after his death. The origin of the saying that the weather on St Swithin's feast-day holds good (or bad) for the next forty days is not known; a similar superstition is associated with other saints elsewhere.

8554 Croydon Lodge of Achievement. Croydon, Surrey.

A circle showing the name of the lodge, within which are four segments of another circle. The centre of the circle is the apex of a triangle, the sides of which overlap the lower part of the circle; the number of the lodge is within the triangle. This triangle is meant to represent a mountain where man 'endeavoured'; the segments are pointers to the summit of the mountain, the apex of the triangle, the 'achievement' of man's endeavours; they also represent the four main points of the compass. The circle represents the sun which, as indicated by the pointers, is always at the meridian with respect to Freemasonry.

8585 Clavis Lodge. Oxford, Oxfordshire.

Hanging from a headstock a large church bell on which is engraved 'Fecit Al 5974; Gloria Deo Soli'.

8594 Danetre Lodge. Daventry, Northamptonshire and Huntingdonshire.

An oak tree on which is a Dane's helmet. The name Danetre is of dubious origin, one theory being that an ancient oak tree that grew on the slopes of Borough Hill was the 'Dane Tree' where the Danes held their tribal meetings, courts, etc. The tree was felled some time ago despite great opposition. The popular theory is that Danetre became corrupted into the present Daventry. Some however consider that Daventry derives from *Dwy afontre*, alleged to mean *the source of two rivers*.

8617 Alfred the Great. Wantage, Berkshire.

A copy of the statue of Alfred the Great which stands in the Market Square, Wantage, the town in which the lodge meets.

8628 Thames Mariner. Marlow, Buckinghamshire.

A mariner's compass in the centre of which is the square and compasses. The lodge meets at Marlow, alongside the River Thames.

8647 Manor of Swanburn Bletchley, Buckinghamshire.

A swan and wavy lines representing a river or burn on which is superimposed a sigma, the eighteenth letter of the Greek alphabet. This letter had been the emblem of the Swanbourne Training Centre which trained railway employees. The sigma is here used to illustrate railway lines.

8650 Brethren in Amity. London.

Hemispheres representing the world, the square and compasses above, a lamp below; the whole within a snake with its tongue in its mouth. The lamp is meant to signify the 'Toc H' movement, an international organization for Christian social service whose members dedicate a reasonable proportion of their leisure time to the service of their fellow men and by including in its membership all men of goodwill.

8662 Kudu Lodge. Radlett, Hertfordshire.

A scout badge between the horns of a kudu, a South African antelope.

8664 Bearwood Lodge. Sindlesham, Berkshire.

The church of St Catherine surrounded by Cedars of Lebanon, Cypress Cedars and pine tree. Standing astride the path is a bear, under the front foot of which is a scroll listing the names of the founders of the lodge.

8680 Lodge of Fellowship and Unity. Orsett, Essex.

An anchor within which are hands clasped in fellowship and unity.

8708 Hinge of Friendship. East Grinstead, Sussex.

Between two pillars, one bearing a terrestrial the other a celestial globe, and within a circle, a stylized rose in the centre of a figure representing the four points of a compass on which is superimposed a ring of ovals forming an unlinked chain. The lodge was formed by members of 41 Club who had to retire from the Round Table Club on reaching the age of 40. The motto of the 41 Club is 'May the hinges of friendship never rust'; hence the name of the lodge.

8743 Lentune Lodge. Lymington, Hampshire and Isle of Wight.

The upper part of the tower of Lymington church showing the clock with the hands at nine o'clock, the time when members of many lodges stop for a moment to think about absent brethren.

8756 Orion Lodge. Slough, Buckinghamshire.

The conspicuous constellation Orion which contains many bright stars; according to Greek legend it represents a giant hunter of Boeotia.

8786 Emmbrook Lodge. Sindlesham, Berkshire.

Within concentric circles, in the upper dexter corner a haystack on stone pillars; in the upper sinister quarter, sheaves of corn; across the centre a shaded area between two lines representing water, and in the lower half seven stars and an Irish water spaniel watching startled wildfowl. The motto below reads 'Sic luceat lux vestra'.

The badge is intended to convey an image of the rural features of the area in such a way as may be translated and understood in the symbolic language of Freemasonry. The concentric circles represent an enclosure or boundary mark which, being unbroken, is symbolic of the bond of friendship and the need for each member to remain in due bounds; the haystack on stone pillars indicates prudence and the corn and water indicate plenty; the dog watching the wildfowl is taken from the sign of the Dog and Duck Inn, where the idea of forming the lodge was first mooted. The seven stars allude to the canopy of Freemasonry Universal.

8830 Tergere Lodge. London.

A shield showing a Greek cross with a wreath of lilies beneath. The motto beneath reads 'Tergere est servare'. The cross is supposed to represent the cross of St George found in the arms of the City of London, the lodge being a City of London Livery Lodge; the lilies are meant to reflect purity, an association with being clean; the lodge was founded by members of the Worshipful Company of Environmental Cleaners.

8850 Lodge of Peace Thame, Oxfordshire.

The Chi Rho monogram, being the first two letters of the Greek word ΧΡΙΣΤΟΣ, meaning Christ. It is depicted as the letter ψηι (X), superimposed on an extended tail of the letter Rho (P).

8893 Fiat Lux. Rainham, East Kent.

The history of the lodge gives the following information.

The Insignia is oval in shape and represents the name of the lodge. The central motif depicts four Volumes of the Sacred Law superimposed upon the terrestrial globe, each open in the form of a square towards a quarter of the globe. The globe is in masonic blue with the lines of latitude and longitude in gold. A scalloped Glory surrounds the globe which itself is superimposed upon a background also in masonic blue. The whole is enclosed and at the bottom centre LODGE 8893, also in gold.

An interpretation of the Insignia is given as: Light shines in all directions both outwardly and inwardly. Through their example may LIGHT shine from the brethren of the lodge to 'the uneducated and popular world' but, at all times, remembering they are able to learn much from that world. LIGHT is shed on our ignorance of Freemasonry by the Rulers of the Craft, and by the brethren on its history and its philosophy through their studies. Over, through, and above all THE GREAT LIGHT OF FREEMASONRY shines out to the four quarters of the world and, in this modern age, to 'the blue canopy of heaven'. Beyond this is 'darkness visible' through which, one prays, LIGHT may shine out from Fiat Lux Lodge 8893. These thoughts have become embodied in the FIAT LUX PRAYER, now used at the opening of the lodge.

'O Thou who hast called us out of darkness to be bearers of light, make us helpers in the world and faithful to the trust that life has put upon us. Prepare our hearts so that we may be partners with the weak, able to serve with the strong, and ready at all times to help our brethren and neighbours with patience, understanding and compassion. By Thy wisdom enlighten our plans and direct our endeavours for the common good that all may share the best they have in thought, in word, and in deed. Establish Thou the work of our hands upon us.'

8954 Chelsea Manor Lodge. London.

A representation of the large manor in Chilchell or Chelcheya (Chelsea) given by Edward the Confessor to the Abbot and Convent of Westminster; below a beehive with bees, a reminder that 'the first class of masonic instruction' was held in the Beehive Tavern, Chelsea Manor Street, London. The motto shown is 'Patientia Industriaque merita sunt'; it was adopted by the founders of the lodge to symbolize the sincerity and keenness with which several brethren persevered in forming The Chelsea Class of Masonic Instruction.

8965 Cadogan Lodge. Caversham, Oxfordshire.

The crest of Earl Cadogan; out of a golden ducal coronet, a green dragon's head. In a scroll beneath, the motto 'Qui invidet minor est'.

8985 Fenny Stratford Lodge. Bletchley, Buckinghamshire.

A 'Fenny Popper', a small cast-iron cannon-like device weighing about twenty pounds. It is charged with gunpowder and fired at regular intervals during the day on 11 November (St Martin's day) each year in memory of Dr Brown-Willis, an eighteenth-century antiquary and benefactor of St Martin's church, the parish church of Fenny Stratford. He left an endowment to fund this 'big bang'.

9035 Forget-me-not Lodge. Ludgershall, Wiltshire.

A blue forget-me-not flower. This badge was adopted by freemasons in Germany in the 1930s when the Nazis were trying to stamp out Freemasonry; the badge was adopted after the war when the Grand Lodge of the Sun was re-opened in Bayreuth; the badge has a special association with military forces serving in the British Army of the Rhine; this lodge is one of those formed mainly for those returning to England after such service.

According to an old German tradition the forget-me-not received its name from the last words of a knight who was drowned in the attempt to procure the flower for his lady.

Another story is that when Adam named the plants in Eden he overlooked the forget-me-not because it was so small. Later he walked through the garden calling all the flowers by name to find if they were accepted, and each plant bowed and whispered its assent; but a voice at his feet asked 'By what name am I called, Adam?', and looking down Adam saw the flower peeping shyly from a shadow. Struck with its beauty and his own forgetfulness, he answered 'As I forgot you before, let me name you in a way to show I shall remember you again; you shall be called "forget-me-not".

It is said that whilst he was in exile Henry IV of England adopted the forget-me-not as his emblem, with the motto 'Remember me.'

9051 Vale of Derwent Lecture Lodge. Consett, Durham.

Within a circle formed by a serpent with its tail in its mouth, a representation of three hills indicating the legend of the Derwent Valley Giants named Con, Ben and Mugg, whose names are perpetuated locally by the names of Consett, Benfield and Muggleswick; below the hills, wavy lines representing water and symbolic of the River Wear; superimposed on the whole, a torch symbolizing education, the purpose of the lodge.

9113 Salvus Securus. London.

A portcullis between two pillars; the portcullis represents security and the pillars, masonry. The founders of the lodge were all connected with the business of security.

9167 Pride of Surrey. Sutton, Surrey.

A Doric, an Ionic and a Corinthian pillar on a chequered pavement supporting a framed square divided diagonally, one half showing a sprig of the plant London Pride, the other an oak leaf and an acorn; these reflect the localities from which the founders came; the oak leaf and the acorn form the emblem of the masonic Province of Surrey.

9187 Trevelyan Lodge. Wokingham, Berkshire.

Within concentric circles showing the motto 'Tyme tryeth troth', two mailed arms holding a bezant, a Turkish coin associated with the Crusades, together with a castle, a bridge over a river, a torch and a letter T which links them together. This is meant to indicate a connection of the Trevelyan family with Windsor and education. Above the circles are the square and compasses between two dolphins from the Trevelyan arms.

The name Trevelyan was adopted as a consequence of the opening of the Trevelyan School, Windsor, by Sir Charles Trevelyan, President of the Board of Education 1924–29.

In Cornish Trevelyan means 'the island of the man from the sea'; Sir Trevelyan, a knight of King Arthur, is said to have swum ashore from St Michael's Mount on a white horse. This finds a reflection in the family armorial bearings which show the upper half of a horse coming out of the water. It will be of interest to note that *DEBRETT* states the name is pronounced 'Trevillian'.

9189 Somerset Provincial Grand Stewards. Weston-super-Mare, Somerset.

A cornucopia with the motto 'We serve'. A cornucopia is the horn of plenty. (See comment under Grand Stewards Lodge.)

9235 Great Ouse Valley Lodge. Olney, Buckinghamshire.

An oval enclosing a scene depicting a meadow alongside the River Ouse, with Olney Church in the background. There are two figures below which are meant to portray Cowper and Newton, hymn writers, representing the mother lodge Cowper and Newton Lodge No. 2244; between these figures is a circle showing crossed keys and a sword, representing the grandmother lodge, St Peter and St Pauls', No. 1410.

9264 Regis Aurigae. Epsom, Surrey.

A representation of a car steering wheel, a crown shown on the central part and an Imperial Crown at the top. The lodge was formed by golfing members of the Royal Automobile Club at Epsom; the steering wheel is meant to indicate the connection with the R.A.C. and the crowns indicate the royal connection with the Club. The name 'Regis Aurigae' was considered as being a rather free transcription of the phrase 'Royal carriages' or 'Royal drivers'.

9275 Lodge of Peace and Friendship. Wokingham, Berkshire.

A white dove of peace within the square and compasses, surrounded by a chain of hands linked in friendship.

9313 Sunnymeads Lodge. Slough, Buckinghamshire.

Within concentric circles showing the number and name of the lodge, the square and compasses on which rest a quartered square depicting the Cross of St George, the Buckinghamshire swan, a sailing boat and rippling water. The circles are surrounded by flames, representing the sun. The sailing boat and rippling water represent the popular sport of sailing on the River Thames at Sunnymeads.

9322 Longueville Lodge. Bletchley, Buckinghamshire.

Standing on a chequered floorcloth and between the three columns of a lodge, a representation of the village church, St Faith's. On either side of the middle column, a wrought-iron hinge as used on the door of the bell-tower of the church.

The church is meant to show the connecting link between the monks of Longueville and the Dukes of Buckingham; the wrought-iron hinges are a reminder that one of the founders was a bell-ringer at the church.

The lodge is named after the village of Longueville in France whence monks came in the eleventh and twelfth centuries to look after and collect the rent from their properties in the locality. After the wars with France the properties came into the hands of the de Giffard family, and then, via the Crown, to the Dukes of Buckingham, who were also Earls of Longueville.

9385 Impeesa Lodge. Downend, Gloucestershire.

A wolf between the square and compasses, the junction of the compasses being in the form of the scout badge. The design is based on the 'Wood badge', the award invented by Lord Baden-Powell, the founder of the scout movement, for leaders who had been trained. 'Impeesa' was the Zulu name for Baden-Powell; it means 'the wolf that never sleeps'.

9405 Forest Villages. Lymington, Hampshire and Isle of Wight.

A shield showing a scene intended to portray the name of the lodge, the approach to a forest village with the church and houses nestling among trees and a forest pony grazing on the green; there is a stream flanked by reeds from which ponies drink to quench their thirst; this is intended to remind brethren of relief and charity; on either side on the base of the shield are branches of two common forest trees, the oak and the holly; the former with its acorns denotes growth and strength, the latter is meant to be a reminder of joy and celebration, for as Freemasons we are taught to 'be happy and communicate happiness'; at the top, within the square and compasses is the Hampshire Rose, representing the Province. Flanking the shield are two pillars, the design of which was taken from the pillars in Thornyhill Church, Bransgore because many of the founders of the lodge lived near or were closely connected with this church.

The badge is unusual in that it was copied from the lodge banner, not, as is generally the case, the other way round. The banner also shows at the top of the shield, but not on the badge, illustrations of three common birds of the forest, the blue tit, the blackbird and the woodpecker.

The designer of the banner intended to convey symbolical meanings as follows; the rose, the only flower represented was to be a reminder of the first degree; the two trees, a reminder of the second degree and the three birds a reminder of the third degree, the three brethren who hold a lodge and all the other 'threes' mentioned in our ritual. Birds and trees are associated together, so if the three birds are added to the two trees, the total, five, should be a reminder of the five points of fellowship, the five orders of architecture and the five brethren who hold a lodge; the total wildlife shown, the flower, the two trees, the three birds and the pony add up to seven, representing the seven liberal arts and sciences and the seven brethren who form a perfect lodge. The church in the centre is meant to be a reminder that God should always be at the centre of our lives.

9441 Nevill Lodge of Installed Masters. Darlington, Durham.

The Nevill shield, on a red background a silver saltire with a red rose in the centre, placed in a porchway or entrance familiar to freemasons, with, arranged behind it, one of the bull supporters from the achievement of the Marquess of Abergavenny, the chain running from its collar in a square-like arrangement forming a framework for the bull supporter between the two pillars; the collar is inscribed with the Nevill motto; 'Ne vile velis'. The translation of the motto, 'Form no mean wish', is shown on another scroll beneath the shield. The badge was designed by RW Bro, Sir Colin Cole, *KCVO, TD*, PJGW, a former Garter Principal King of Arms.

Mottoes

Many lodge badges incorporate a motto, some of which are used with the armorial bearings of the person after whom the lodge has been named; others have an obvious association with the name or history of the lodge, and some have been devised by the founders, occasionally using rather dubious Latin! Some mottoes given below have had obvious printing errors corrected.

In England mottoes are not hereditary; they are sometimes mentioned or alluded to in a grant of impersonal arms, but not in a grant to an individual. The officers of arms will allow a motto chosen by the grantee to be painted on the grant and noted in their records, but that does not stop the armiger changing the motto at his pleasure; nor does it stop anyone else from using the same motto. Things are different in Scotland where much stricter rules apply, and similarly, to some extent, in Ireland.

Examples of some of the mottoes used are given in this section; the examples are shown in order of lodge precedence. The English translation (where appropriate) together with other information, has come from one of the following sources; the lodge secretary; *Elvin's Mottoes Revised* (Heraldry Today); Debrett's *Peerage*;

Registered Badges (Maj. J.F. Edwards, *MBE FRHistSoc.; A Dictionary of Mottoes*, (Pine, Routledge and Kegan Paul, London, 1983), or from W.Bro. Graham Redman, PJGD. Assistant Grand Secretary.

No.	NAME OF LODGE	Const	*Motto and translation*
6	LODGE OF FRIENDSHIP	1721	*Vera amicita.* True friendship.
9	ALBION	1762	*Audi, vide, tace.* Hear, see, be silent. This is the motto shown on the scroll of the armorial bearings of the United Grand Lodge of England. The words are part of a rhyming motto fashionable many years ago; 'Audi, vide, tace, si vis vivere in pace' translatable as 'Hear, see, silent be, if you would live peacefully!'; another free translation sometimes found is 'Hear, see, hold your tongue, if in peace you would live on.' In his paper 'English Craft Certificates' (*AQC* 82; 189) Bro. T.O. Haunch states he found four examples of the use of this motto by freemasons before the Union of the two Grand Lodges in 1813. The following is taken from a footnote to his paper: The first part [of the motto] is found (rendered 'Vide, Aude, Tace') as the motto to an emblematical plate used as the frontispiece to the 1776 edition of *Jachin and Boaz*. It also appears (in its correct form) on the title page of the *Free-Masons Calendar* from 1777 (the second issue) to 1785 inclusive, in an allegorical design showing the three principal Orders and the three Graces. Other examples of its occurrence (again as 'Vide, Aude, Tace') are in the allegorical frontispiece to *The Free-Masons' Magazine*, Vol. 1, 1793, and in a copy of the latter in an Irish periodical. *The Sentimental and Masonic Magazine*, Vol. VI, 1795. One of the plates accompanying the paper shows a certificate dated 6 September, 1795, issued by a lodge owing allegiance to the Grand Lodge of the Antients; on one of the columns are the words 'Vide, Aude, Tace', Bro. Sir Lionel Brett, referring to this in his comment on the paper, tells us that as written here the phrase means 'See, dare, be silent'. The motto (in its correct form) was adopted by United Grand Lodge and shown on their seal in use from 1815.
18	OLD DUNDEE	1723	In the Lord is all our trust. *Job* 13;15). Motto used by Masons Company in 1472.
46	OLD UNION	1735	*In unitate stabilis.* Firm in unity.
91	LODGE OF REGULARITY	1755	*Jam ducentos floruit annos.* Now (i.e. already) it has flourished for two hundred years.
114	BRITISH UNION	1762	*Sic tria juncta virent.* So three in harmony are vigorous. The 'three in harmony' are England, Scotland and Ireland, the national emblems of each being shown in the lodge badge.
185	TRANQUILLITY	1787	*Tranquillitas heri hodie in aeternum.* Tranquillity yesterday, today and for ever.
259	PRINCE OF WALES'S	1787	*Honi soit qui mal y pense.* Evil be to him who evil thinks of it. This is the motto of The Most Noble Order of the Garter which was founded by Edward III of England in 1348 (earlier dates mentioned have been officially discounted). The supposed origin of the motto, unproven, is that the king retrieved a lady's garter that had dropped at some court festivity.
739	TEMPERANCE LODGE	1858	*Nulla pallescere culpa.* To turn pale from no guilt. (From Horace: *Letters* Bk 1; 1; line 61; in sense of having no guilt to make one turn pale.)
754	HIGH CROSS	1858	*Dieu pour la Tranchée qui contre.* (If) God (be) for the Tranches, who is against them?
767	UNION	1858	*Vis una fortior.* A single force is the stronger.
788	CRESCENT	1859	*Crescens.* Increasing.

No.	NAME OF LODGE	Const	*Motto and translation*
804	CARNARVON	1859	*Unc je servira.* One I serve.
840	SCIENTIFIC	1860	Mind moves the mass.
873	LODGE OF INDUSTRY	1861	*Industria et labore.* By industry and labour.
879	SOUTHWARK	1861	*Antiquum obtinens.* Possessing our ancient honour.
902	BURGOYNE	1862	*Peritia potius quam vi.* By skill rather than by strength.
1017	MONTEFIORE	1864	Think and Thank.
1147	ST DAVID'S	1867	*Y ddraig goch ddyry gychwyn.* The Red Dragon shall lead. (The Red Dragon is an emblem used by Wales.)
1250	GILBERT GREENALL	1869	*Alta peto.* I seek to rise.
1310	HARROW	1870	*Stet fortuna domus.* May the fortune of our house endure, (Motto of the Harrow School.)
1328	GRANITE	1870	*Frangas non flectas.* You may break but shall not bend me.
1400	CURWEN	1871	*Si je n'estoy.* If I were not.
1404	SAINT VINCENT	1872	*Patiendo vincens.* Conquering through endurance.
1413	MAYO	1872	*A cruce salus.* Salvation from the cross.
1491	ATHENAEUM	1874	*Sapientia summa felicitas.* The greatest happiness is wisdom. The badge of the lodge shows Athena, the Greek goddess of Wisdom.
1556	ADDISCOME LODGE	1875	*Auspicio regis et senatus Angliae.* Under the auspices of the sovereign and senate of England Motto of the East India Company.
1575	CLIVE LODGE	1875	*Audacter et sincere.* Boldly and sincerely.
1597	MUSGRAVE	1876	*Fortiter.* Bravely.
1621	CASTLE LODGE	1876	*Fidelitas urbis salus regis.* The fidelity of the city is the safety of the king.
1625	TREDEGAR	1876	*Si Deus nobiscum quis contra nos?* If God be with us, who can be against us? (See *Romans* 8:31)
1637	UNITY	1876	*Unitas et fidelitas.* Unity and fidelity.
1662	BEACONSFIELD	1876	*Forti nihil difficile.* Nothing is difficult to the strong (or brave).
1743	LODGE OF PERSEVERANCE	1878	*Excelsior.* Higher.
1894	HERSCHEL	1881	*Coelis exploratis.* For the heavens explored. This motto was granted to Sir William Herschel for his great astronomical discoveries, and in the arms are a telescope and the symbol of the planet Uranus which he discovered.
1899	WELLESLEY	1881	Fortune is the companion of valour. This is the English translation of the Latin motto 'Virtutis fortuna comes' shown on the arms used by the Duke of Wellington (Wellesley was his family surname). According to *Elvin's Mottoes Revised*: 'This motto is one of the many which, without having any special reference to the family coat-of-arms, are assumed by some member of a family who has added fresh honours to those already possessed by the stock from which he is descended. Thus the motto of the Duke of Wellington is peculiarly suited to express the success of the first Duke which waited on his valour in the field, and his genius in the senate; and moreover, alludes to the rewards with which a grateful nation requited his achievements.'
1932	WHITWORTH	1881	*Per ignem pro cruce.* Through fire for the cross.
1984	EARL OF CLARENDON	1882	*Fidei coticula crux.* The Cross, the sign of faith.
2048	HENRY LEVANDER	1884	*Tendit in ardua virtus.* Virtue reaches the heights.
2108	EMPIRE	1889	*Coelum non regem.* Heaven not the king.
2140	HUGUENOT	1886	*Lux lucit in tenebris.* Light shines in darkness. The lodge badge shows a lighted candle surrounded by seven stars.
2153	LODGE OF HOPE	1886	*In Deo spes nostra.* In God is our hope.

No.	Name of lodge	Const	*Motto and translation*
2191	Anglo-American	1886	*Dieu et mon droit.* God and my right. Motto of British sovereigns (see remarks under lodge No. 3343). *E pluribus unum.* One out of many. Motto of the United States of America since 1782.
2202	Regent's Park	1887	Merit and ability.
2233	Old Westminsters'	1887	*Dat Deus incrementum.* God gives the increase. (Motto of Westminster School.)
2420	Fernidand de Rothschild	1891	*Concordia integritas industria.* Concord, integrity, industry.
2421	Carrington	1891	*Tenax in fide.* Steadfast in faith.
2533	Fitzwilliam	1894	*Appetitus rationi pareat.* Let your desire obey your reason.
2571	Holmes	1895	*Deus mihi adjutor.* God is my helper.
2622	Beach	1896	All in good time.
2674	Ravensworth	1897	*Fama semper vivit.* Our renown lives forever
2683	Addington	1897	*Alta petens.* Seeking higher things.
2693	Pellipar	1898	To God only be all glory. Motto of The Worshipful Company of Skinners.
2752	Marlow	1899	*Palmam qui meruit ferat.* Let him who has earned it bear the palm. This is the motto used by Horatio, Lord Nelson. *Elvin's Mottoes* includes the following note which is taken from Burke's *Peerage*: 'The words of this motto are from an Ode to the Winds in the *Lusus Poetici* of Dr Jortin, the author of the *Life of Erasmus*, and were applied by Lord Grenville to Nelson. The whole passage is; Et nobis faciles parcite et hostibus; Concurrent paribus cum ratibus rates; Spectent numina ponti, et Palmam qui meruit, ferat. O winds! breath calmly o'er us and our foes! Let ship with ship alone contending close. And while the sea-gods watch above the fray, Let him who merits bear the palm away. It is presumed that, unlike Lord Nelson who, by his actions, was justified in claiming the last line as an apt motto, the founders of the lodge adopted the motto as an aspiration hopefully to be achieved by their members in the future.
2885	Charterhouse Deo Dante Dedi	1901	*Ædes Carthusianæ.* The Carthusian House.
3058	Loyd Lindsay	1904	*Astra castra lumen numen.* The stars are my camp, (Thy) divine will my light.
3089	Stephens	1905	*Honeste audax.* Honourably bold.
3098	Chelsea	1905	*Nisi Dominus frustra.* It is vain without the Lord. This motto is derived from the second verse of Psalm 127, the first two verses of which are: Nisi Dominus aedificaverit domum, in vanum laboraverunt qui aedificant eam. Nisi Dominus custodierit civitatem, frustra vigilat qui custodit eam. This is translated in the *Book of Common Prayer* as: Except the Lord build the house; their labour is but lost that build it. Except the Lord keep the city; the watchman waketh but in vain. The Prayer Book version forms the basis of the final anthem currently used in London in the ceremony for the Consecration of a new lodge (or chapter). A setting of the same anthem was specially composed by the then Grand Organist, Dr Henry Goss Custard, for the dedication of Freemasons' Hall, London, in 1933.
3200	Lord Desborough	1907	Loyal devoir. Loyal duty.

No.	Name of lodge	Const	*Motto and translation*
3213	City of London St Olave's	1907	*Auld lang syne*. Old times' sake.
3343	Duke of Sussex Lodge	1908	Dieu et mon droit. God and my right. Motto of the English and later British sovereigns. It is said to have originated in 1198 following the victory of Richard I over Philip Augustus, King of France at the battle of Gisors. After the victory Richard wrote 'It is not we who have done it, but God and our right through us.'
3343	*Duke of Sussex Chapter*	1940	*A Deo lux nostra*. Our light is from God. *God, Light Himself*, dwells awfully retir'd From mortal eye, or angel's purer ken; Whose single smile has, from the first of time, Fill'd, overflowing, all those lamps of heaven, That beam for ever thro' the boundless sky.
3439	Joseph Lancaster	1910	*Floreat apis*. May the bee flourish.
3509	Victory	1911	England expects every man to do his duty. Based on Nelson's famous signal at the battle of Trafalgar, 1805
3510	George Green	1911	*Fideliter*. Faithfully.
3525	Guild of Freemen	1911	*Domine, dirige nos*. O Lord, direct us. (Motto of City of London).
3547	Old Fraternity	1911	*Ad finem esto fidelis*. Stay faithful to the (very) end. The lodge badge depicts bluebells which denote constancy.
3592	Civitas	1912	*Loquere domine quia audit servus tuus*. Speak, Lord, for thy servant heareth. (See 1 *Samuel* 3;9.)
3604	Bromley Priory	1912	*Resuscitatio*. Renewal of life.
3613	Archimedian	1912	*Labor omnia vincit*. Labour conquers all things.
3700	Commercial Travellers	1913	*Ubique. Per mare per terra. Nulla dies sine linea*. Everywhere. By sea and land. No day without limit.
3720	Neeld	1914	*Nomen extendere factis*. To promote one's name by deeds.
3749	Hale	1915	*A ma puissance*. According to my power.
3916	Pax Magna	1919	*Vivit post funera virtus*. Virtue lives after death.
3924	Earl of Mount Edgecumbe	1919	*Au plaisir fort de Dieu*. At the all-powerful disposal of God.
4041	Corium	1919	*Fraternus amor maneto*. Let brotherly love continue.
4158	Sabrina	1920	*Floreat Salopia*. Let Shropshire flourish.
4222	Vespasian	1920	*Servabo fidem*. I will keep faith.
4238	Inglefield	1921	The sun my compass.
4335	St Austin	1921	*Danti Deus dat*. God gives to the giver.
4586	Joppa	1924	*Je tiens*. I hold. *Je tiendrai*. I will hold you. The lodge badge shows a man holding the hand of another man attempting to scale a cliff.
4625	Rodney	1924	*Non generant aquilae columbas*. Eagles do not beget doves.
4717	Whitsters'	1925	*Proxima munditia pietati*. Cleanliness is next to Godliness. The lodge was formed by members of the National Federation of Launderers.
4790	Old Salopian	1925	*Intus et recte ne labora*. Right within, toil not.
4821	Laus deo	1926	Praise God for all.
4868	Southall-Norwood	1926	*Experimentum annorum sustinebo*. I shall attempt a new understanding.
4919	Earl of Malmesbury	1927	*Ubique patriam reminisci*. Everywhere to remember one's country.
4949	Moorfields	1927	*Absque labore nihil*. Nothing without effort.
5009	Isma	1928	*Cura communis venditoris venditori*. Care is owed by one salesman to another.
5191	Aldworth	1930	*Veritas omnia vincit*. Truth conquers all things.

No.	Name of lodge	Const	*Motto and translation*
5304	Ansgar	1931	*E labore dulcedo.* Pleasure arises out of labour.
5368	Old Ellesmerian	1932	*Pro patria dimicans.* Fighting for our country.
5381	Liverpool Epworth	1932	*Vive hodie.* Live today.
5481	Old Wrekinian	1934	*Aut vincere aut mori.* Victory or death.
5655	Parsifal	1937	*Victor mannae occultae sumet.* The victor shall take (or eat) of the hidden manna. This reflects the achievements of Wagner's operatic hero after whom the lodge was named.
5688	West Croydon	1937	*Mens sana in corpore sano.* A healthy mind in a healthy body. Juvenal *Satires*, x, 356; said to be one of the most famous of proverbial Latin sayings.
5876	Penn and Tyler's Green	1943	God guard thee.
5894	Whiteknights	1943	*Absit invidia.* Let envy be absent.
5902	Norma	1943	*Quadra Euclidis.* Euclid's square.
5987	Old Sunning	1944	*Fraternitas flumen sempiternum.* Brotherhood, the everlasting stream.
6007	Red Rose	1944	*Veritas sub rosa.* Truth beneath the rose.
6091	Good Companions	1945	*Fidelis et constans.* Faithful and constant.
6154	Burke	1945	Do good and suppress evil.
6216	Borlase	1946	*Te digna sequere.* Follow things worthy of you.
6243	Roden	1946	*De novo ab initio.* New and fresh from the beginning
6308	Hughenden	1946	*Fraternitas perfecta architectorum.* A complete brotherhood of architects.
6485	Uranus	1947	*Sic vos non vobis.* Thus not for yourselves. *Elvin's Mottoes* states: Virgil, when someone had wrongly claimed a couplet in honour of Augustus, which he had written on the palace door, put up on the same door the above commencement of a verse which, when no-one else could finish it, he completed as follows; 'Hos ego versiculos feci, tulit alter honores. Sic vos non vobis nidificatis aves. Sic vos non vobis vellera fertis oves. Sic vos non vobis mellificatis apes. Sic vos non vobis fertis aratra boves.' Bro. Graham Redman translates this as follows: These little verses *I* wrote, but another has taken the kudos. Just so, not for yourselves, birds, do you raise up your nests. Just so, not for yourselves, sheep, do you carry your wool. Just so, not for yourselves, bees, do you honey produce. Just so, not for yourselves, oxen, the plough do you bear.
6586	Honor per onus	1947	Honour through burden.
6602	Old Wilsonians	1947	*Non sibi sed omnibus.* Not for himself but for all.
6608	Cambrensis	1948	*More majorum.* By the custom of our forefathers.
6609	Excelsior	1948	*Altus altior.* High, higher.
6613	Magnum Bonum	1948	*Vestigia nulla retrorsum.* No steps backwards. (From Horace, *Letters*, Book 1; 1; lines 74–5).
6618	Square and Level	1948	*Unitas et fidelitas.* Unity and fidelity.
6647	Poulton Hall	1948	*Pulsante operictur [sic].* The intention of the founders of the lodge was to have a Latin motto giving the meaning 'Knock, and it shall open.' There may have been a printing mistake right from the start, for the Latin used is erroneous. Bro. Graham Redman thinks the original may have been 'Pulsanti aperietur' meaning 'It will (shall) be opened for one who pounds.'

No.	Name of lodge	Const	*Motto and translation*
6648	Old Chigwellian	1948	*Aut viam inveniam aut faciam.* If I cannot find a way, I'll make one.
6674	Cestreham	1948	*Fidelis.* Faithful.
6742	South Africa	1948	*Eendrag maak kag.* (Afrikaans) Unity makes strength.
6771	Menevia	1948	*Spes mea in Deo est.* My hope is in God.
6782	Gateacre	1948	*Pro bono omnium.* For the good of all.
6797	Old Helean	1948	*Tentando superabimus.* We shall overcome.
6807	Lovekyn Chantry	1948	*Bene agere ac laetari.* Do well and rejoice.
6809	Christopher Wren	1948	*In omnibus rectum rebus.* Upright in all things [affairs].
6822	Perfect Cube	1949	*Pacem servias fidelity. [sic]* May you serve peace (with) fidelity.
6846	Ivel	1949	*Caritas benevolentia veritas.* Charity, benevolence, truth. This motto reflects the three Grand Principles upon which our Order is founded, namely Brotherly Love, Relief and Truth.
6850	Lodge of Justice	1949	Truth shall prevail. The lodge badge shows the figure of Justice as seen on the Old Bailey.
6853	Lodge of Faith for Duty.	1949	*Foy pour devoir.* Faith for duty.
6866	Ordinges	1949	*Omnino frugifer.* Entirely fruitful.
6884	Gunfleet	1949	*Sit lux et lux fuit.* Let there be light and there was light. *Genesis* 1; 3.
6901	Crowley	1949	*Labore et honore.* By industry and honour. *More majorum.* After the manner of our ancestors
7064	Mentor	1951	*Æmulari ad amussim.* Emulate exactly. The motto is intended to be freely translated 'Imitate zealously that which is correct'; this refers to the open book shown in the lodge badge which is meant to serve the double purpose of the Volume of the Sacred Law and the Emulation book of ritual.
7181	Old Paludians	1952	*Ad astra.* To the stars.
7236	Torch	1952	*Semper prospiciamus.* Let us always look forward.
7345	Heatherden	1954	Truth, honour, virtue.
7367	Boteler	1954	*Deus spes nostra.* God is our hope.
7469	Teddington St. Mary's	1956	*Ora et labora.* Pray and labour.
7596	Hundred of Elthorne	1958	*Ad propagandum scientiam comparatum.* Brought together to spread wisdom.
7725	Old Bloxhamist	1960	*Justorum semita lux splendens.* (*Vulgate* version of *Proverbs* 4; 18.) The path of the just is as a shining light.
7731	Philip Bull	1960	God is courteous.
7943	Bourne End	1964	*Aqua praeterita mola non molit.* The mill cannot grind with water that is past. This motto reflects the history of the watering mills, both corn and paper, of the meeting place of the lodge, Bourne End, Buckinghamshire.
7955	Lodge of Orleans	1963	Benevolence and fidelity.
8145	Staplehurst Lodge	1966	*Deo regi et fratribus, honor fidelitas benevolentia.* To God, the King and the brethren be honour, fidelity [and] benevolence. (See *1 Peter* 2; 17). With the exception of the additional word 'et', the wording shown on the lodge badge is identical to the wording on the reverse of the Royal Arch breast jewel.
8172	Harrow Green	1967.	*Gradatim.* Gradually.
8255	Kenelm	1968	*Alta petens.* Seeking the heights.
8345	Hundred of Stoke	1970	*In Deo confido.* I trust in God.
8386	Fortescue	1971	*Deus forte scutum.* God is a strong shield.

No.	Name of lodge	Const	*Motto and translation*
8549	Berkshire St David's	1973	*Gwrando edrych tewi.* See, hear, be silent.
8554	Croydon Lodge of Achievement	1973	*Confectio per contentio [sic].* Achievement through endeavour.
8668	Justice and Peace	1975	*Sine metu aut benefice.* Without fear or favour.
8786	Emmbrook	1977	*Sic luceat lux vestra.* So may your light shine.
8812	Hillcliffe	1977	*Levavi Oculos.* I lifted up mine eyes. (*Psalm* 121; 1.)
8830	Tergere	1978	*Tergere est servare.* To clean is to preserve (the motto of The Worshipful Company of Environmental Cleaners).
8849	Verney	1978	*Ung sent ung sol.* One faith, one sun.
8954	Chelsea Manor	1980	*Patientia industriaque merita sunt [sic].* It is understood this is meant to mean 'Things are earned by patience and industry'; virtues referred to in the traditional history of the third degree.
8965	Cadogan	1980	*Qui invidet minor est.* He who envies is inferior.
8974	Marlow Valley	1980	*Collegium vallis amicum.* The loving fraternity of the valley.
9178	Claydon	1985	*Servata fides cineri.* The promise made to the ashes (i.e. of my forefathers) has been kept. This is one of the mottoes found in the arms of Sir Ralph Verney *Bt. KBE, DL*, Prov. GM Buckinghamshire 1970–6; the baronetcy was created in 1818, and Claydon House is the family seat. The motto is also used used by the Earl of Harrowby. According to *Elvin's Mottoes*: Sir Dudley Ryder, Lord Chief Justice of the King's Bench, had kissed the King's hands on 24 May 1756, on his elevation to the peerage; but he dying within a few days, the patent was not completed, and the promise was not fulfilled in favour of his son Nathaniel, first Baron Harrowby, till the year 1776, when this motto was adopted to record the circumstances.
9187	Trevelyan	1986	*Time tryeth troth.*
9189	Somerset Provincial Grand Stewards	1986	We serve.
9206	Phoenix Lodge of Installed Masters	1986	In the end is my beginning.
9279	Fiennes Cornwallis	1988	*Virtus vincit invidiam.* Virtue overcomes envy.
9441	Nevill Lodge of Installed Masters	1991	*Ne vile velis.* Form no mean wish. This motto forms a play on the name Neville; Ne vile . . .

PART 4:

BANNERS

General

MANY lodges have their own banner; it usually takes the form of a badge or emblem embroidered on a cloth suspended from a cross-bar. The word used in the Middle Ages to describe such a banner is 'gonfalon': it was used by Milton in *Paradise Lost* (Book V; 589):

Ten thousand thousand Ensigns, high advanc't,
Standards and Gonfalons twixt Van and Reare
Streame in the Air, and for distinction serve 590
Of Hierarchies, of Orders, and Degrees;

Grand Lodge and many Provincial Grand Lodges have their own distinctive banners, which are carried in some ceremonial processions. These banners may be in the style of a gonfalon, but quite often they are in the form of a conventional flag, where one side of the banner is attached to a pole or, in heraldic terms, the hoist.

Other banners met with in masonic ceremonial processions are the personal standards of the Grand Master and, where they have them, the Pro. Grand Master, and Provincial or District Grand Masters; these are generally in the form of a conventional flag.

Early-known evidence of banners in masonic processions

The earliest evidence we have pointing to the carrying of masonic banners is of an indirect nature; it is found in a somewhat scurrilous engraving printed in 1742. This purports to depict

A Geometrical view of the Grand Procession of Scald Miserable Masons, design'd as they were Drawn up over against Somerset House, . . .

Amongst the items carried in the procession were banners bearing

Three great Lights, the Sun Hieroglyphical to Rule the Day, the Moon Emblematical to Rule the Night, a Master Mason Political to Rule his Lodge.
The Entered Prentice's Token.
The letter G famous for differencing the Fellow-Craft's Lodge from that of Prentices.
The Funeral of a Grand Master according to ye rites of ye Order, with the 15 Loving Brethren.

This of course was all part of 'mock masonry' as seen by the humorist; one assumes there must have been banners carried in masonic processions for the humorist to mock.

There is more reliable evidence to indicate the details of the Procession around the Hall before the proclamation of a new Grand Master. This is found in the following extract from Anderson's 1738 edition of the *Constitutions*.

ASSEMBLY and *Feast* at *Merchant-Taylors-Hall* on 24 *June* 1724.

DALKEITH *Grand Master* with his *Deputy* and *Wardens* waited on Brother *Richmond* in the Morning at *Whitehall* . . . [the procession went]

On the *Left* Hand	On the right Hand
The *Sword* carried by the *Master* of the Lodge to which the *Sword* belong'd.	The Book of *Constitutions* on a Cushion carried by the *Master* of the *Senior Lodge*.
RICHMOND *Grand Master* Elect.	DALKEITH *Grand Master*.

During the *Procession*, 3 Times round the *Tables* the Brethren stood up and fac'd about with the *regular* Salutations; and when return'd

Brother *Dalkeith* stood up, and bowing to the *Assembly*, thank'd em for the Honour he had of being their *Grand Master*, and then proclaim'd aloud the most noble Prince and our Brother

IV. CHARLES LENNOS Duke of *Richmond* and *Lennox*
GRAND MASTER of *Masons*!

The *Duke* having bow'd to the *Assembly*, Brother DALKEITH invested him with the proper *Ensigns* and *Badges* of his Office and Authority, install'd him in *Solomon's* Chair, and wishing him all the Prosperity, sat down on his Right Hand. Upon which the Assembly join'd in due Homage, affectionate Congratulations and other Signs of Joy.

It will be noted that there is no reference to banners being carried.

Similar details are found in later pages of the *Constitutions*. Unfortunately we do not know the details of 'the proper *Ensigns* and *Badges*' with which the Grand Master was invested immediately before he was 'install'd in *Solomon's* Chair'. It is worth noting that Preston used the same terms in the second edition (1775) of his *Illustrations of Masonry*, in the section dealing with the Installation ceremony. For the Senior Warden he writes:

I appoint you Senior Warden of this lodge; and invest you with the ensigns of your office*.'

The asterisk refers to a footnote which reads: 'Here specify its moral excellence.' For the Junior Warden he uses the word 'badge' instead of 'ensigns', and refers to the same footnote. Preston was apparently giving the two words the same meaning, probably referring to the emblems of office, namely the level and plumb rule respectively.

Public processions

The following extract from the Minutes of the premier Grand Lodge confirms that public processions of freemasons wearing their regalia *did* take place.

At the Braundshead Tavern New Bond Street on Thursday the 3d day of May 1739

Present
The Marquis of Carnarvon G:M
John Ward Esq[r] D:G:M
Lord George Graham S:G:W
Andrew Robinson Esq[r] J:G:W
The Earl of Loudon)
The Earl of Darnly) L.G.M.
The Duke of Gordon
the twelve Stewards

Together with a great number of former G[d] Officers & other Brethren properly cloathed Who proceeded in a regular manner in Coaches and Chariots to Fishmongers hall in Thames Street having several Setts of Musick playing before them . . .

There are other entries of a similar nature.

One would not expect the Grand Lodge Minute to make reference to banners being carried in the procession, but the presence of banners in the 'mock masonry' engravings of the 'scald miserables', of which mention was made earlier, would tend to confirm that banners of one sort or another *were* being carried in masonic processions.

According to Noorthouck's *Constitutions* of 1784, on 3 April 1747 Grand Lodge

'decided to discontinue for the future the usual public procession of the society on the feast day.

The occasion of this prudent regulation was, that some unfaithful brethren, disappointed in their expectations of the high offices and honours of the society, had joined a number of buffoons of the day, in a scheme to exhibit a mockery of the public procession to the grand feast. This, as may be widely supposed, furnished mirth to the gaping croud, [sic] and disgust to the fraternity; who wisely recollecting themselves, determined in the future, to confine their operations within the limits of their own assembly.

For the future, then, the wearing of masonic regalia in a public procession was banned by Grand Lodge unless (according to the *Constitutions*) by the special licence of the Grand Master. The granting of such dispensation was later extended to include Provincial and District Grand Masters. Items in Provincial and private lodge histories, as well as in newspapers show that dispensation was given on various occasions.

Generally speaking the public processions when brethren were in masonic regalia were in connection with Provincial Grand Lodge business, usually a procession to a local Cathedral or church and then on to the place where a banquet was to be held; a stone-laying ceremony, or occasionally to attend a masonic funeral of one of their members. Each of these will be briefly discussed.

Provincial Grand Lodge meetings

The first of two examples chosen to illustrate public processions in connection with a Provincial Grand Lodge meeting is taken from *Freemasonry in Warwickshire, 1728–1978*, (The Warwickshire Peace Memorial Temple Limited, Birmingham, 1978). The relevant extract reads:

The Provincial Grand Lodge was held at the Castle Inn the following day [26 September 1827], presided over by the Right Hon. Earl Ferrers, when a band of ten performers was engaged to lead the procession to church, and several men were also engaged to carry banners. The Minute Book contains a note that a record of the proceedings is contained in the Minute Book of the Provincial Grand Lodge, but unfortunately this particular book has been lost. As this was the first meeting of the Provincial Grand Lodge after his appointment, there are some grounds for assuming that Earl Ferrers was installed at this meeting.

It would have been of particular interest to know more about the banners that were carried; as the word is in the plural, it is reasonable to assume that it was not just the banner of the Provincial Grand Lodge; presumably the other banners were those of the respective lodges taking part in the procession. This might well have been an example of brethren being 'ranged under their respective banners', (of which more later on).

The other example is mentioned in Lee's *Craft Freemasonry in Derbyshire.* The author writes that on 12 September 1826 the Provincial Grand Secretary sent the following letter to various local lodges.

I have received orders from the Very Worshipful Prov. Deputy Grand Master to inform you that he purposes holding a Provincial Grand Lodge, at the Kings Arms County Tavern, Derby, on tuesday the 26th at ½ past nine o'clock a.m. for the purpose of his installation and any other Masonic business, when the attendance of yourself and officers with as many of the Brethren as can make it convenient to attend is requested to assist on that solemn occasion.

After the signature there was the following:

N.B. You are requested to appear in full Masonic clothing, & to bring with you your Jewels, Banners, &c, and to appoint two past masters to officiate as Stewards, who are to be provided with proper collars and aprons.

Two other extracts are worth quoting:

In anticipation of the day of installation of the DEP, Prov. G.M., the Duke of Devonshire, Prov. G.M., and George Beaumont each presented his banner to the Tyrian Lodge, the cost of the latter banner being £9 14s., and these were first displayed on the occasion. . . .

An account of the proceedings appeared in the local newspapers, which reported that the Prov. G.L. was held at the King's Arms county Tavern at 10 o'clock a.m., after which the Tyrian Lodge was opened, at 11 o'clock the Lodges proceeded in order, with the Derby Militia Band playing before them, to All Saints' Church. Their appropriate banners were displayed, among them being the superb flag presented by the Most Noble the Duke of Devonshire to the Tyrian Lodge (still in its possession), and the insignia were borne by the proper officers. At 5 O'clock the Lodge, with its visitors, sat down to dinner at the King's Arms Tavern, after which appropriate toasts were drunk, and the evening was spent in a way that might truly be said would bear the morning's reflection.

Stone-laying ceremonies

In his 1775 edition of *Illustrations of Masonry* Preston gives details of the ceremony for the laying of a foundation stone, including the order of the procession, but there is no reference to a banner or standard being borne. There is likewise no such reference in Noorthouck's description (in his *Constitutions*) of laying the foundation stone of Freemasons' Hall, a ceremony which took place in 1775 or a year later when he described the procession in connection with the dedication of the new Hall.

Masonic stone-laying ceremonies were reported in the newspapers of the day and are occasionally mentioned in lodge histories. One such processsion is recorded in *History of Freemasonry in Oxfordshire*, (Col. A.J. Kerry, *OBE* privately printed). The date was 30 October, 1861, the occasion the laying of the foundation stone of the Corn Exchange in the City of Oxford. The order of procession began with 'Flags and banners'; towards the end of the procession came the banner of the Provincial Grand Master.

Such processions were probably infrequent; in *A Short History of the Province of Cheshire 1725–1975* (O.W. Hope, Phoenix Press, Sale, ud.) the author gives a list headed 'Foundation Stones Laid' by Provincial Grand Masters. It is as follows:

1768 Corner Stone, Eastgate, Chester.
1782 New Bridge Gate (laid by Deputy)
1816 Delamere Church
1843 Keystone in window at Church at Over
1867 St Thomas' Church, Hyde
1871 St Paul's School, Stalybridge
1872 Extension of St Paul's Church, Stalybridge
1873 Collegiate School, Knutsford
1883 Fulshaw Memorial School
1892 Corner Stone of Randle Holme Porch, St Mary on the Hill, Chester
1892 St George's Church, Stockport

1895 Church School, Ashton-on-Mersey
1897 Masonic Hall, Nantwich
1908 Masonic Hall, Chester
1911 Wallasey Masonic Hall
1911 Birkenhead Masonic Hall

The fact that they are recorded in this manner suggests care was taken to ensure that all such ceremonies were included. Nevertheless in a period of 143 years there are only sixteen entries, and half of those were spread over the last thirty years of the nineteenth century! No doubt similar figures could be ascertained by other masonic provinces.

The stone-laying ceremony was included in the first (1815) edition of the *Book of Constitutions* of the United Grand Lodge of England; it is also found in all subsequent editions up to and including that issued in 1917. In all of these, however, there *is* a reference to a place in the procession for a 'Grand Standard Bearer with the Banner of the Grand Lodge' and another 'Grand Standard Bearer with the Standard of the Grand Master'.

Masonic funerals

There is evidence that on occasions brethren wearing their regalia attended a masonic funeral of one of their members. A masonic funeral service is given in Preston's 1775 edition of *Illustrations of Masonry*. There is nothing mentioned, however, about the carrying of a lodge banner.

The masonic funeral ceremony has never been included in the *Book of Constitutions*. However, in the editions from 1815 to 1873 inclusive there was a section dealing with this matter; it read as follows:

> No mason can be interred with the formalities of the order, unless it be at his own special request, nor unless he has been advanced to the degree of a master mason. When the wish of the deceased shall have been communicated to the master of the lodge of which he died a member, the master may apply to the grand master or provincial grand master for a dispension.
>
> A dispensation having been obtained, the master may invite other lodges to attend in form, but the whole ceremony, unless the grand master or his deputy, or the provincial grand master or his deputy, be present, must be under the direction of the master of the lodge to which the deceased had belonged; and he is accountable for the regularity and conduct of the whole proceeding.
>
> The lodges rank according to seniority, the junior preceding (except the lodge to which the deceased belonged, which in every case is to go to the last) and each lodge forms one division.

During the 1950s much attention was given by masonic authorities to attacks from some members of the Church. The following quotation from *Grand Lodge 1717–1967* (Oxford University Press, 1967, pp. 201–2) deals with the subject matter of this particular matter.

> It was, however, clearly desirable that the opponents of Freemasonry should be given the least opportunity for attack. Such attacks seemed likely where the paths of Religion and Freemasonry most nearly came together, in funeral services of deceased members, in attendance at other religious services in masonic dress, and to a lesser extent, in the incorporation of masonic ceremonies of elements clearly derived from sectarian religious ceremonies.

In 1962 the Board of General Purposes produced, and Grand Lodge accepted, a statement headed *The Relationship of Masonry and Religion*. Items (iii) and (iv) read:

> (iii) that there be no active participation by Masons, as such, in any part of the burial service or cremation of a Brother and that there be no Masonic prayers, readings or exhortations either then or at the graveside subsequent to the interment, since the final obsequies of any human being, Mason or not, are complete in themselves and do not call in the case of a Freemason for any additional ministrations. That if it is wished to recall and allude to his Masonic life and actions, this can appropriately be done at the next Lodge Meeting in the presence of his Brethren, or at a specifically arranged Memorial Service;
> (iv) but that while no obstacle should be put in the way of Masons wishing to take part in an act of corporate worship, only in rare and exceptional cases should they be granted dispensation to do so wearing regalia; moreover that the order of service should in all cases be such as the officiating Minister or his superior consider to be appropriate to the occasion.

An Especial Grand Lodge Meeting

An interesting instance of banners being carried in public masonic processions is recorded in *History of Freemasonry in Norfolk*, pp. 279–80. It gives the 'official account of the ceremony ... taken from the printed proceedings of Grand Lodge'. The heading is as follows:

> At an Especial Grand Lodge Holden at the Assembly Rooms in the City of Norwich on Monday, the 23 day of August, 1819.

Amongst those present were His Royal Highness the Duke of Sussex, M.W. Grand Master and R.W. Bro. Thomas William Coke, M.P., Provincial Grand Master for Norfolk. After dealing with the proceedings of the Especial Grand Lodge it gives the detail of the procession then formed which moved to the Cathedral Church of Norwich and later returned to the Assembly Rooms. In the procession were carried:

the standard of the Provincial Grand Lodge of Norfolk;
the banner of the United Grand Lodge of England;
the standard of the Provincial Grand Master for Norfolk;
the banner of the Grand Master, the Duke of Sussex, and
the standard of the Prince Regent, Grand Patron.

Banners and Standards

Note the apparent arbitrary use of the terms 'banner' and 'standard' in the quotation just given. *An Encyclopaedic Dictionary of Heraldry* (Julian Franklyn and John Tanner, illustrated by Violetta Keeble, Pergamon Press, Aylesbury, 1970) defines 'banner' as

'a rectangular flag, fringed of the colours, originally measuring in the dip [i.e. the depth of the flag] about twice the length of the fly [i.e. the width of the flag]; now roughly square and emblazoned with the armorial devices that distinguish the shield of an armiger; exterior decoration not included.

It defines 'standard' as

a large flag, generally about six times as long from hoist (i.e. the side of the flag attached to the mast] to fly, as in the dip, tapering, and bifurcated in the fly, fringed of the colours.

(Incidentally, this book also refers to the sovereign's Household Badge being miscalled the Royal Standard.)

The following extracts come from *The General Armory of England, Scotland, Ireland and Wales* (Sir Bernard Burke, *CB, LL.D* Ulster King of Arms, London, Harrison, 1884, pp. xx–xxl)

The Banner is coeval with the introduction of Heraldry, and dates consequently from the twelfth century. It was of nearly a square form, exhibiting the owner's arms, and it served as the rallying point of the several divisions of which the army was composed. . . .

The right to bear a banner was confined to bannerets and persons of a higher rank. . . .

The Standard was long and narrow, and split at the end. In the upper part of the English standard appeared the Cross of St George, the remainder being charged with the motto, crest, or badge, but never with the arms. It is difficult to determine the qualifications which constituted a right to a standard, but there is reason to believe that no [person under the rank of a knight could use one. . . .

The length of the standard, varied according to the rank of the bearer; the King's was from eight to nine yards in length; that of a Duke, seven yards; of a Marquess, six yards and a half; of an Earl, six yards; of a Viscount, five yards and a half; of a Baron, five yards; of a Banneret, four yards and a half; and of a Knight, four yards.

So far as present-day Freemasonry is concerned the term 'standard' seems to refer to the 'flag' belonging to the Grand Master or the Pro Grand Master which is carried by a Grand Standard Bearer into and out of Grand Lodge. The tem 'banner' seems to refer to the 'flags' used by the lodge, whether it be Grand Lodge, Provincial or District Grand Lodge or by a private lodge. Generally speaking those of Grand Lodge and Provincial or District Grand Lodges are of the conventional flag type, attached to a hoist; whilst private lodge banners are of the gonfalon type, hanging from a cross-bar. This is a generalization; there are always exceptions. One particularly well-known exception is the Grand Lodge banner displayed at the Especial Grand Lodge held at the Albert Hall in 1967 at which HRH the Duke of Kent was installed as Grand Master. The banner was more like a very large 'altar-cloth', too heavy to be carried; it was draped over the front of the organ, behind the seating at the back of the throne.

Those attending the Quarterly Communications of Grand Lodge today will see the standard of the Grand (or Pro. Grand) Master and the standard of Grand Lodge being carried in by Grand Standard Bearers; a similar procedure applies to Provincial and District Grand Lodges.

There are some private lodges that carry their lodge banner in the procession into and out of the lodge room, but the practice is uncommon. When it is done it is usually on a special occasion. One such occasion was the Sesquicentennial Meeting of Cecil Lodge No. 449 on 21 May 1988 at which the lodge banner was dedicated. Item 5 of the Order of Ceremony printed on the lodge summons reads; 'The Brethren of the Lodge will process the Banner into the Lodge Room, . . .'

Banner designs

Once the members of a lodge decide to have a banner, there is usually a meeting of the Lodge Committee to decide what emblems are to be depicted on the banner. More often than not, the banner will be decorated with the badge adopted by the lodge.

Although there is nothing in the *Book of Constitutions* calling for the approval of the design to be depicted on a banner, there is nevertheless a long-standing convention that the design be approved by the Grand Master. The Notes on 'Lodge and Chapter badges' issued by the Grand Secretary's office serve equally as well for guidance on lodge banners.

Dedication of banners

When the banner has been made, the members of the lodge usually ask for it to be dedicated. This is not necessarily done by a Chaplain; quite often the ceremony is presided over by a senior masonic personality such as a Provincial Grand Master, his Deputy or his Assistant.

If the ceremony is in a Province, the core of the Order of Procedure is likely to be along the following lines. Similar (though probably shorter) arrangements are likely to be followed, with the necessary appropriate changes, if the ceremony were in London or a District.

The Banner is collected from outside the lodge room; the Banner Deputation passes round the lodge and displays the Banner to the assembled brethren.

The Presiding Officer calls upon the Chaplain for the Dedication prayer. This is likely to be along the following lines:

O Lord, our Heavenly Father, Architect and Ruler of the Universe, who dost from Thy Throne behold all the dwellers upon earth; we beseech Thee to bless and hallow this Banner which we here dedicate as a symbol of our Masonic Fellowship, and to the honour and glory of Thy Holy Name. Grant to all who gather beneath its shadow, wisdom to teach, humility to learn and grace to fulfil their obligations. Pour down upon them, and upon all members of our fraternity, the continual dew of Thy Blessing, that we may daily increase in love of Thee and of each other, and when earth's fitful day is past, grant us a glorious entry into Thy heavenly temple, where, amid the company of Thy faithful people, we may shine as the stars for ever and ever. S.M.I.B.

The Presiding Officer then causes the Banner to be carried to the East.

The Presiding Officer then delivers the Banner into the keeping of the Master, on behalf of the lodge.

The Master accepts the Banner and requests permission from the Presiding Officer for it to be placed on its stand in the East.

The Banner deputation resume their seats.

An Oration suitable for the occasion is given by the Chaplain.

The Oration will depend upon the Chaplain. There will probably be a reference to the history of the lodge, some comment on the design depicted on the banner, its association with symbolism generally and the lodge in particular, together with a reference to the pride and honour the members of the lodge should feel about Freemasonry in general and their lodge in particular. Finally there will be a suitable inspirational message.

'... ranged under their respective banners.'

In the opening of Grand Lodge the Grand Master asks the Grand Pursuivant what his duty is. His reply includes 'to see that [the brethren] are ... ranged under their respective banners'. When asked if this is so, he gives a qualified affirmative answer. Provincial and District Grand lodges follow a similar procedure. We cannot be sure when the practice of asking this question was first started. The possibility is that it was introduced following the revision of the Opening and Closing ceremonies at the time of the Union of the two Grand Lodges. Despite a thorough search it has not been possible to identify the source of the phrase we use.

It is quite possible that at one time members meeting in Grand Lodge or Provincial or District Grand Lodges *were* ranged under a banner with which they could identify. For Grand Lodge meetings it might have been the banner of the Province or District, but one is left with the impression that the phrase 'under their respective banners' was meant to apply to private lodges. This would seem to be confirmed by the fact that those called to Grand Lodge are summoned individually, Grand Officers as members of Grand Lodge and other brethren in their capacity as master, wardens and past masters of one or more lodges. Similar comments, with the appropriate changes, apply to Provincial and District Grand Lodges. The theory was probably that members attending were expected to arrange themselves in a block of seats allocated to different lodges, each block being identified by the banner of the lodge.

If the phrase *was* introduced at the time of the Union, it is reasonable to assume that lodge banners were then in general use. But had they been so, one would have expected some reference to them in the *Book of Constitutions*; there is not, either pre- or post-Union.

An interesting item on page 283 of *History of Freemasonry in Norfolk* (H. Le Strange; Norwich, 1896) refers to a Provincial Grand Lodge meeting during which the Provincial Grand Secretary stated he would be visiting every lodge in the Province and would be asking the Worshipful Masters to ensure their respective Lodges had a banner. Whether it was the general practice of lodges to have a banner is uncertain; there is no such requirement in the *Book of Constitutions*.

There is a picture of the Installation of the Marquess of Hartington (later the Duke of Devonshire *KG*) as Provincial Grand Master, Derbyshire. This appears in *Craft Masonry in Derbyshire* (G. Trevelyan Lee, Derby, Bemrose and Sons Ltd. 1926) some of the brethren attending the assembly are holding banners, presumably their lodge banners. (This identical picture has been reproduced with the caption 'Installation of the Duke of Newcastle at the Mechanics' Hall, Nottingham, as Prov. G.M. of the Freemasons of Nottinghamshire . . .', the date 1860 having been added).

More evidence of banners in a Provincial Grand Lodge is found in the collection of prints in the Library at Freemasons' Hall, Great Queen Street, London, where there is a copy of a photograph of the Installation of the Earl of Lathom as Provincial Grand Master of West Lancashire, the date being 1899; the banners, presumably lodge banners, are hanging from a bar between the floor and balcony seating.

Present-day procedure

Today brethren attending a Quarterly Communication of the United Grand Lodge of England are not 'arranged under their respective banners' (though members of Grand Stewards' Lodge occupy the special seats reserved for those Past Grand Stewards who are not Past Grand Officers – Rule 37, *Book of Constitutions*). However, at the Luncheon held after the meeting, some of the Provinces arrange for specific places to be reserved for some of their members so that they may sit together; they may be said to be 'ranged' together, but not under a banner.

The procedure in Provincial Grand Lodge meetings varies, as will be seen from the following. In some cases the meeting will be arranged 'under the banner of . . . Lodge.' This lodge has been selected by the Provincial Grand Master beforehand; it is responsible for making some of the arrangements required for holding the meeting. If lodge banners are displayed, it is usually given pride of place. Such a lodge is referred to below as the 'host' lodge.

The Province of Bedfordshire

Every lodge has a banner; a replica is brought along to the meeting and hung from a rail, pride of place being given to the 'host' lodge. It is understood that this procedure started when RW Bro. Sir Gilbert Inglefield was Provincial Grand Master (1958–78); he wanted to give some meaning to the phrase 'ranged under their respective banners'.

The Province of Bristol

All lodges assemble in the places allocated to them under their respective lodge numbers, but without banners; the only banner present on that occasion is the Provincial Banner.

The Province of Cambridgeshire

Most (if not all) the lodges have a banner which is brought along to the meeting. The banners are displayed around the lodge in seniority, with the exception of the 'host' lodge, which, with the master, is given pride of place, in the east.

The Province of Oxfordshire

The Provincial Grand Lodge meeting is held in the Town Hall. All but one of the lodges has a banner. When the room is being prepared the banners are are placed on a rail between the ground floor and the balcony, in seniority, the brethren of the lodge sitting as near as possible to the banner of their respective lodge. This Province does not use the 'host' system.

The Province of Sussex

A representative number of lodge banners are displayed, the master of the lodges chosen being ranged with their banner.

The Province of Warwickshire

The banners of the lodges are displayed around the room in which the meeting is being held.

The Province of Derbyshire

At one time the procedure in this Province was similar to that described for Oxfordshire, but later the banners were replaced by cards bearing the name of the lodge, indicating the area in which the members of each lodge should sit. However, this practice did not last long.

In the events leading up to the celebration of the bi-centenary of the Province, Derbyshire adopted an idea suggested by their Grand Director of Ceremonies, Bro. John Wallace. This was to have at each Provincial Grand Lodge meeting a spectacular display of the Provincial banner and of all the lodge banners; the idea was to encourage the attendance not only of the master and wardens, who are called to be there, but also other qualified brethren. The idea seems to have worked well.

Such an idea, though, is only practical where there is sufficient room – and a great deal of room is necessary! – and where most of the lodges have banners, and it has to be remembered that with the high cost of making banners, not all lodges are willing to meet that expense. The Province of Derbyshire is fortunate in this respect; in 1991 fifty-eight of the seventy-one lodges have banners that could be paraded; a few others have banners that are too fragile to be carried in procession.

Brief details of the display, reproduced here with permission from the Province, are as follows:

Whilst the room is being prepared for the meeting, the banner bearer of each lodge places a stand for his banner (which he has to bring with him) beside the chair reserved for him. These chairs are arranged around the room, those in the east being behind the dais, in the south behind the junior warden, in the west behind the senior warden and in the north behind the secretary.

Before the proceedings begin the banner-bearing parties are formed in two processional columns in order of seniority. Each party consists of the master and wardens of the lodge together with the banner bearer with his banner; they enter the hall, when called, two by two.

At the appropriate part of the proceedings the Provincial Grand Master calls for the Reports from each lodge and for the banner display. The Provincial Grand Master then takes his place in the east at the foot of the dais; the Deputy and Assistant Provincial Grand Masters take a position, side by side, in the centre of the room in line with the junior warden and secretary. The Provincial Grand Director of Ceremonies stands in the west.

The Provincial Grand Director of Ceremonies then announces the names of the lodges, two by two. As their names are called the banner parties enter by their respective doors and advance to the east, the master of each lodge veering to the Deputy/Assistant Provincial Grand Master, handing over their Reports in passing before proceeding eastward to be greeted by the Provincial Grand Master; they then make their way to the seats reserved for them. The wardens and the banner bearer with the banner continue in direct line to the east before branching off to their respective seats. Whilst the banner is being paraded the members of the relevant lodge stand.

At the end of the procession, when the master and wardens are seated and the banner bearers are standing by their respective chairs in the east, south, west and north, the main lights are dimmed and the banners are floodlit.

The Officers resume their seats and the Provincial Grand Master then directs that the Banner of the Province be displayed to the brethren. Once again the Provincial Grand Director of Ceremonies and his Deputy go to the centre of the room. The Provincial Grand Director of Ceremonies then calls for the Provincial Grand Standard Bearer who brings the (gonfalon type) banner to the centre.

Once in position the Provincial Grand Director of Ceremonies says:

> And the Lord commanded all the men of the children of Israel to pitch by their own standard, each with the ensign of their father's house.

The Provincial Deputy Grand Director of Ceremonies and the Provincial Grand Standard Bearer take a few paces to the east and then the Deputy says; 'Brethren of the Province of Derbyshire in the east, upstanding.' The Provincial Grand Standard Bearer raises high the banner and then the Provincial Grand Director of Ceremonies says: 'On the east side towards the rising sun shall they of the camp of Judah stand with Issachar and Zebulun.' The Deputy then instructs the brethren to be seated.

He and the Provincial Grand Standard Bearer then make their way to a position facing south and the process is repeated with the appropriate change of wording. A similar display, again with an appropriate change in wording, is given to the west and north.

The Provincial Grand Director of Ceremonies then says: 'And the Children of Israel did all that the Lord had commanded, and so they pitched their standards. The rectangle of banners we have formed can be said to represent their encampment. To quote from Psalm 20: 'We will rejoice in Thy salvation, and in the Name of God we will set up our banner; and may the Lord fulfil our petitions. Some put their trust in chariots and some in horses, but we remember the Name of the Lord our God.'

The Provincial Grand Director of Ceremonies then instructs the Provincial Grand Standard Bearer to set up the Banner in the east. Having done so, a fanfare is played. The Provincial Grand Director of Ceremonies then resumes his seat and the rest of the Provincial Grand Lodge business is proceeded with.

Amongst the Provinces that do not display lodge banners at a Provincial Grand Lodge meeting are Durham, Essex, East Kent, Hampshire and Isle of Wight, Yorkshire, West Riding, Cheshire, South Wales, Eastern Division, East Lancashire, and Cumberland and Westmorland. In the last-named Province the lodges were ranged under their respective banners many years ago, each lodge having a replica of its banner painted on a board attached to a pole; many of these are now lost.

Grand Standard Bearers

In the 1815 edition of the *Book of Constitutions* the Rule regarding Grand Standard Bearers read;

> Grand standard bearers may be appointed by the grand master, as occasions shall require; they must be master masons, and are to carry the standards of the grand lodge, grand master, and past grand masters, on all grand ceremonies. They are not, however, by their appointment, members of the grand lodge, nor are they to wear the clothing of a grand officer.
>
> Any grand officer, entitled to have a standard, may appoint a standard bearer whenever it shall be necessary, who must be a master mason.

[This might have caused problems. Under the *Book of Constitutions* a master mason was not a member of Grand Lodge, nor could he represent a master or a warden 'unable to attend his duty in Grand Lodge'. The problem could not arise if the words 'duly qualified to attend Grand Lodge' had been included after the words 'master mason'.]

The wording quoted above remained unchanged until the 1884 edition, when the ranks of Grand Standard Bearer and Past Grand Standard Bearer were shown in the precedence of members of Grand Lodge as numbers 33 and 34 respectively.

Personal standards

If the Grand Master is going to preside in Grand Lodge, his personal standard is carried in the procession entering and leaving the temple. That of the present Grand Master, H.R.H. The Duke of Kent, shows The Royal Arms differenced with a label of five points silver, the first, third and fifth points each charged with a blue anchor and the second and fourth with the Cross of St George.

In the absence of the Grand Master, the personal standard of the officer who is going to preside (if he has one) is carried. Both the present Pro Grand Master, Right Honourable Lord Farnham, and Right Honourable Lord Cornwallis, Past Pro Grand Master, have such standards.

Some Provincial Grand Masters may have personal standards; these may be carried into the Provincial Grand Lodge over which they are presiding.

The Grand Lodge banner

The Arms of Grand Lodge shown on the Grand Lodge banner are a combination of the coats of Arms of the premier Grand Lodge and those of the Grand Lodge of the Antients. The former, founded in 1717, adopted the Arms granted in 1473 to the Freemasons' Company of London (the three castles, chevron and compasses). The latter, formed in 1751, adopted the Arms (the man, the lion, the ox and the eagle) alleged to have been designed by Jacob Jehuda Leoni, a brother who flourished towards the end of the seventeenth century. The two coats were combined, by impalement [i.e. a vertical central line by which the shield is parted] at the Union of the two Grand Lodges in 1813, with the addition of the Crest (a representation of the Ark of the Covenant) and the two cherubs which were taken from the Arms of the Antients. These combined Arms had not been authorized by the College of Arms, but in 1919 the matter was regularized by a formal Grant of Arms and, to mark the long and close association of the Royal House with our Institution, a border showing eight gold lions on a red background was added. (Note: the information concerning the border found in *Freemasons' Guide and Compendium* (p. 552, Bernard E. Jones, Harrap, London) is incorrect.)

The relevant wording of the Grant is:

Per pale gules and quarterly azure and or dexter, on a chevron between three castles argent a pair of compasses extended of the third, sinister a cross quarterly of the fourth and vert between, in the first quarter a lion rampant of the third, in the second an ox passant sable, in the third a man with hands elevated proper vested of the fifth the robe crimson lined with ermine, and in the fourth an eagle displayed also of the third, the whole within a bordure of the first charged with eight lions passant guardant of the third. For the Crest, on a wreath of the colours a representation of an ark supported on either side by a cherub proper with the motto over in Hebrew characters 'Holiness to the Lord', and for supporters, on either side a cherub proper.

The colours are referred to as 'of the first' ('second' etc.); they can be more easily identifiable by reference to the following.

'of the first'	gules	red
'of the second'	azure	blue
'of the third'	or	gold
'of the fourth'	argent	silver
'of the fifth'	vert	green
'of the sixth'	sable	black

Banners of Provincial and District Grand Lodges

Not every Province or District has a banner; those that do fall roughly into two classes. There are those that have taken advantage of a scheme which has the approval of the present Garter Principal King of Arms, Sir Colin Cole, *KCVO, TD,* PJGW. This scheme enables the Province or District to obtain the requisite authority to use the same basic coat of Arms as Grand Lodge but with a different bordure, thereby emphasizing the unity of the constitution of the United Grand Lodge of England whilst distinguishing the individual Province or District.

Other Provinces or Districts use Arms or a device associated with their Province. It is known that in many cases the relevant approval for permission to use the Arms has been given.

Examples of some Provincial Grand Lodge banners are given below. Where the Grant of Arms is basically the same as that of Grand Lodge, only the details of the bordure are given, the 'official' wording being used. Colours can be easily identified from the note above; other heraldic terms, unless already explained, are explained after each example given. The reason for the charge shown on the bordure is also given.

Buckinghamshire: as Grand Lodge, 'the whole within a bordure per pale of the sixth and first charged with six swans rising of the fourth each gorged with a ducal coronet gold.' ('per pale' = an imaginary vertical line on the shield; 'gorged' = neck encircled). The swans appear on the Arms of the County.

Cheshire: as Grand Lodge, 'the whole within a bordure of the second charged with six garbs also gold'. The garbs, or sheaves of corn, are shown on the Arms of the County.

Durham: as Grand Lodge, 'within a bordure of the second charged with a cross between eight lions rampant of the third'. ('rampant' = standing on hind-paw, facing right).

Gloucester: as Grand Lodge, 'within a bordure of the fifth charged with eight horseshoes of the fourth'.

Isle of Man: Within concentric circles bearing the words 'Isle of Man Province' a sword, point uppermost, on which is superimposed a viking ship; on the dexter side, the square and compasses; on the sinister side, the emblem of the Isle of Man, namely three legs conjoined.

West Kent: as Grand Lodge, within a red and green bordure charged at the top with a white horse between two acorns; in the lower part between two acorns, a golden saxon crown on a fountain; and on both the dexter and sinister side, a mill-rind on a bezant. A bezant is a roundel like a coin; a mill-rind is the iron affixed to the centre of a mill-stone.

East Lancashire: as Grand Lodge, 'within a bordure vair charged with two stags' head caboshed of the third and two roses of the first'. ('vair' = representing squirrel fur; 'caboshed' = facing forward, head cut off to show no part of neck).

West Lancashire: as Grand Lodge, 'within a bordure per pale of the second and third semé of fleur-de-lys gold and roses of the first'. ('semé' = scattered).

Leicestershire and Rutland: Three shields, one above, two below, between the words 'PROVINCIAL GRAND LODGE' and 'LEICESTERSHIRE AND RUTLAND. The shield at the top bears the arms of the county of Leicestershire; in the first quarter on a white background and within a red circle a silver cinqefoil covered in ermine representing the Beaumont Earls of Leicester; in the second quarter on a red background a white double-tailed lion rampant, representing the two Simons de Montfort, father and son; in the third quarter on a red background, a white ostrich feather with ermine tails, one of the personal badges of John of Gaunt, and in the fourth quarter on a white background a black maunch or sleeve, taken from the arms of the Hastings family. On the lower (dexter) shield, the arms of the city of Leicester, on a red background, a silver cinqefoil covered in ermine. On the lower (sinister) shield, the arms of the county of Rutland; on a green background a horseshoe amongst a scattering of acorns, all gold.

Middlesex: as Grand Lodge, 'within a bordure of the first charged with a Saxon Crown in chief likewise of the third and three seaxes two erect in fesse and one fessewise in base also proper pomels and hilts gold,' ('in chief' = top of shield; 'seaxes' = scimitars; 'fesse' = imaginary horizontal line on shield; 'fessewise' = horizontally).

Nottinghamshire: An oval wreath of acacia in gold enframing the old Nottingham Town Arms: gules (red), issuant from the base a ragged green cross between, in the upper part, two golden ducal coronets, the lower limb of the cross being partially covered with another golden ducal coronet. On the wreath at the top are the arms of Newark-on-Trent; on the dexter side, the arms of East Retfold, and on the sinister side, the arms of Mansfield. (When the banner was designed, Worksop had not received its Charter). Beneath, on a scroll, the words 'AUDI VIDE TACE'; at the top of the design a scroll bearing the words 'PROVINCIAL GRAND LODGE' at the bottom, on a scroll, the word 'NOTTINGHAMSHIRE', below which is a square and compasses.

Oxfordshire: as Grand Lodge, 'within a Bordure Azure charged with four Crowns or and as many Ox Heads caboshed Argent armed gold.' ('armed gold' = horns gold.)

Northumberland: On a shield with a white background, a castle; the motto 'Libertas et natale solum' (Liberty and my native soil) is shown beneath. The castle represents the Norman castle built in 1080 by Robert, eldest son of William the Conqueror, and replaced by the existing castle between 1172 and 1177, and from which the name Newcastle is derived.

Shropshire: the arms of Grand Lodge but without the bordure of lions, impaling the arms of Shrewsbury Town, three leopards' heads caboshed.

Staffordshire: as Grand Lodge, 'within a bordure of the second charged with eight Stafford knots gold'.

Surrey: as Grand Lodge, 'within a bordure quarterly of the second and sixth charged with a representation of King Edgar's crown in chief gold, two ostrich feathers erect in fesse argent and an oak sprig in base of the last', King Edgar's crown and the sprig of oak are found on the Arms of the County; the ostrich feathers are emblems of Edward, Prince of Wales, Grand Master of the Province 1924–36.

North Wales: Within concentric circles bearing the words 'Provincial Grand Lodge, North Wales', the arms of Grand Lodge with the Welsh Dragon on a shield superimposed in the centre.

Banner Lodges

Old Union Lodge No. 46 is known as a 'banner lodge'; that is a lodge in which the master 'presents his banner to the lodge'. This particular custom started in November 1827. A Committee of the lodge reported:

> it was recommended and carried unanimously that every master of the Lodge should present his Banner on his Installation of the form and with the ornaments thereafter to be agreed upon, and also that a Banner of the Lodge should be agreed upon and procured.

By-law No. VII of the lodge reads:

> BANNER OF THE MASTER. VII. — Every Master shall, on being installed, present his banner to the Lodge, of such form, and with such ornaments as shall be approved by the Past Masters.

This lodge has been fortunate in having had amongst its members heralds from the College of Arms, including more than one Garter King of Arms. The Past Masters of the lodge could be sure of sound advice when they were asked to present banners in accordance with the By-law just quoted. The following extracts have been taken from *A Continuation of the Short History of the Old Union Lodge, No. 46 on the Roll of the United Grand Lodge of the Antient Fraternity of Free and Accepted Masons of England. 1935–1985* (Bro. Graham Redman PG Steward, P.M.)

> (pp. 11–12.) The meeting on 24th January, 1956 was notable as the last occasion on which a banner was presented to the Lodge in accordance – albeit somewhat belatedly – with By-Law VII. During the War, this practice of successive Masters presenting their banners to the Lodge had had perforce to be abandoned, the last banner being presented by Bro. Frank Pritchard who was Master in 1941; and rationing and other post-war conditions had not been conducive to its resumption. Now that it was once more possible to obtain suitable materials, Bro. Major R.L. Loyd took the opportunity to present his banner as a 'token of the happiness and pleasure he had enjoyed during his years of Membership of the Lodge.' He was the last to do so, and it seems now likely that changing conditions have brought about the demise of the custom, save perhaps in exceptional circumstances.
>
> (p. 16) A committee appointed to survey the banners presented by Past Masters under By-Law VII, and to make recommendations regarding their repair and display, duly reported, and advised that the practice of displaying the banners at meetings should continue as in the past, those to be displayed being those of eminent masons, and those members still living. Banners in these categories in imperfect condition, but not beyond economic repair, should be renovated, and all should be kept between meetings in a cupboard, which would allow them to be stored in such a way as to minimize the risk of damage. Subsequently, in the early 1980s, these banners were framed as a further measure to ensure their preservation.

Some framed banners are now on loan to the Café Royal, London, and are displayed in their masonic suite in the basement.

Pattison Lodge No. 913 in the Province of West Kent is another lodge known as a banner lodge. Their earliest banner was presented by Bro. Everett H. Denton, the first secretary of the lodge, and bears the date 1861–2. The lodge has a record of the details and designs of each banner, each of which has been photographed and an album containing eighty coloured photographs is kept in the bank. Because of the great increase in costs, the custom of presenting a banner has died out.

Though not strictly a banner lodge (they have only one personal banner presented by the master of the lodge in 1892), the Lodge of Fortitude and Old Cumberland No. 12 is probably unique in having a set of silk banners each of which bears the emblem of an officer of the lodge. The set comprises banners for the master, wardens, treasurer, secretary, deacons and inner guard. Sadly, because of their age, these banners are in a delicate state, beyond renovation; the lodge is considering having replicas reproduced in woven form, though for what purpose is not known.

Reference has already been made to the banners of Tyrian Lodge, No. 253 being displayed in a church procession. This lodge does not claim to be a 'banner' lodge, but over the years it collected a total of seventeen banners! Unfortunately four seem to have been lost. A Report in the minutes of the lodge under the date 22 May 1888 indicate the following;

> one banner was thought to be presented by a Provincial Grand Master of the Province;
> three other banners were presented by Deputy Provincial Grand Masters;
> six banners were presented to the lodge by noblemen, one in 1820, four in 1826 and one in 1829;
> three banners bearing 'the arms of the Tyrian Lodge', one of which was presented on 4 May 1826 by the Duke of Devonshire, Provincial Grand Master;
> four other entries are found in the minutes regarding the presentation of banners but the banners themselves have not been found.

Addiscombe Lodge No. 1556 was also a banner lodge. The first master gave a banner bearing his arms; each succeeding master likewise presented a banner to the lodge but the design shown on the banners is not known; nor is it known whether the masters were in fact armigerous; the custom continued until the Jubilee year in 1925. A record of that year says 'The lodge possesses a very beautiful and interesting collection of banners which were displayed at every meeting of the lodge.' In 1930 it was resolved to discontinue the practice and the banners were returned to the families of the donors.

No doubt there are other lodges which can claim to be a 'banner lodge'.

Making banners

The cost of making a lodge or chapter banner is quite high; it is often met by a gift from one or more of the members or possibly the families of members of the lodge.

To get the best value for money to be spent on the banner much care and attention should be given to the design to be shown on the banner (the simpler the better); the size of the banner; the material to be used; the colours to be employed; how the banner is to hang; the use of lining; the quality of fringing and whether the work is to be done by machine, by hand, painted or hand-embroidered, the latter being by far the better investment. Some banner makers now use a computer to assist in the working of the design to be used.

Masonic outfitters are usually able to provide all the necessary facilities for the making of banners; so too is the Royal School of Needlework which specializes in all kinds of embroidery, especially royal, military, ecclesiastical and masonic. It must also be said that many lodge and chapter banners have been beautifully made by the womenfolk of lodge or chapter members; and it is not unknown for members themselves to design and make banners of merit and distinction! One such case is a brother in Lancashire who has made many banners for local lodges and chapters; another is a distinguished brother who was a Grand Superintendent for many years; being a Reverend Canon he also dedicates the banner! Banners are also made by seamstresses at Freemasons' Hall.

Examples of lodge banners

Some examples of lodge banners are now given. In most cases the motif on the banner is the same as the badge of the lodge, though some are different. Many of the lodges whose badge has already been described will have a banner, some of which may be found in the following entries.

An acknowledgement has already been made to the kindness of Bros. L.R. Harborne and R.L.W. White in allowing me to quote from their excellent book *The History of Freemasonry in Berkshire and Buckinghamshire*; a further acknowledgement is made here for their permission to reproduce some of the photographs of lodge banners they used. These photographs were taken by Bro. Iain Parker of Parker Photography, Wendover. Their kindness in allowing me to use them is much appreciated.

114 British Union Lodge. Ipswich, Suffolk. The Union flag; on the horizontal section of the Cross of St George is the name of the lodge; in the upper part of the vertical section of the Cross are the square and compasses, and on the lower part, the number of the lodge.

117 Salopian Lodge of Charity. Shrewsbury, Shropshire. A shield showing three leopards' faces as engraved on the arms of the Borough of Shrewsbury; above the shield the Centenary Jewel approved by Grand Lodge, namely the letter C in the centre of a rope enclosing a serpent; the word 'Salopian' in a scroll above and the words 'Lodge of Charity' in a scroll below; underneath is the number of the lodge.

The leopards' faces were at one time called 'loggerheads'. The letter 'C' in the Centenary Jewel represents the Roman method of expressing one hundred; the rope indicates the binding together of the past and the present, and the serpent, with its tail in its mouth, represents wisdom.

148 Lodge of Lights. Warrington, West Lancashire. Within a circular strap on which is written 'The three great though emblematical lights of Freemasonry' an open bible upon which rest the square and compasses; there is an All-seeing eye above, an irradiated sun at the dexter side and a moon and seven stars on the sinister side; on a scroll between two torches are the words 'Warrington Lancashire, W. Division,'; the red rose of Lancashire is beneath.

591 Buckingham Lodge. Aylesbury, Buckinghamshire. A red and blue shield on which is depicted the Buckinghamshire swan, around its neck a crown to which a golden chain is attached.

601 St John's. Wellington, Shropshire. The figure of St John holding an open book in his left hand and in his right a chalice from which issues a snake. The book is said to be the Gospel According to St John; the cup relates to a tradition that a priest of the temple of Diana of Ephesus gave John a poisoned cup to drink as a test of the power of his faith. Two condemned men had already drunk of the cup and died; John not only survived unharmed but restored the other two to life. From medieval times the emblem had a symbolic meaning, the chalice standing for the Christian faith, the snake for Satan (*Hall's Dictionary of Subjects and Symbols in Art.*)

948 Lodge of St Barnabas. Linslade, Buckinghamshire. A figure representing St Barnabas holding a staff in his right hand and an open book, representing the Gospels, in the left hand. St Barnabas, 'a good man, full of the Holy Ghost and of faith' (*Acts*, 11; 24) was a Cypriot Jew, remembered for his close association with St Paul. He is said to have been martyred at the Cyprian port of Salamis, but this is not recorded in the bible. The local church is dedicated to this saint, and this is the probable reason why the lodge took the name.

1068 Bulwer Lodge of Cairo. Slough, Buckinghamshire. An ornamental shield showing, in the first and fourth quarters the arms of Sir Henry Bulwer, District Grand Master of Turkey, who consecrated the lodge, a red shield with a silver chevron showing three five-pointed stars between three eagle reguardant (i.e. the head turned round, looking back); in the second quarter the arms of the Company of Masons, a black shield with a silver chevron showing a pair of golden compasses between three castles, and in the third quarter, a desert scene showing pyramids. The word 'Cairo', where the lodge was consecrated, appearing beneath the ornamental shield. Sir Henry Bulwer was the British Minister Plenipotentiary to the Ottoman Empire at Constantinople, Egypt then being under Turkish domination. Freemasonry was banned in Egypt in 1956; the lodge then transferred to London and in 1980 moved into the Province of Buckinghamshire.

1120 Lodge of St Milburga. Wellington, Shropshire. St Milburga holding a stem of barley; on the dexter side the ruins of Buildwas Abbey within a circlet of laurel leaves; on the sinister side a representation of the Iron Bridge in a similar circlet, these two being two well-known local landmarks; below the dexter circlet, the date 662, the year of the saint's birth, and below the other circlet the date 725, the date of her death.

The saint was one of the three daughters of Merewald, brother of Wulfhere, the first Christian king of Mercia; she was a foundress and abbess of Wenlock Abbey and reputed to be a very beautiful and holy woman possessing miraculous powers. One legend has it that she once caused barley, sown in the morning, to ripen by midday and be reaped in the evening. In the background of the banner behind the saint can be seen flying wild geese which had eaten some of the newly sown grain; she bade these 'be gone, and never again to trespass on her land'.

1250 Gilbert Greenall Lodge. Warrington, West Lancashire. Per pale (a shield divided vertically); dexter, on a gold background three green buglehorns on a bend nebuly plain cotised (a diagonal key-shaped pattern between two thin lines), the hand of Ulster in a small shield at the top; sinister, on a blue background, a sword point uppermost, hilt golden. The motto beneath, Alta Peto.

1432 Fitz Alan Lodge. Oswestry, Shropshire. A shield showing the crest of the Fitazalan arms, a galloping horse with a branch in its mouth; the square and compasses, the level, and a sprig of acacia are also shown.

1501 Wycombe Lodge. Marlow, Buckinghamshire. Within concentric circles the Buckinghamshire swan, duly gorged (having a coronet around the neck) and chained, standing on a mound; outside the circles, a wreath composed of a sprig of acacia and an ear of corn, conjoined at the bottom with the square and compasses.

1540 Chaucer Lodge. London. A sky-blue banner showing a shield with a white background. In the first quarter of the shield is a tabard; in the second quarter is said to be the arms of the City of London (but the sword has been omitted); in the third quarter seven stars with the letter T in the centre and in the fourth quarter the mosaic pavement of a lodge and a working tool from each of the three degrees, namely a gavel, square and the compasses. Various other masonic emblems surround the shield.

The symbolical explanation given in a leaflet says the sky-blue is symbolical of the heavens, that roof of the great Temple of the Universe under which we all have our being and above which we believe the Great Architect of the Universe reigns for ever.

The white ground of the shield reminds us of the badge of innocence with which we were invested at our initiation. The tabard reminds us of the Tabard Inn in Southwark from which the Canterbury Pilgrims set forth on their journey; it is intended to show a link between the lodge, consecrated in Southwark in 1875, and Chaucer, after whom the lodge is named and whose *Canterbury Tales* tell us of the pilgrims and the inn.

The arms of the City of London are shown as a link with that city where so many of the lodge members carry out their daily avocations.

The seven stars represent the number to form a perfect lodge; they have a further allusion to the seven liberal arts and sciences, as explained in the fourth part of the second Lecture. The T in the centre represents the square and the influence and authority of the Worshipful Master.

The items in the fourth quarter remind us of the lessons conveyed in the relevant parts of the ritual.

The leaflet goes on to explain in some detail the symbolical nature (as seen by the author) of the other masonic emblems shown on the banner, including 'a rose surcharged with the letter G in rays of light'; the rose is said to represent 'the source of our common origin, depicted in the earlier days by the V.P., which symbol is still retained in our lodges in the form of the collars worn by our officers, but which has been more or less superseded by the Rose, exemplified on our aprons.' There is also a reference to the rose of Sharon and other mystical matters. It is not known what the letters 'V.P.' are meant to signify.

The references here are so obscure as to be meaningless to many; the symbolical explanation given in the leaflet is likely to have a somewhat limited appeal.

1621 Castle Lodge. Bridgnorth, Shropshire. A castle with the motto of the town of Bridgnorth beneath, 'Fidelitas urbis salus regis.' The square and compasses are also shown together with the name and number of the lodge and the word 'Centenary'. The banner is handwoven on canvas in woollen cross-stitch; approximately 75,000 stitches were needed to complete the banner.

1899 Wellesley Lodge. Sindlesham, Berkshire. The armorial bearings of the Duke of Wellington; in the first and fourth quarter a white cross on a red background, in each of the quarters formed thereby five plates in saltire; in the second and third quarters, on a gold background, a red lion rampant with a ducal collar around its neck; over all, in the centre, as an augmentation or honourable addition to the arms, the union badge of the United Kingdom, being the combined crosses of St George, St Andrew and St Patrick. The crest is also shown; out of a golden ducal coronet the upper part of a red lion holding a forked pennant bearing the cross of St George. The motto 'Virtutis fortuna comes' is shown beneath. The banner does not show the supporters.

2114 Lodge of Prudence. Woolton, West Lancashire. The figure of Prudence holding in her left hand a staff topped by a cross around which a snake is entwined; her right hand holds a pair of compasses, their open points resting on a box showing a square and a circle at the front; above, on the dexter side, an irradiated star, and on the sinister side, a cornucopia. The words 'Let Prudence direct you' are shown below.

Prudence is one of the four cardinal virtues signifying not just caution, but wise conduct. The snake is derived from *Matthew* 10; 16; 'be ye wise as serpents'; the compasses are meant to refer to her measured judgement.

The reason for the other emblems is not known; in Christian art vices and virtues are often depicted together; the cornucopia may be in this category, indicating over-indulgence or greed.

2262 Dagmar Lodge Slough, Buckinghamshire. Within concentric circles showing the name and number of the lodge four red hearts between a cross pattée (each limb expanding as it progresses outwards from the centre, like the shape of the Victoria Cross). This reflects the charitable work, particularly in the field of hospitals, education and relief work, carried out by Princess Dagmar (1847–1928), after whom the lodge was named; she was a Danish princess and the younger sister of Queen Alexandra. The design for the original lodge banner was, almost without variation, the Danish Royal Arms; however this did not receive the approval of the Grand Master. An ornate design of a golden lion rampant appears above a scroll showing the words 'Province of Buckinghamshire'; this crest was associated with the Royal Danish Arms. Below is another scroll showing the words 'Hall Stone Lodge', beneath this, a chequered pavement showing the square and compasses and the dates 1888–1988, the latter year being the date the new banner was dedicated.

2309 Christopher Lodge. Slough, Buckinghamshire. A golden griffin on a blue background; above a helm, a crest of a unicorn's head. The design appears to have been taken from charges on arms adopted without permission by a Brother George Garner, the prime mover in the formation of the lodge and after whom the lodge was originally named. Later the lodge moved to the Christopher Hotel, Eton and in 1895 the name of the lodge was changed to Christopher Lodge.

2414 Wychwood Lodge. Burford, Oxfordshire. An oval bearing the name and number of the lodge and enclosing a chequered floorcloth as a centrepiece on which appears a representation of the entrance to the lodge premises, an arch beneath which are two doors; on seven of the white squares of the chequered cloth is a tree shaped like an elm, one of the trees with pliant branches to which the prefix wych (or witch) is sometimes attached; this is probably meant to be a punning reference to the name of the lodge. The trees represent the Wychwood forest; the centrepiece accurately reflects the entrance to the lodge courtyard.

2421 Carrington Lodge. Marlow, Buckinghamshire. The Carrington arms, blazones as 'quarterly of six', that is six 'compartments'. In the first, on a gold background, is a chevron bordered by a thin line between three black demi-griffins; in the second on a green background, three golden shields each enclosing a silver shield; in the third on a white background, three battering rams; in the fourth, a blue criss-cross pattern on a gold background; in the fifth, on a white background a red cross patonce, that is the end of each limb looking like a very shallow fleur-de-lys, and in the sixth, three red wavy bars on a gold background. For supporters, black griffons, the dexter charged with gold fleur-de-lys, the sinister charged with gold trefoils; the crest, an elephant's head with three fleur-de-lys on the neck. The Motto shown is 'Tenex in fide'.

2430 Runymede Lodge. Slough, Buckinghamshire. The banner shows an important episode in the history of England, King John signing the Magna Carta at Runymede in 1215; the king is seated in a field amongst barons and knights, many of whom carry a standard. Beneath the frame showing the scene is the Volume of the Sacred Law flanked by the square and compasses and an All-Seeing Eye.

2435 Wineslai Lodge. Winslow, Buckinghamshire. Beneath the saxon crown of King Offa who had a camp at Winslow, a representation of a gridiron on which St Lawrence was burnt; the local church is dedicated to this saint; a floral wreath surrounds the gridiron. A garlanded scroll above shows the name of the lodge, the number appears on a panel beneath. An All-Seeing Eye in a Glory is shown at the top between the square and compasses on one side and a pentalpha on the other.

2492 Concordia. Aylesbury, Buckinghamshire. The banner is based on the Rothschild arms; quarterly. In the first quarter a black double-headed eagle displayed on a gold background (the Rothschild arms show an eagle displayed); in the second and third quarters on a blue background, a bent arm holding five golden arrows, and in the fourth quarter on a gold background, a red lion rampant; overall, in the centre, an escutcheon or shield, with a red background showing a white band from the lower dexter corner to the upper sinister corner, in the middle of which is a target (the Rothshchild arms has an escutcheon, red, thereon a target the point to the dexter); the Buckinghamshire swan, gorged and chained, is shown as the crest (the Rothschild arms has a black eagle). The supporters are, on the dexter side a lion and on the sinister side a unicorn. The first word of the motto on the Rothschild arms is 'Concordia'. This lodge has no apparent connection with the Rothschild family other than that both it and the Ferdinand de Rothschild Lodge No. 2420 were sponsored by Buckingham Lodge, No. 591, Baron Ferdinand de Rothschild was to be the first master of the lodge bearing his name, but being unable to be present at the Consecration, was subsequently installed as second master.

2651 Lodge of Charity. Warrington, West Lancashire. The figure of Charity with two children at the end of a chequered floorcloth showing various masonic emblems; the floorcloth is flanked by two pillars on top of which are the usual globes; the names of the lodge founders are engraven on the columns; above the figure of Charity is an irradiated triangle enclosing an All-seeing eye.

2683 Addington Lodge. Slough, Buckinghamshire. The armorial bearing of Rt Hon, Lord Addington, Provincial Grand Master, Buckinghamshire at the time the lodge was founded. On a green background, a silver chevron with a narrow green band near the edges which are in the form of a continuing line of semi-circles joined together by a short straight line; above the chevron are two silver eagle heads and another appears below the chevron; the necks of the eagles are covered by a red collar bearing a fleur-de-lys design. There is a similar design as the crest and the supporters are eagles similarly collared bearing a shield charged with a red rose and fur. The motto beneath is Alta Petens. An All-Seeing Eye, the square and compasses and a pentalpha are shown above.

2812 St Martin's Lodge. Bletchley, Buckinghamshire. A representation of the bishop who became known as St Martin of Tours. Whilst serving as a soldier he gave half his cloak to a naked beggar. This led to a firm belief in Christianity and he was baptized soon afterwards. He left the army and became an active missionary. He was one of the first holy men who was not a martyr to be publicly venerated as a saint and his influence was felt far and wide. Many churches in England were dedicated to him, including St Martin's-in-the-Fields, London; so too was the parish church in Fenny Stratford, where the lodge was formed. In the corner of the banner is a shield showing what is known as a carbuncle; it is believed that English armorists assigned these arms to him, having been misled by a similarity of his name to that of a well-known French family.

2816 Bowen Lodge. Beaconsfield, Buckinghamshire. A shield impaling the arms of the Company of Masons with those of Buckinghamshire; the square and compasses with a pentalpha is above together with a scroll showing the name of the lodge; below a scroll shows the lodge number and beneath that a monogram of the letters J, E, B, the initials of W. Bro. J.E. Bowen, Deputy Provincial Grand Master of Buckinghamshire; he consecrated the lodge.

2849 Beaconsfield. Slough, Buckinghamshire. Below an All-Seeing Eye, pillars showing the names of the founders and the usual globes; on the base of the dexter pillar are the square and compasses, and on the base of the dexter pillar there is a pentalpha. Between the pillars is a shield impaling the Buckinghamshire swan, gorged and chained on a red and blue background, and one of the quarters from the arms of Lord Burnham, namely a golden voided saltire, fretted, on a red background between two rams' heads and an augmentation of the badge of Ulster, being a red, open upright palm, erect.

2963 Lodge of Friendship. Warrington, West Lancashire. A black hand clasping a white hand in a gesture of friendship.

3213 City of London St Olave's Lodge. London. A stave of music showing the notation and words of the song 'Auld Lang Syne'. The lodge was formed by members of an amateur musical association within the boundaries of St Olave's.

3287 St Elphin Lodge. Warrington, West Lancashire. A portrayal of St Elphin's church; an All-seeing eye; the bible, the square and compasses and the pentalpha decorate the four corners.

3401 St Michael's Temperance Lodge. Woolton, West Lancashire, St Michael slaying the dragon; below, the pedestals of the master and wardens, on the former an open bible with the square and compasses. On either side, a panel with the names of the founders of the lodge.

3596 James T. Callow Lodge. Woolton, West Lancashire. A castle between an ear of corn and a sprig of acacia. Above the castle is an All-seeing eye. It has been suggested that the castle is meant to represent the Temple.

3597 Lodge of Rectitude. Warrington, West Lancashire. Between pillars one of which is topped by a terrestrial and the other a celestial globe, and beneath the square and compasses enclosing an All-seeing eye, the arms of Warrington, the town in which the lodge meets. The founders' names are on the pillars.

3651 Bombay Lodge. Radlett, Hertfordshire. Within concentric circles showing the name and number of the lodge, the flags of St George in saltire, above which are the square and compasses, and below which is an anchor. An Imperial crown sits above the square and compasses. The lodge was consecrated in Bombay and known originally as Army and Navy Lodge, hence the badge. Following the formation of the Grand Lodge of India, the lodge was transferred to London. An 'Army and Navy Lodge' already existed in London, so with the approval of the Grand

Master the name was changed to Bombay Lodge; permission was given to retain the original badge. The lodge banner shows on one side the badge with the original name of the lodge, and on the other, the badge with the new name.

3693 Fallowfield Lodge. Chorlton-cum-Hardy, West Lancashire. On a blue background, a portal, behind which is a chequered pavement on which stands, at the back, a pediment supported by five columns. On the entablature is an open book on which is written V.S. LAW; above, on a red background the words QUADRAGESIMUS SEPTIMUS: a red rose is shown on the front of the pavement.

The two columns of the portal are meant to represent the two pillars at the entrance of King Solomon's Temple; the five columns, the five orders of architecture; the red rose is a symbol of Lancashire, the Province in which the lodge meets; the Latin phrase, meaning Forty-seven, is a reference to the 47th proposition of Euclid and the emblem of the jewel worn by Past Masters.

3874 Red Triangle Lodge. Woolton, West Lancashire. An All-seeing eye within a red triangle, base uppermost; the square and compasses, level, plumb-rule and Volume of the Sacred Law surround the triangle.

3916. Pax Magna Lodge. Nottingham, Nottinghamshire. Between pillars topped by a terrestrial globe (on the dexter side) and a celestial globe (on the sinister side) an ornate circle showing a background of the rising sun dispelling the clouds of night and a flying dove bearing an olive branch; the pillars show scrolls bearing the names of the founders of the lodge. A scroll above shows the name and number of the lodge; above the scroll, in the centre, is an irradiated All-seeing eye, and below, closing the circle, the square and compasses. The columns rest upon a chequered floorcloth; below the circle is a broken sword and an olive branch in saltire. Pendent from the centre of the floorcloth is a shield showing the arms of the County of Nottingham, the city in which the lodge meets, with the motto 'Vivit post funera virtus'. The lodge was consecrated in 1919, shortly after the Peace Treaty which ended the Great War of 1914–18; hence the emblems of peace.

4002 Minerva Lodge. Liverpool, West Lancashire. The head of the Roman goddess Minerva, wearing a helmet; she was known as the goddess of wisdom and is identified with the Greek goddess Athena.

4103 Aigburth Lodge. Liverpool, West Lancashire. Beneath an All-seeing eye and between pillars one of which bears a terrestrial and the other a celestial globe, a scene of the village of Aigburth in the thirteenth century; the Volume of the Sacred Law on which rests the square and compasses is shown beneath; the dexter pillar bears the square, the sinister the plumb-rule.

4158 Sabrina Lodge. Shrewsbury, Shropshire. The maid Sabrina sitting on a raft floating on the River Severn. A member of the lodge, which meets at Shrewsbury, has given the following explanation:

> About 1400 BC Locrin possessed the middle part of our island; he obtained from his brother Kamber, a prisoner taken in battle with the king of the Huns. This prisoner was Estrilidas, the beautiful daughter of that king. Locrin fell in love with her, but he was already engaged to a daughter of Corineus, Gwendoloena, whom he was forced to marry. He secretly visited Estilidis for several years and in the process of time, following the death of Corineus, divorced his wife and advanced Estilidis to be Queen.
>
> Gwendoloena was provoked beyond measure and after retiring to Cornwall assembled the forces of that kingdom and joined battle with Locrin near the River Sture. Locrin was killed and Gwendoloena took over the government of the kingdom.
>
> Estilidis and her beautiful daughter by Locrin, named Sabre, were captured and Gwendoloena ordered that they be thrown into the river which in future was to bear the damsel's name, hoping by this to perpetuate her memory and that of the infamous Locrin. In time the name became somewhat corrupted and although known as the River Severn, it is also referred to as Sabrina.

This version is a little different from that given in *The Dictionary of Phrase and Fable* (Brewer) which says that Sabrina 'fled from the battle and jumped into the river. Nereus took pity on her, and made her "goddess of the Severn" which is poetically called Sabrina.'

Milton refers to the incident in his poem 'Comus'.

4335 St Austin Lodge. Warrington, West Lancashire. An Austin Friar in front of a representation of St Austin's Friary in Warrington which was disbanded at the Reformation; beneath the motto 'Danti Deus dat'. The square and compasses with the triad 'Relief, Brotherly Love, Truth' is shown below. Above, on the dexter side the armorial bearings of the town of Warrington are shown, whilst on the sinister side are the armorial bearings of Greenall (though these appear to be back-to-front; the charges should go from top left to bottom right, not top right to bottom left, as shown).

The name Austin is a reduction of Augustin.

4530 Heaton Moor Lodge. Heaton Moor, West Lancashire. On a chequered floorcloth and between the usual pillars, and beneath an All-seeing eye, a Spread-eagle; other masonic emblems are also shown.

4634 Chilterns Lodge Slough, Buckinghamshire. Beneath the name of the lodge and at the head of a Roll of Masters from 1924–1949, a cartouche showing a painting of the Chiltern Hills.

4679 Travellers Lodge. Warrington, West Lancashire. An ark on water, above which is a dove carrying a sprig in its beak; the lodge was founded for commercial travellers and the design shown was to symbolize these men returning home after their travels to attend the peaceful haven of a lodge.
4877 Longmynd Lodge. Church Stretton, Shropshire. A circle depicting the hills after which the lodge was named.
5115 Upton Manor Lodge. Slough, Buckinghamshire. A scene depicting the giving of the Manor of Uptone (recorded in the Domesday Book as Opetone) by Paganus de Beauchamp to a representative of the monastery of the Augustinian Canons of Merton who had come to Upton in the twelfth century; an All-Seeing Eye is above two pillars showing the names of past masters of the lodge. The pillars are topped by the usual terrestrial and celestial globes.
5128 Ashmole Lodge. Warrington, West Lancashire. A portrait of Elias Ashmole, 1617–92, the antiquary and genealogist who founded the Ashmolean Museum at Oxford. As stated at the start of this book, his diary records that he was made a freemason at Warrington on 16 October 1646. Above the portrait is the red rose of Lancashire and above that an open bible.
5170 St Oswald Lodge. Warrington, West Lancashire. An illustration of St Oswald Church, Winwick.
5368 Old Ellesmerian. Ellesmere, Shropshire. An adaptation of the arms of St Oswald's School, Ellesmere, showing a cross between two celestial crowns; in a triangle below, a raven with a ring in its beak; this also appears as a crest above the shield. Below is the motto 'Pro patria dimicans'.

The reference is to St Oswald, King and martyr, the crowns representing the two kingdoms over which he ruled. In Christian art the raven is an emblem of God's providence, an allusion to the ravens which fed Elijah (1 *Kings* 17; 4). St Oswald is often depicted as holding in his hand a raven with a ring in its mouth.
5481 Old Wrekinian Lodge. Wellington, Shropshire. A shield showing a crowned lion rampant, above which is the motto 'Aut vincere aut mori'. This is not quite the same design as the badge of the lodge which appears to show the armorial bearings of Wrekin College, namely a lion rampant (uncrowned) with an escutcheon showing a stem of seven bay leaves.
5486 Lodge of Success. London. Between pillars bearing respectively a terrestrial and a celestial globe, the figure of Pythagoras elucidating his theorum, subsequently incorporated as the 47th problem of the First Book of Euclid, an event which is said to have given the great philosopher intense personal satisfaction and increased the respect in which he was held by the learned men of the period.
5568 Hundred of Burnham Lodge. Slough, Buckinghamshire. A scene depicting the wooded area known as Burnham Beeches; the name of the lodge is taken from one of the eighteen Saxon 'Hundreds' of the County of Buckingham; their duty was to supply men for the Buckingham garrison in time of war. The courts governing the Hundred levied taxes, looked after roads and bridges, and tried and punished criminals.
5622 Semper Sursum Lodge. Barrow-in-Furness, West Lancashire. On a chequered floorcloth bearing the rough and perfect ashlars against which lean the level and plumb rule, and between two pillars the dexter bearing a terrestrial globe, the sinister a celestial globe, the arms of Barrow in Furness, the town in which the lodge meets; these are, on a golden bend between a coiled serpent and a stag on a red background, a bee and an arrow, point uppermost; in the upper part of the shield, on a white background, a paddle-wheel steamship on the move under steam and canvas; the crest is a battlement from which emerges a ram's head wearing a golden collar. An All-seeing eye, radiated, is above the crest; the lower fringe of the banner shows the square and compasses. The founders decided to use the motto of the town as the name of their lodge.
5637 Pegasus Lodge. Aylesbury, Buckinghamshire. Facing sinister and standing on its hind legs on top of a globe representing the world, the winged horse Pegasus of Greek mythology; six stars are also shown, together with the usual pillars. The lodge was formed by freemasons from R.A.F. Halton.
5724 Uxacona. Wellington, Shropshire. A view through a brick built archway straddling a road; a hill and two oak trees are shown in the field on one side of the road which is meant to represent the Roman road which passed through Usc-Con and the Wrekin on its way to Uriconium.

The name Uxacona is a Romanized form of the older Celtic name Usc-Con; Usk means water; Con (from Cond) means junction (of a stream with a pool or lake).
5840 Sarnia-Riduna Lodge. London. On a salmon-coloured background (representing the sails of the old fishing vessels) and within concentric circles, the three Islands of Guernsey, Alderney and Jersey on an azure background (representing the sea); within the concentric circles at the top, the word LONDON (being the meeting place of the lodge), at the base the figures 5840 (being the number of the lodge), on the dexter side a Greek cross bearing the word VEGA (representing the hospital ship that brought Red Cross parcels and letters to the Islands after the war), and on the sinister side a Guernsey lily. Below the circles, three shields, the first bearing the arms of Guernsey, the second the arms of Jersey and the third the arms of Alderney. Above the shields a scroll showing the consecration date of the lodge.
5939 Great Sankey Lodge. Warrington, West Lancashire. A portrayal of the local St Mary's Church in the vestry of which the founders met to form the lodge, the vicar being one of them.

6200 Pax Vera Lodge. Sale, Cheshire. Between pillars showing the names of the founders of the lodge, the dexter bearing a terrestrial and the sinister a celestial globe, an open bible upon which rest the square and compasses; above a dove of peace wings outstretched, head downwards, holding an olive branch in its beak.

6243 Roden Lodge. Whitchurch, Shropshire. Superimposed on a flaming torch a circle enclosing a battlement above blue and wave lines indicating a river; above the battlements, a hawk. The consecrating elements of corn, wine and oil are interwoven in the decorative surround of the banner; below is the motto 'De novo ab initio'.

It is said that the history of the town of Wem forms the basis of the design. The hawk is a reminder that the Domesday Book (1086) records the district was noted for its extensive woodlands with a large aviary of hawks; an eleventh century medieval castle was the centre of the siege of Wem in 1643 and its garrison helped to capture Shrewsbury for the Parliamentarians in 1645; the castle overlooked and guarded the River Roden, the name selected by the founders for the lodge; the torch is a reference to the Great Fire of Wem in 1677.

6288 Newton Lodge. Warrington, West Lancashire. Between pillars on which are seen the names of the founders and on top of which are the usual globes, a scene depicting the lake below the church at Newton-le-Willows; above, the crest from the arms of the Legh family residing at Haydock and Newton, namely a ram's head arising from a coronet.

6308 Hughenden Lodge. Marlow. Buckinghamshire. An illustration of St Michael's and All Angels Church in Hughenden Park, close to Hughenden Manor, the home of the Victorian statesman Benjamin Disraeli, the first Earl of Beaconsfield. The motto 'Fraternitas perfecta architectorum' appears above, together with the swan of Buckinghamshire, gorged and chained.

6483 Hampden Lodge. Aylesbury, Buckinghamshire. Between pillars, the dexter bearing a celestial globe and the sinister a terrestrial globe, the arms of the Hamden family; silver, a red saltire (St Andrew's cross) between four blue eagles displayed; above, a talbot (dog) for the crest and below, the motto 'Vestigia nulla retrorsum'; this motto is also used by Magnum Bonum Lodge, No. 6613. (The globes are more often than not shown the other way round.)

6507 Weyland Lodge. Bicester, Oxfordshire. A circle enclosing a stylised fleur-de-lys based on the design shown in the Seal of the Priory of Bicester; it is shown between the usual two pillars with their globes; there is an All-seeing eye above and a chequered floorcloth below on which are many masonic emblems.

The use of the design of the fleur-de-lys in Bicester appears to have been because of the close association of the town with the Priory which was founded in 1182 by a local baron, Gilbert Basset; the Priory was dissolved in 1536 by Henry VIII. An examination of three ancient seals of the Priory shows one bearing a stylised fleur-de-lys, an important emblem used by the Priory which dominated the life of Bicester throughout the Middle Ages. The fleur-de-lys is said to derive from a royal gift.

6632 Vale Lodge. Aylesbury, Buckinghamshire. Between columns bearing the usual pillars, a representation of St Mary's Church, that being the symbolic centre of the Vale of Aylesbury from which the lodge takes its name.

6647 Poulton Hall Lodge. Morecambe and Heysham, West Lancashire. Within the square and compasses an illustration of the doorway of the old Poulton Hall; this is flanked by the usual two pillars with their respective globes; beneath is the motto 'Pulsante operictur'. (See comments under this lodge in the section headed 'Mottoes'.)

6674 Cestreham Lodge. Beaconsfield, Buckinghamshire. The main item on the banner is a portrayal of the Lollard, Thomas Harding, a dissenter who was burned at the stake in Chesham in May 1532 for the heinous crime of being caught reading religious tracts; he stands in martyr's robes with flames at his feet; in the background is St Mary's Church, Chesham where, in a small room above the south door, he was imprisoned the night before his execution; behind are the rolling Chiltern Hills; surrounding all are the leaves and mast of the beech tree commonly found in the Chilterns. Cestreham was the Saxon name for Chesham when the Domesday Book was being written; the name has been translated as 'camp home'.

6687 Montem Lodge Slough, Buckinghamshire. Between the usual two pillars, a scene depicting a field with two hills in the background, one topped by a flag bearing the Cross of St George, the other a castle; at the foot of the hills are a large crowd and tents, giving the impression of a fairground; in the foreground a horse-drawn carriage occupied by two men and a lady, talking to two children. Quoting from *The History of Freemasonry in Berkshire and Buckinghamshire*:

> The name Montem is derived from an isolated hillock, Salt Hill, which became famous as the site of a unique festival. How the custom of 'Ad Montem' began, history does not record; suffice it to say it was long before the time of Malim who ruled over the scholars at Eton in the mid-sixteenth century, for it was he who recorded how, on or about the feast of the Conversion of St Paul, the scholars set out in procession 'ad Montem' to recite Latin verse and to initiate novices. Over the decades the date and the nature of the ceremony changed, bringing with it the masses out of London and around, on pleasure bent, until in 1847, Eton's headmaster appealed to Queen Victoria for permission to end the celebrations before the situation became completely beyond control. Its full history makes fascinating reading and the lodge emblem perpetuates the memory of a part of the history of this corner of Berks, and Bucks.

6754 Old Wycombiensian Lodge. Marlow, Buckinghamshire. Within concentric circles bearing the name and number of the lodge, the Buckinghamshire swan, gorged and chained, against a background of blue and red and standing on a green field, holding in its beak the arms of the Royal Grammar School.
6782 Gateacre Lodge. Woolton, West Lancashire. Within concentric circles bearing the motto 'Pro bono omnium', a pastoral scene showing a three-barred gate, fields, hedges and hills and the rising sun.
6968 Brickhill Lodge. Bletchley, Buckinghamshire. A representation of a country scene which includes the local church at Brickhill, the home of a prominent local business man and first master of the lodge, WBro. Hedley C. Clarke. The original name Brichella is also shown.
7345 Heatherden Lodge Slough, Buckinghamshire. Within an oval topped by the square and compasses a formal representation of the entrance of Heatherden Hall. The motto 'Truth, honour, virtue' is shown beneath. The Hall was one of the largest mansions in the district and was, in 1954, the headquarters of Pinewood Film Studios with which many of the founders and later initiates were connected.
7367 Boteler Lodge. Warrington, West Lancashire. Within concentric circles bearing the name and number of the lodge, the arms of the Boteler family who for four hundred years were Lords of Warrington; on a blue background a silver bend between six covered cups; the crest is a white unicorn; the crest rests on a panel showing the names of the founders of the lodge; the motto 'Deus spes nostra' is shown below. The name Boteler was derived from the high and important office of butler to the king, a post held by the family.
7438 Stokenchurch Lodge. Marlow, Buckinghamshire. A wheelback chair beneath a beech tree, the chair being the product of four local factories and made from locally grown beech trees.
7719 Shelburne Lodge. Marlow, Buckinghamshire. Within a wreath a representation of the guildhall built by John, Earl of Sherburne in the early 1700s, which remains today as an outstanding feature at the west end of the High Street. It was erected in a style universally used in England at the time, to the design of the architect Henry Keene, Surveyor of Westminster Abbey. A pair of pillars, topped by the usual globes, flank the picture; an All-seeing eye is shown above.
7755 Setantia Lodge of Installed Masters. Preston, West Lancashire. A Roman soldier and a Roman 'civil servant' holding Ptolemy's map of Lancashire. Setantia was the name of a local tribe in Roman times.
7761 Norman Arches Lodge. Marlow, Buckinghamshire. Within a circle a representation of Norman arches in a woodland setting; the square and compasses are shown beneath together with a chequered floorcloth flanked by the usual two pillars.
7775 Cheiron Lodge. Aylesbury, Buckinghamshire. Between the usual two pillars, the figure of Cheiron, the wisest and noblest of the Centaurs, holding the torch of Learning. It was he who trained and educated the heroes of ancient Greece and sent them out to combat evil in the world. He symbolises the union of the spiritual and the animal in man, the spiritual having dominion over the animal.
7917 Wolverton Trinity Lodge. Wolverton, Buckinghamshire. Flanked by the usual columns showing the terrestrial and celestial globes, an oval containing a representation of Wulfhere, an Anglo-Saxon chief from whom it is believed the name Wolverton is derived. The church of the Holy Trinity is shown in the background; the columns stand on a chequered pavement together with the rough and perfect ashlars.
7943 Bourne End Lodge. Marlow, Buckinghamshire. Within an oval, a river scene showing a water-mill and a flying swan; an ear of corn is inset on the dexter side and a scroll of paper on the sinister side; these refer to both the corn and paper mills bound up in the history of Bourne End. The flying swan represents the swan found in the armorial bearings of the county. The motto beneath is 'Aqua praeterita, mola non molit'; there are the usual columns, a chequered pavement and ashlars as described in the banner for Wolverton Trinity Lodge.
8142 Planet Lodge. Slough, Buckinghamshire. Within concentric circles bearing the name and number of the lodge the square and compasses enclosing the astronomical symbols of Uranus and Saturn.
8258 Lodge of Good Endeavour. Warrington, West Lancashire. Between the usual two pillars found on so many banners, and within concentric circles bearing the name and number of the lodge, the armorial bearings of the town of Warrington, the lions of the de Vilars, first Lords of Warrington and the cups of the Botelers. There is an irradiated letter G above and an open bible below upon which rests the square and compasses.
8555 St Giles Lodge. Stony Stratford, Buckinghamshire. The figure of St Giles with his pet hind standing under an arch, in front of which there is a chequered floorcloth on which rest various masonic implements.
8572 Cae Glas Lodge. Oswestry, Shropshire. The Minutes of the lodge describing the banner (May, 1980) record:

> In the centre, above the square and compasses is shown a square pavement in perspective flanked by two great pillars of the Temple. The pavement is reflected in gold above, implying the rays of the rising sun at the opening of the lodge and those of the setting at its closing.
>
> Above the pavement we may gaze out of the lodge, past an ear of corn, at a scene of green fields crossed by a stream, reminding us of the origin of the name of the lodge and of the beauty of the Province of Shropshire. In the distance, mountains remind us of Oswestry's connection with Wales, the origin of our Province, and our brotherhood with our near neighbours.

The All-seeing eye is displayed in such a position in the ogee quatrefoil which serves as a window that it may observe without as well as within. Above the quatrefoil the name and number of the lodge are displayed against a background of the sky as a reminder of the heights to which the members should endeavour to lift the honour and reputation of the lodge.

The lodge takes its name from the site of an open green space called Cae Glas, one meaning of which is thought to be 'Greenfield' which, as the designer of the banner points out, 'suggests a "fresh start", a "new beginning"'.

8616 Marlow Bridge. Marlow, Buckinghamshire. A representation of the suspension bridge over the River Thames at Marlow; above, within concentric circles in the form of a strap with a buckle, the Buckinghamshire swan, gorged and chained; the strap shows the motto 'Juncti in concordia.' On either side the usual columns with globes; beneath an open book recording the names of the founders of the lodge.

8629 St Lawrence Lodge Marlow, Buckinghamshire. The tower and golden ball of St Lawrence Church, a prominent landmark at the top of the hill at West Wycombe. This is surrounded by concentric circles bearing the name and number of the lodge and square and compasses; the banner also shows the names of the founders of the lodge.

8687 Prior Walter Lodge. London. Between two pillars whose capitals are decorated with cinquefoils and St John's crosses, the Maltese cross of St John, in the centre of which is a kneeling figure of Prior Walter holding a Patriarchal cross, an emblem associated with founders of monasteries. Each pillar bears a globe; an architrave shows the name of the lodge. Above the architrave are the square and compasses together with two shield, each bearing a St George's cross.

Prior Walter was the first Prior of the Hospitaller Order of St John of Jerusalem; he was responsible for the building of the Great Priory buildings in Clerkenwell on land given by John de Briset who came to England with William the Conqueror. St John's Gate in Clerkenwell is all that is left of the Great Priory which was destroyed by fire at the time of the Peasant's Revolt led by Wat Tyler.

The lodge was formed by members of the Order of St John of Jerusalem and by members of the St John Ambulance Brigade. The Order still maintains in Jerusalem an Ophthalmic Hospital for the treatment of diseases of the eye, and for research into the causes of eye disorders. This is in keeping with the traditions of the Order; at the time of the first Crusade to the Holy Land they maintained a hospital for sick and wounded pilgrims.

8849 Verney Lodge. Buckingham, Buckinghamshire. A phoenix rising from flames, the crest of the armorial bearings of Sir Ralph Verney PProvGM Buckinghamshire; the motto 'Vng sent ung sol' is also shown.

8812 Hillcliffe Lodge. Warrington, West Lancashire. A stylized design representing a country scene with a hill and cliffs; above, hands clasped in friendship, representing the sponsoring lodge, Friendship; above that the crest from the arms of Colonel Lyon, the owner of the hill; the lion carries a flag on which is depicted the Lancashire rose and the Cheshire wheatsheaf.

8974 Marlow Valley Lodge. Marlow, Buckinghamshire. Between sheaves of wheat a country scene including the tower and steeple of Marlow Church; the Buckinghamshire swan, gorged and chained, is seen on the river Thames; below, the motto 'Collegium vallis amigum' and an open book recording the names of masters of the lodge. On either side, the usual two columns around which is a blue band recording the names of the founders of the lodge.

8985 Fenny Stratford Lodge. Bletchley, Buckinghamshire. The 'Fenny Popper', a small cast-iron cannon-like device weighing about twenty pounds; it is charged with gunpowder and fired at regular intervals during the day on 11 November each year – St Martin's day. The ceremony is in memory of Dr Brown-Willis, an eighteenth century antiquary and benefactor of St Martin's Church, the parish church of Fenny Stratford; he left an endowment to fund this annual 'big bang'. The Buckinghamshire swan, gorged and chained, is shown above.

9206 Phoenix Lodge of Installed Masters. Leyland, West Lancashire. Outer concentric circles bearing the words 'In my end is my beginning'; inner circles showing the name and number of the lodge and within that circle a phoenix.

9222 Buckinghamshire Provincial Grand Stewards Lodge. Beaconsfield, Buckinghamshire. Within concentric circles showing the name and number of the lodge, the Buckinghamshire swan, gorged and chained, between the legs of a pair of compasses; alongside is a cornucopia overflowing with fruit.

9277 Milton Keynes Lodge. Wolverton, Buckinghamshire. On a chequered pavement showing the compass points, the outline of the new town Milton Keynes, and on which is a triangle enclosing the letter G. Over all, the square and compasses; scrolls show the name and number of the lodge.

PART 5:

ROYAL ARCH CHAPTERS

General

THE rules and procedure governing Royal Arch chapter numbers, names, badges and banners are generally the same as those governing Craft lodges. This is because the Royal Arch is not a fourth degree; rather it is an Order that has grown out of, and is dependent upon, the Craft. In support of this statement it can be said that brethren holding certain senior appointments in the Craft have to hold comparable offices in the Royal Arch, provided of course they are duly qualified Royal Arch masons; further, the Royal Arch Regulations make it clear that any matter not covered therein is considered as being covered by the Book of Constitutions.

This was not always the case. For that reason some historical facts and other interesting matters relating to the Royal Arch are dealt with in this section.

The Excellent Grand and Royal Chapter

The premier Grand Lodge did not recognize the Royal Arch as part of Craft masonry; it had no objections to it as long as it was considered a separate and distinct Society. Some of its members had taken the degree. Indeed a few of them, acting in their private capacity, had set up a Grand Chapter, known as The Excellent Grand and Royal Chapter from which our present Supreme Grand Chapter is descended. The document setting up this first Grand Chapter is known as the Charter of Compact; it is dated 1766.

The Grand and Royal Chapter of Jerusalem

The first Abstract of Laws for the Society of Royal Arch Masons was published by this Grand Chapter in 1778; it gave the name as The Grand and Royal Chapter of Jerusalem. Regulation IX dealt with the mode of application for a charter which, amongst other things, had to specify 'the title they would chuse to have their chapter known by'.

A 'List of Regular Chapters' formed by the Grand Chapter is attached to the 1786 edition of their Laws and Regulations; there are 106 of them. Just before the Union of the two Grand Lodges in 1813, this Grand Chapter granted its 183rd charter.

The Grand Lodge of the Antients

Unlike the premier Grand Lodge, the Grand Lodge of the Antients actively encouraged the Royal Arch degree. Their Grand Secretary, Laurence Dermott, called it 'the Root, Heart and Marrow of Freemasonry'. There is no firm evidence though, that they ever set up a separate Grand Chapter; rather, it seems, their Grand Lodge controlled the degree. They considered that the warrants they issued to their lodges were sufficient enough authority for the conferment of the Royal Arch degree. There was, therefore, no separate Roll of Royal Arch Chapters; the chapters were known by the name and number of the lodge in which they worked.

In 1807 this Grand Lodge published its Laws and Regulations for the Instruction and Government of the Holy Royal Arch. These stipulated 'That no Chapter of Holy Royal Arch shall be held . . . unless the party composing such Chapter shall possess a regular subsisting Warrant of Craft Masonry, granted by this Grand Lodge [i.e. the Grand Lodge of the Antients], or a Charter of Constitution, specially granted for that purpose . . .'.

Supreme Grand Chapter

The recognition of the Royal Arch was an essential part of the Union of the two Grand Lodges. It was made possible by the acceptance of what is now the preamble to our Book of Constitutions, namely that pure antient masonry consists of the three degrees, Entered Apprentice, Fellowcraft and Master Mason, including the Royal Arch. This gave rise to the wording we use today, that the Royal Arch is not a fourth degree, but the Master Mason's completed.

The Regulations for the Royal Arch after the Union of the two Grand Lodges were first published in 1817. From these it is clear that; a) all chapters which existed before 1813 had to attach themselves to a regular lodge if they had not already done so; b) they had to notify Grand Chapter of the lodge to which they were attached, and c) that for the future no lodge would be authorized to form a chapter unless it had previously obtained a charter which was to be attached to the lodge warrant.

The next edition of the Royal Arch Regulations was issued in 1843. This included a sentence dealing with the situation where a lodge to which a chapter was attached was suspended or erased. In such cases the chapter could, with the authority of Grand Chapter, attach itself to another lodge.

It was not until the 1956 edition of the Regulations that reference was made to a chapter, at the request of its members, being allowed to transfer from one lodge to another, again with the prior approval of Grand Chapter. This does not mean such action had not previously taken place; presumably the inclusion of the statement was to make the position quite clear.

Age and Precedence of Chapters

The age of a chapter is generally determined in the same way as the age of a lodge, that is by the date of its Constitution. Similar rules also apply to Bi-Centenary Charters in respect of those Chapters brought into being by the first Grand and Royal Arch Chapter and for which records are available. However, there are problems with chapters which worked in a lodge under the Grand Lodge of the Antients; no separate list exists for these. Only when they can prove a continuous, uninterrupted run for 200 years from an entry proving their existence can they receive the Bi-Centenary Charter.

There are a few chapters that are older than the lodge to which they are attached; examples are given below. Unless otherwise stated the name of the lodge is the same as that of the chapter.

Chapter				Lodge			
Caledonian	No. 204	constituted	1797;		lodge	constituted	1802
Friendship	No. 257	constituted	1769;	Phoenix	Lodge	constituted	1786
Britannia	No. 312	constituted	1783;	Lion	Lodge	constituted	1797
Salisbury	No. 435	constituted	1833;		lodge	constituted	1836.
Bushey Park	No. 2381	constituted	1874;		lodge	constituted	1890.

The reason for this is that in some cases the chapter was formed before the constitution of the lodge to which it became attached in accordance with the Regulations issued after the Union of the two Grand Lodges; in other cases the chapter, for one reason or another, parted from the lodge to which it was originally attached and became attached to another lodge Constituted at a later date.

The precedence of a chapter is determined by the number it bears, which is the same as the lodge to which it is attached. This means that in some instances a chapter attached to an old-established lodge will rank higher in precedence than a chapter which has already celebrated its centenary! The following list gives some examples. An asterisk against the name indicates the chapter has celebrated its centenary.

Name of Chapter	Chapter Const'd.	Number	Lodge constituted and date of precedency – both lodge & chapter
Chapter of St James's*	1788	2	T.I.
Royal Somerset House and Inverness	1892	4	T.I.
United Chapter of Prudence*	1808	12	T.I.
Old Dundee	1963	18	1723
Egyptian	1944	27	1811
United Mariners	1930	30	1753

NAME OF CHAPTER	Chapter Const'd.	Number	Lodge constituted and date of precedency – both lodge & chapter
ST JOHN THE BAPTIST	1932	39	1732
CHAPTER OF FRIENDSHIP	1945	44	1803
KNIGHTS OF MALTA	1972	50	1803
CRICHTON	1921	1641	1873
BROOKE*	1887	2005	1883
JUBILEE*	1887	2013	1883
ST GEORGE*	1886	2025	1883
WILBERFORCE*	1889	2134	1885
JERSEY*	1875	2163	1886
STERNDALE BENNETT*	1889	2182	1886
REGENT'S PARK*	1889	2202	1887
BUSHEY PARK*	1874	2381	1890

Chapter names

The 1817 edition of Royal Arch *Regulations* did not specify that a chapter must bear the same name as the lodge to which it was attached. For chapters already in existence, whether or not they were attached to a lodge before 1817, it was presumably difficult for Grand Chapter to be insistent on this matter and arrangements were no doubt left to individual chapters.

After 1817 it was the lodge which had to seek permission to form a new chapter; the charter that would be granted was to be attached to the lodge warrant. This meant that the lodge and the chapter would be considered as being united. It follows that the identity of the chapter, that is its number and its name should, generally speaking, be the same as that of the lodge.

The 1843 edition of Royal Arch *Regulations* included for the first time a specific statement that any chapter transferred from one lodge to another had to take not only the number but, unless the First Grand Principal shall decide otherwise, the name of the lodge to which it is transferred.

The first published Form of Petition for a Chapter is found in the 1879 Royal Arch *Regulations*; it included the phrase 'to be named The . . . . . . Chapter'. In the 1970 edition of the Regulations the definite article preceding the name was omitted from the printed form.

Not every chapter on the current Roll of Supreme Grand Chapter bears the same name as the lodge to which it is attached. Appendix E lists those chapters formed before the Union of the two Grand Lodges in 1813 and which are still on the Roll; over sixty per cent of these have names that are different from the lodge to which they are attached. Examples of other chapters in a similar position, formed after 1817, are shown in Appendix F.

Badges

Many chapters do not have a badge; of those that do, many use Royal Arch emblems such as the triple tau or the interlaced triangles, whilst others use the Jewel of the Order, usually without the ribbon attached. Where the Jewel is concerned there is no consistency as to the side shown, possibly because, unlike the *Laws and Constitutions* of the Supreme Grand Chapter of Royal Arch Freemasons of Scotland, the current (1993) *Regulations* of our Supreme Grand Chapter do not indicate which is the obverse and which is the reverse side of the Jewel.

The side generally considered to be the obverse is the side which shows the motto: 'Si talia jungere possis sit tibi scire satis' which can be loosely translated as 'If you understand this you know enough'.

The reason why this is generally considered the obverse side is that it is the same as the representation of the Jewel shown in the margin of the Charter of Compact (1766), the document setting up the first Grand Chapter. Further it corresponds with the oldest extant Royal Arch breast jewel, dated 1765, which belonged to Dr. John James Rouby and which is now in the museum at Freemasons' Hall. London. This jewel is engraven on one side only, that with the motto.

In many cases the chapter uses the same badge as that used by the lodge to which it is attached, except that Royal Arch emblems replace Craft emblems.

There are some chapters, however, that use a badge that is quite different from the badge used by the lodge to which the chapter is attached. In most cases the reason for this is that the chapter has always borne a different name from the lodge to which it is attached and the badge reflects the name of the chapter rather than that of the lodge. In a few cases the chapter may have transferred its allegiance to another lodge and, although it may have adopted the name of the lodge, it still retains its original badge.

Examples of Badges of Private Chapters

Examples of chapter badges that differ from the badge of the lodge to which the chapter is attached are included in the list below. In every case a description of the lodge badge has already been given, though care must be taken when looking for the lodge for it might bear a different name, but the number will be the same. In some instances it would appear that there is no longer any essential difference in the Craft and Chapter badges, though the date when the change was made is not known. Such examples are included here as a matter of interest.

1 Grand Master's Chapter. London. A shield heraldically described as 'quarterly of six'. The shield is partitioned horizontally by two wavy lines above and below which there are three compartments. In the first and third above the lines are a stylized fleur-de-lys and in the middle one a mullet; in the middle lower compartment is a triangle; the other two are without a charge.

This badge appears on the Invitation Card to the Centenary celebrations of the Grand Master's Lodge in 1859, on which is also shown the badge used by the lodge. The badge described above has been used by the chapter since its consecration in 1886. Its origin is not known, nor is the reason for the charges used, although the triangle was presumably used to show a connection with the Royal Arch. The triangle also forms part of the Jewel worn by the Grand Master; the mullet, an heraldic term denoting a five-pointed star-like figure, may have been used to represent a pentalpha which forms part of the Jewel worn by the Deputy Grand Master and was also used extensively by the Royal Arch section of the Grand Lodge of the Antients.

The Grand Master's Lodge was formerly on the Roll of the Grand Lodge of the Antients and worked the Royal Arch ceremony in the lodge. It is believed to have continued doing so for a while after 1817, but not for long; the present chapter was constituted in 1886.

143 Mount Moriah Chapter (attached to Middlesex Lodge). London. A background of the sceptres of the three principals in the same order as they sit in chapter; superimposed thereon the arms used by Westminster Abbey or, to give the correct title, the Collegiate Church of St Peter, namely the arms said to be attributable to Edward the Confessor, a blue cross patonce (a very shallow fleur-de-lys) between five gold martlets; at the top of the shield the arms of England as used in the fifteenth and sixteenth centuries (namely France in the first and fourth quarters and England in the second and third quarters) between two united roses of York and Lancaster; resting upon these arms is a shield showing the arms of Middlesex, three seaxes. Scrolls surrounding the whole show the name and number of the chapter and the date of its constitution, together with 'Amalgam^{d} S. Peter, Westminster.

Lodge No. 1537, St Peter Westminster, amalgamated with Middlesex Lodge No. 143 on 17 March 1947; the history of the latter says 'St Peter Westminster preserved its identity upon the summons . . .'; this is the explanation of part of the wording on the scroll referred to above. Mount Moriah chapter had a long association with Middlesex Lodge, but it was not until 15 October 1889 that at an Emergency Meeting of the lodge it was agreed that the chapter should be 'legally attached to the lodge'.

The badge of Middlesex Lodge is now a circle showing the arms of Middlesex; the lodge is a London lodge.

1625 Tredegar Chapter. London. Superimposed on interlaced triangles concentric circles showing the name and number of the chapter and enclosing the sceptres borne by the Principals of a Chapter and the word 'LONDON' on a central scroll.

1677 Crusaders Chapter. London. An interlaced cord joined at the top by a scroll enclosing a Maltese cross surmounted by a triangle within which is a shield, surmounted by an Imperial crown, showing a cross potent.

1752 Atholl Chapter (attached to Ogmore Lodge). Bridgend, South Wales, Eastern Division. The armorial bearing of the Duke of Atholl with the motto 'Furth fortune and fill the fetters'.

1816 Victoria Park. London. Superimposed on interlaced triangles concentric circles enclosing a park scene.

1817 St Andrew's. Southend-on-Sea, Essex. Superimposed on concentric circles a triangle on which rests a framed representation of a church.

1962 London Rifle Brigade. London. On a pair of rifles in saltire concentric circles within which are the Royal Arms, the whole surrounded by scrolls bearing the names of battle honours and surmounted by an Imperial crown. Below, between a scroll bearing the motto 'Primus in urbe' and concentric circles within which are interlaced triangles and the triple tau, and a shield bearing the arms of the City of London.

1967 Macartney Chapter (attached to Beacon Court Lodge). Gillingham, East Kent. Concentric circles on which rests a triangle enclosing the crest from the Macartney arms. Beacon Court (the name and badge of the lodge) and a saxon crown.

1983 St Edmund's Chapter (attached to Martyn Lodge). Southwold, Suffolk. Within interlaced triangles an oval enclosing St Edmund.

2127 Drury Lane. London. On interlaced triangles a strap enclosing a lyre.

2170 Hercules Chapter. Colombo, Sri Lanka (attached to St. George Lodge). The figure of Hercules standing beside the Nemean lion he killed, the first of his twelve labours.

2202 Regent's Park. London. A triple tau.

Above
The Grand Lodge Banner and the personal standard of the Grand Master in saltire. This is the design adopted for use on the jewel of the office worn by Grand Standard Bearers. Unfortunately most such jewels are heraldically wrong, possibly because the illustration in the *Book of Constitutions* is incorrect. The arms on the dexter side of a shield should always be nearest the staff; the illustration shows the sinister side of Grand Lodge arms (i.e. the four apocalyptic figures) in this position – it should be the three castles and the compasses, as correctly shown above.

Left
Provincial Grand Lodge, Isle of Man; a circle containing interlaced triangles showing a viking ship, the Isle of Man emblem, i.e. three legs conjoined, the square and compasses and a sword, point uppermost (see page 98).

Provincial Grand Lodge of Leicestershire and Rutland; the armorial bearings are those of the county of Leicestershire, the arms of the city of Leicester and the arms of the county of Rutland (page 98).

Provincial Grand Lodge of Oxfordshire, being the Grand Lodge banner within a bordure of four gold crowns and four ox heads cut off at the neck, associated with the Oxford (page 98).

Provincial Grand Lodge of Surrey; being the Grand Lodge banner within a bordure charged with a representation of King Edgar's crown, two ostrich feathers and a sprig of oak. The crown and sprig of oak are found in the Arms of the County of Surrey; the ostrich feathers are emblems of Edward, Prince of Wales, Grand Master of the Province 1924-36 (page 98).

Provincial Grand Chapter of Derbyshire, the design shown here incorporates the rose and Imperial crown found in the arms granted to Derbyshire County Council (page 115).

Provincial Grand Chapter of Devonshire; in the upper half a stylized ancient sailing ship and, in the lower half, emblems and furnishings associated with the Royal Arch (page 115).

Provincial Grand Chapter of Northamptonshire and Huntingdonshire; the white rose on the red background represents the county of Northampton; the arms on the other shield are those of Huntingdonshire County Council (page 115).

Provincial Grand Chapter of Jersey showing the arms of Grand Lodge with an escutcheon in the centre bearing the arms of Jersey; the triple tau within a triangle indicates the Royal Arch (page 115).

Provincial Grand Chapter of Monmouthshire showing a design taken from the reverse side of the Royal Arch Jewel of the Order; a comparison with the illustration in the *Book of Constitutions* will indicate the differences (page 115).

Light of Lights, No. 148, Warrington, West Lancashire, showing the three great lights of Freemasonry together with the sun, the moon and the All-seeing eye (page 100)

Ancient Union Lodge, No. 203 Liverpool, West Lancashire, showing the three great lights of Freemasonry together with the sun, the moon and All-seeing-eye.

Salopian Lodge, No. 262, Shrewsbury, Shropshire, showing three leopard's heads, as seen in the arms of the Borough of Shrewsbury.

Lodge of St Barnabas, No. 948, Linslade, Buckinghamshire; the local church is dedicated to this saint (page 100).

St Oswald Lodge, No. 1124, Oswestry, Shropshire showing King Oswald seated on a throne, a sword in his right hand and a branch in his left hand. The town of Oswestry is named after this king (page 61).

Fitzalan Lodge No. 1432, Oswestry, Shropshire, showing the crest of the Fitzalan arms; some masonic emblems are also shown on the banner. The Fitzalan family were Lords of Oswestry in the twelfth century (page 61).

Wycombe Lodge, No. 1501, Marlow, Buckinghamshire; it shows the Buckinghamshire swan, duly gorged (having a coronet round its neck) and chained, standing on a mound. A sprig of acacia and the square and compasses are also shown (page 101).

Castle Lodge, No. 1621, Bridgnorth, Shropshire showing a castle with the motto of Bridgnorth beneath. The motto means 'The fidelity of the city is the safety of the king.' (Note; the definite article preceding the name on the banner is not part of the official name of the Lodge) (page 101).

The banner used by Earl of Clarendon Lodge, No. 1984, Watford, Hertfordshire, showing the arms and motto of the earl; the motto means 'The Cross, the sign of faith' (page 63).

Dagmar Lodge, No. 2262, Slough, Buckinghamshire; the four red hearts between a cross reflect the charitable work, particularly in the field of hospitals, education and relief work, carried out by Princess Dagmar after whom the lodge was named; she was a Danish princess and the younger sister of Queen Alexandra (page 102).

Christopher Lodge No. 2309, Slough, Buckinghamshire. The design appears to have been taken from charges on arms adopted without permission by Brother George Gardner, the prime mover in the formation of the lodge and after whom it was named. Later the lodge moved to Christopher Hotel, Eton and the name of the lodge was changed to Christopher Lodge in 1895 (page 102).

Wychwood Lodge, No. 2414, Burford, Oxfordshire showing on a chequered floorcloth a representation of the entrance to the lodge premises; stylized wych (or witch) elm trees are shown on white squares; these represent a wood, a punning reference to the name of the lodge (page 102).

Carrington Lodge, No. 2421, Marlow, Buckinghamshire, named after Lord Carrington, first Marquess of Lincolnshire, the first Provincial Grand Master of the new Province of Buckinghamshire; the banner shows his arms (page 102).

Runymede Lodge No. 2430, Slough, Buckinghamshire; the scene King John at Runnymede signing the great charter of liberty, known as the Magna Carta, which the barons of England obtained from him in 1215 (page 102).

Wineslai Lodge, No. 2435, Winslow, Buckinghamshire. The crown refers to King Offa who had a camp at Winslow; the emblem below the crown is a representation of the gridiron on which St Lawrence was burnt; the local church is named after him (page 102).

Concordia Lodge, No. 2492, Aylesbury, Buckinghamshire; the design is based on the Rothschild arms. The first word of their motto is 'Concordia'; the lodge has no apparent connection with that family, other than both it and the Ferdinand de Rothschild Lodge No. 2420 were sponsored by Buckingham Lodge No. 591 (page 102).

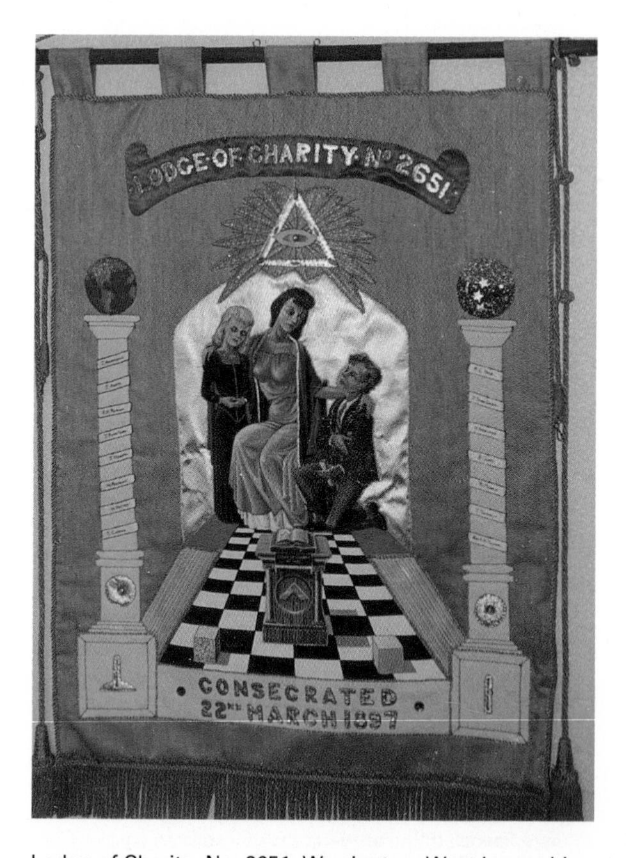

Lodge of Charity, No. 2651, Warrington, West Lancashire. The figure of Charity with two children; various masonic emblems are also shown (page 103).

Bowen Lodge, No. 2816, Beaconsfield, Buckinghamshire showing the arms of the Company of Masons impaled with those of the county of Buckinghamshire. The monogram J E B shows the initials of WBro. J. E. Bowen, Deputy Provincial Grand Master of the Province, after whom the lodge was named and who consecrated it (page 103).

Fallowfield Lodge, No. 3693, Chorlton-cum-Hardy, West Lancashire. The two columns of the portal are meant to represent the entrance to King Solomon's Temple; the five columns, the five orders of architecture; the red rose is a symbol of Lancashire, the Province in which the lodge meets; the Latin phrase meaning Forty-seven, is a reference to the jewel worn by Past Masters (page 104).

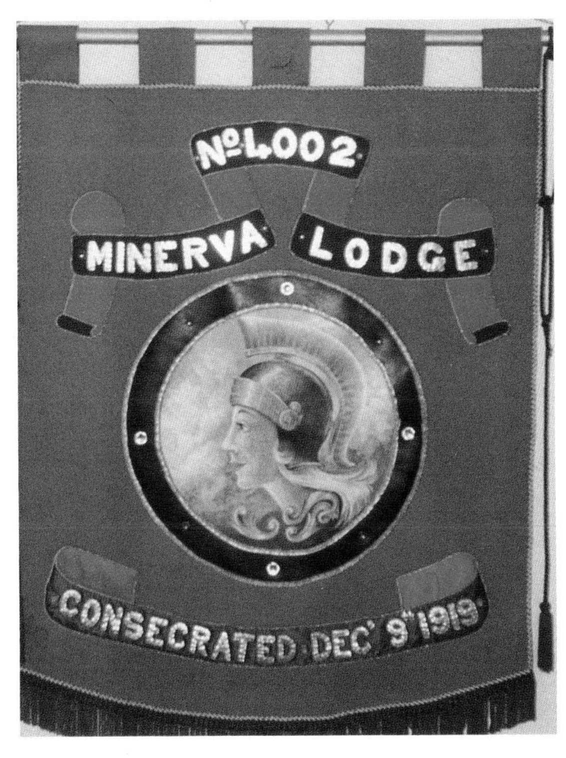

Minerva Lodge, No. 4002, Liverpool, West Lancashire; it shows the head of the Roman goddess Minerva, wearing a helmet; she was the goddess of wisdom and is identified with the Greek goddess Athena (page 104).

Sabrina Lodge, No. 4158, Shrewsbury, Shropshire; the maid Sabrina is seen sitting on raft floating on the River Severn which is poetically called Sabrina. The motto means 'Let Shropshire flourish' (page 104).

Inglefield Lodge, No. 4238, Slough, Buckinghamshire, depicting the arms of the Provincial Grand Master who consecrated the Lodge and who presented the banner, RWBro. Rear-Admiral Sir E. F. Inglefield, *KBE*.

Heaton Moor Lodge, No. 4530, Heaton Moor, West Lancashire. In the centre of this banner is a spread-eagle, but the main components are two pillars, one topped by a celestial and the other by a terrestrial globe; an All-seeing-eye, and various other masonic emblems, all of which are common to many lodge banners (page 104).

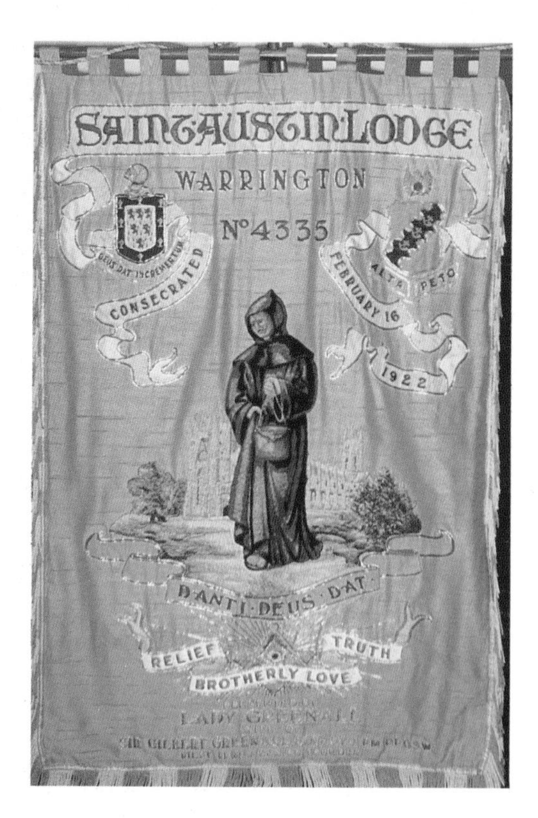

St Austin Lodge, No. 4335, Warrington, West Lancashire. The friar represents St Austin's Friary in Warrington which was disbanded at the Reformation. The arms of the town of Warrington are shown; so too are the arms of Greenhall (though they appear to be back-to front). The motto 'Danti Deus dat' means 'God gives to the giver' (page 104).

Travellers Chapter, No. 4679, Warrington, West Lancashire. It shows an ark on water, above which is a dove carrying a sprig in its beak; Royal Arch emblems are also shown. The chapter was founded for commercial travellers. Only a few chapters have 'identifying' banners (page 105 discussing lodge banner).

Upton Manor Lodge, No. 5115, Slough, Buckinghamshire, showing a scene depicting the giving of the Manor of Upton to a representative of the monastery of the Augustinian Canons of Merton who had come to Upton in the twelfth century (page 105).

Ashmole Lodge, No. 5128, Warrington, West Lancashire, showing the features of Elias Ashmole, the antiquary and genealogist who founded the Ashmolean Museum, Oxford. His diary records him being made a freemason at Warrington on 16 October, 1646 (page 105).

Old Wrekinian Lodge, No. 5481, Wellington, Shropshire. The design on the shield is similar to, but not the same as, the badge of the lodge, which appears to show the armorial bearkings of Wrekin College. The motto 'Aut vincere aut mori' means 'Victory or death' (page 105).

Lodge of Success, No. 5486, London. This shows the figure of Pythagorus between two pillars, elucidating his theorium, subsequently incorporated as the 47th problem of the First Book of Euclid (page 105).

Pegasus Lodge, No. 5637, Aylesbury, Buckinghamshire. The winged horse of Pegasus standing on the top of the globe representing the world, and seven stars, all between pillars (page 105).

Uxacona Lodge, No. 5724, Wellington, Shropshire, showing a view through a brick built archway straddling a road which passed through Usc-Con and the Wrekin on its way to Uriconium. The name Uxacona is a Roman form of the older Celtic name Usc-Con; Usk means water; Con (from Cond) means junction of a stream with a pool or lake (page 105).

Shropshire Installed Masters Lodge, No. 6262, Shrewsbury, Shrophire. In addition to the masters' emblem, the square, and the pentalpha, part of the jewel worn by the Provincial Grand Master, this banner also includes a huntsman's bugle horn from the arms of Lord Forester who was Provincial Grand Master, Shropshire 1938-77 and the first master of the lodge (page 72)

Weyland Lodge, No. 6507, Bicester, Oxfordshire. The design is a stylized fleur-de-lys; the fleur-de-lys was used extensively as a decoration by the Priory which dominated the life of those in Bicester through the Middle Ages (page 106).

Montem Lodge, No. 6687, Slough, Buckinghamshire. A historical scene recording part of the history of the area (page 106).

Boteler Lodge, No. 7367, Warrington, West Lancashire showing the arms of the Boteler family, who for four hundred years were Lords of Warrington. The name was derived from the high and important office of butler to the king, a post held by the family. The motto 'Deus spes nostra' means 'God is our hope' (page 107).

Brickhill Lodge, No. 6968, Bletchley, Buckinghamshire. The design depicted represents a country scene which includes the local church, the home of a prominent business man and the first master of the lodge. The original name of the village, Brichella, is also shown (page 107).

Stokenchurch Lodge, No. 7438, Marlow, Buckinghamshire. On this banner is depicted a wheelback chair beneath a beech tree, the chair being the product of four local factories and made from locally grown beech trees (page 107).

Setantia Lodge of Installed Masters, No. 7755, Preston, West Lancashire, showing a Roman soldier and a Roman 'civil servant' holding Ptolemy's map of Lancashire, Setantia was the name of a local tribe in Roman times (page 107).

Cheiron Lodge, No. 7775, Aylesbury, Buckinghamshire. The figure of Cheiron, the wisest and the noblest of the Centaurs, holding the torch of Learning (page 107).

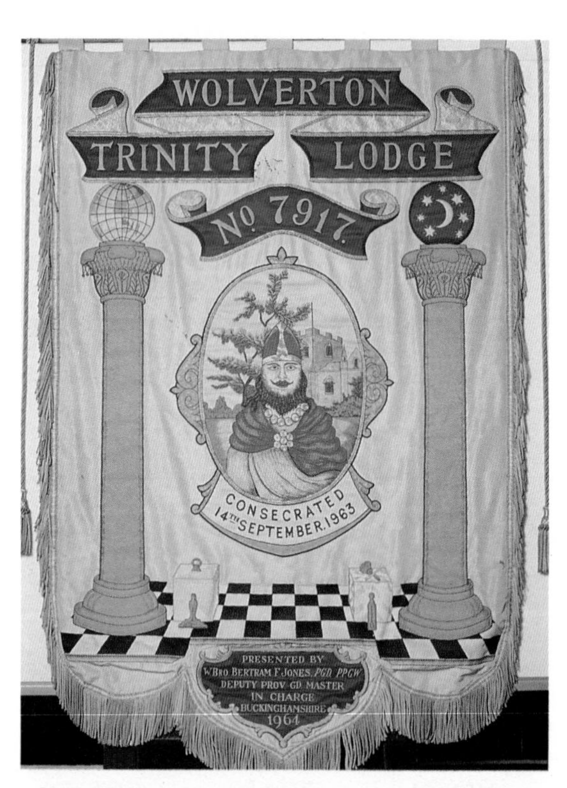

Wolverton Trinity Lodge, No. 7917, Wolverton, Buckinghamshire. A representation of Wulfhere, an Anglo-Saxon chief from whom it is believed the name Wolverton is derived. The church of the Holy Trinity is shown in the background (page 107).

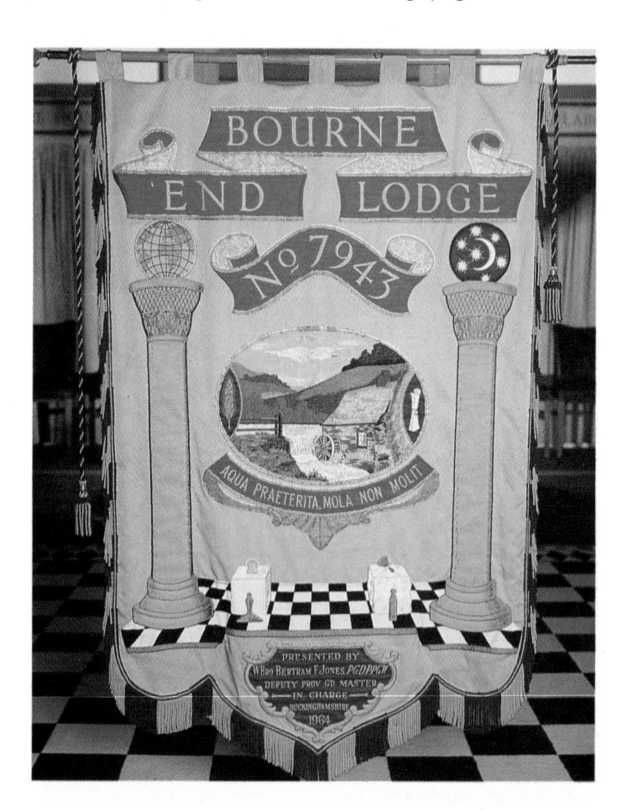

Bourne End Lodge, No. 7943, Marlow, Buckinghamshire. The scene alludes to the corn and paper mills bound up in the history of Bourne End. The motto means 'The mill cannot grind with water that is past' (page 107).

Cae Glas Lodge, No. 8572, Oswestry, Shropshire; the chequered pavement is reflected in gold in the upper part of the scene, implying the rays of the rising and setting sun at the opening and closing of the lodge; the scene in the centre indicates the beauty of the area and is also a reference to the name of the lodge, one meaning of which is thought to be 'Greenfield.' The All-seeing eye is also shown (page 105).

Prior Walter Lodge, No. 8687, London. The figure of Prior Walter holding a Patriarchal cross, an emblem associated with founders of monasteries. The Maltese Cross of St. John represents the Order of St John of Jerusalem and members of the St John's Brigade; the founders of the lodge were all members of that Order (page 108).

Fenny Stratford Lodge, No. 8985, Bletchley, Buckinghamshire. The 'Fenny Popper', a small cast iron cannon device-like charged with gunpowder and fired at regular intervals during the day on 11 November each year – St Martin's day (page 108).

Milton Keynes Lodge, No. 9277, Wolverton, Buckinghamshire. This shows, on a chequered floor-cloth, the outline of the new city of Milton Keynes (page 108).

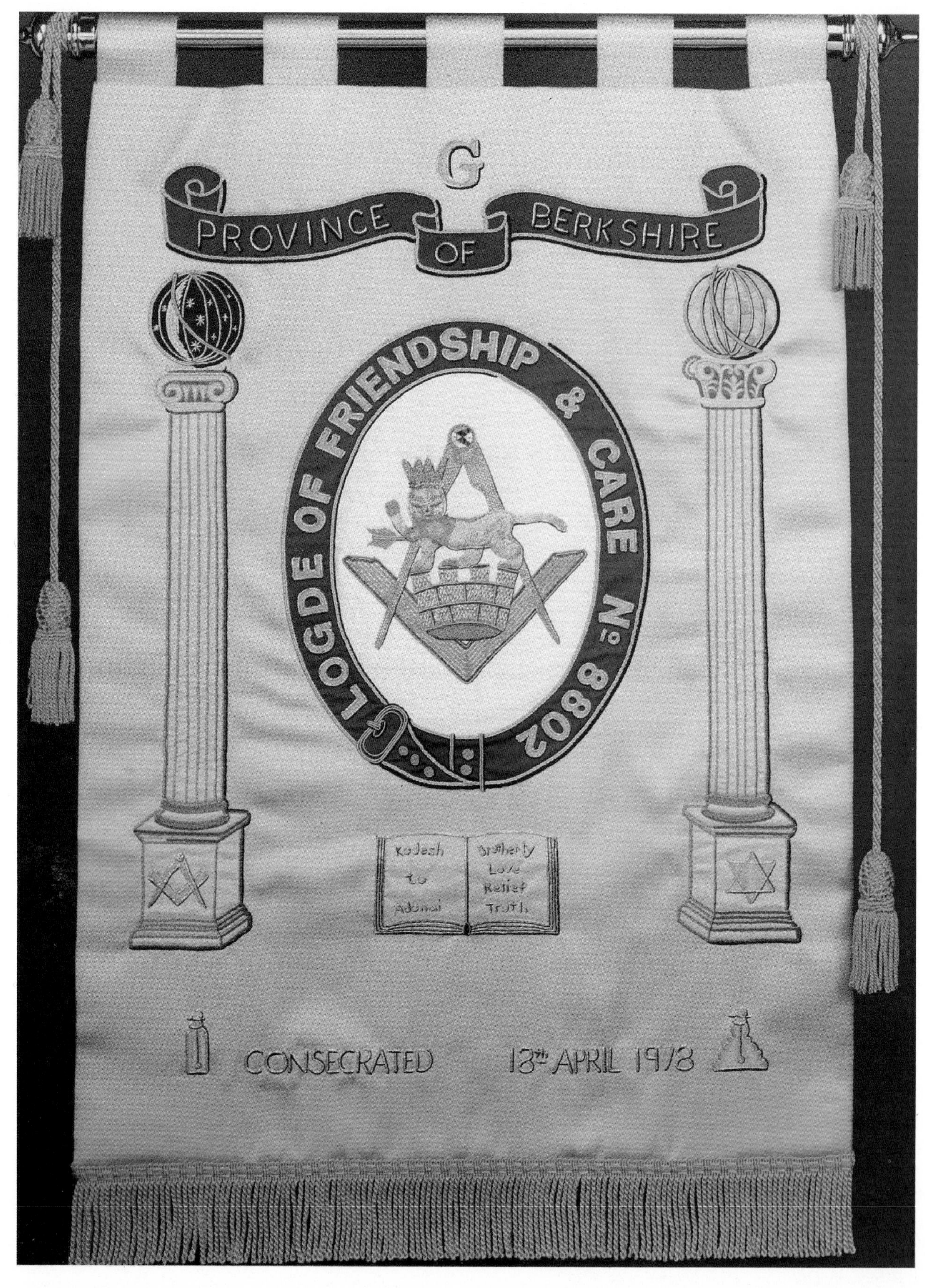

Lodge of Friendship and Care, No. 8802, Sindlesham, Berkshire. This shows, between the usual two pillars and resting on the square, the crest of the arms belonging to the Rt Hon. Lord Harris, *CBE, MC, DL,* OSM, PJGW after whom the RMBI home at Sindlesham is named.

2226 St David's. Rhymney, Monmouth. A figure of St David in concentric triangles resting on interlaced triangles.
2233 Public Schools Chapter (attached to Old Westminsters' Lodge). London. Shields showing the armorial bearings of Westminster, Charterhouse, Cheltenham, Sherborne and Clifton Schools.
2271 St Pancras Chapter. London. A stylized arrangement of some Craft and Royal Arch emblems.
2302 St Mary's. Nottingham, Nottinghamshire. A banner showing Craft and Royal Arch emblems and a picture of St Mary.
2475 Beach Chapter (attached to Border Lodge). Camberley, Hampshire and Isle of Wight. The crest of the Beach armorial bearings; below, a scroll bearing the motto 'Tout en bon heure'.
2533 Gildenberg Chapter (attached to Fitzwilliam Lodge). Peterborough, Northamptonshire and Huntingdonshire. Concentric circles bearing concentric triangles enclosing a shield per pale; dexter, the arms used by the See of Peterborough, namely two keys placed back-to-back in saltire between four cross crosslets fitchée, sinister the arms used by Dean and Chapter of Peterborough, two swords in saltire, point uppermost, between four cross crosslets fitchée. (Cross crosslets have a short cross-piece on each limb; fitchée means the lower limb tapers to a point). Gildenberg means Golden Borough, an early name for Peterborough.
2571 Addison Potter Chapter (attached to Sancta Maria Lodge). Newcastle upon Tyne, Northumberland. A seahorse, the Potter crest. Beneath, the motto 'Spero bene agere'.
2654 Arter Chapter. King's Heath, Worcestershire. On interlaced triangles, concentric circles enclosing a shield showing a chevron between three martlets.
2656 Campbell Chapter (attached to Adam's Peak Lodge). Talawakelle, Sri Lanka. On a triangle, a shield bearing quarterly first and fourth a gyronny of eight; second a dagger, and third a castle.
2682 William Harvey Chapter (attached to Sancta Maria Lodge). London. Concentric circles bearing the name and number of the chapter, enclosing the arms of William Harvey, the discoverer of the circulation of the blood.
2728 Muswell Hill Chapter. London. A representation of the founders' jewel.
2862 Ruhuna Chapter (attached to Grant Lodge, Sri Lanka). Galle, Sri Lanka. Equilateral triangles interlaced by concentric circles enclosing a cock.
2885 Carthusian Chapter (attached to Charterhouse Deo Dante Dedi Lodge). London. Above a representation of the building housing the Charterhouse Mission in Surrey, and within concentric circles with the words Floreat Æternum Carthusiana Domus, a triangle enclosing a triple tau. The wording is the last two lines of the Carmen Carthusianum – May His everlasting blessing rest upon Charterhouse.
2913 Junior Engineers' Chapter. London. Within concentric circles bearing the name and number of the chapter, and superimposed on interlaced triangles; dexter, a draughtsman, sinister, an artisan, in chief, a theodolite and in base, a blacksmith. The inner side of the concentric smaller circle has 'teeth', indicating a cogged wheel.
2941 Lambeth Borough Council Chapter. London. Interlaced triangles upon which are superimposed concentric circles enclosing a lamb bearing a banner on which is meant to be the Hebrew letter Beth, thus creating canting arms, lam(b) – beth. The Hebrew letter has been incorrectly illustrated; the eleventh letter of the Hebrew alphabet (Caph) is shown. This closely resembles the Beth, the difference being that the lower right hand corner of the Caph is rounded whilst the lower right hand corner of the Beth is square with the base line extending slightly beyond the downward stroke.
3092 Elstree Chapter. Radlett, Hertfordshire. A representation of an oak tree, known as Eadwulf's tree.
3221 Wessex Chapter (attached to London Dorset Lodge). London. Interlaced triangles upon which is superimposed a circle enclosing a dragon facing sinister. There seems to be some doubt about the dragon; no-one was sure why it was used. The heraldic beast more often associated with Wessex (and used as a badge by the Wessex Regiment in the Second World War) is a wyvern; this is depicted as having two legs only, which are those of an eagle; the beast is usually depicted as being supported by its tail only. The membership of the chapter was originally drawn from the counties of Berkshire, Devon, Dorset, Gloucestershire, Hampshire and the Isle of Wight, Somerset and Wiltshire, the counties making up the old Kingdom of Wessex.

Among the non-heraldic experts confusion exists between the fictitious beasts known as the dragon, the wyvern and the cockatrice, especially where the attitude is different from that usually adopted. The following definitions are taken from *An Encyclopaedic Dictionary of Heraldry* (Julian Franklyn and John Tanner, Pergamon Press 1970):

cockatrice: a composite fictitious beast, hatched from an egg laid by a cock, having a cock's head and legs, a pair of wings either feathered or membraneous, the body bird-shape tapering to a long, curling snake-like tail, terminating in a barb ...

dragon: a composite fictitious beast, part serpent, part crocodile, having four short legs terminating in eagle-like claws, a long curled tail terminating in a barb and a pair of membraneous wings ...

wyvern; a composite fictitious beast having a pug dog-like head with a short, backward curved horn on the snout, a bird-like neck, and breast covered with scales instead of feathers and the body tapering away in a long snakelike tail, curving towards the end, and terminating in a barb.

In 1612 Henry Peacham published his *Minerva Britanna*; one of the plates, indicating beauty is only skin deep, shows a naked woman on one of these beasts. As can be seen from the verse underneath the picture, given here, the beast is described as a dragon, but that description hardly fits the definition given above, especially as the creature has only two legs!

A virgin naked, on a Dragon sits,
One hand out-stretch'd, a christall glasse doth show;
The other beares a dart, that deadly hits;
Upon her head, a garland white as snow,
Of print and Lillies, Beauty most desir'd
Were I her painter, should be thus attired.

As a matter of interest the plates from this book form part of the decorative ceiling of the Long Gallery at Blickling Hall, Norfolk.

3252 King Edward VII Chapter. Chatham, East Kent. A triangle on which is superimposed a circle showing the head of King Edward VII facing sinister.

3261 Broadsmith Chapter (attached to Randle Holme Lodge). Whitby, Cheshire, Concentric circles bearing the (presumed) arms of Frederick Broadsmith, a founder-member of the chapter who was, at that time, Provincial Grand Scribe E, Cheshire.

3343 Duke of Sussex Chapter London. Below interlaced triangles, an oval showing a pastoral scene above the motto 'A Deo lux nostra' (Our light is from God).

5560 Silver Jubilee Chapter (attached to Lodge of Unity). Sao Paulo, South America, Northern Division. The busts of King George V and Queen Mary on interlaced triangles.

5719 King David Chapter. London, Concentric circles enclosing a representation of an enthroned King David.

6648 Essex Schools Chapter (Attached to Old Chigwellian Lodge). London. Within a wreath quartered by a cross, elements of the badges used by the founding lodges, oak leaves and acorns in the first quarter (Old Foresters Lodge No. 7726, a bishop's mitre in the second (Old Chigwellian Lodge No. 6648), a chevron between three cross crosslets in the third (Old Felstedian Lodge No. 3662) and three triple crowns in the fourth (Old Bancroftians Lodge No. 5619); in the centre a circle enclosing three seaxes.

Banners

When reference is made to banners in a chapter under the English constitution, it is the four Principal Banners that immediately come to mind. In addition to these, some may consider the triple tau hanging with the Principal Banners in the east and the ensigns of the twelve tribes of Israel displayed in the centre of the chapter, as well as the three 'Judah' banners found in the west in some chapters, the latter representing the three sojourners.

But none of these is the main subject of this book; the reference here is to a banner identifying the chapter in the same way as the lodge banner identifies the lodge.

The rules and practice governing chapter banners are the same as those governing lodge banners.

Not many chapters have a chapter banner; for those that do, the emblems used are usually the same as those used for the lodge banner, apart from the obvious exception that Royal Arch emblems replace Craft emblems.

Supreme Grand Chapter

Supreme Grand Chapter does not have its own particular banner. This is possibly because the Preliminary Declaration in the *Book of Constitutions* states that 'pure Antient Masonry' includes 'the Supreme Order of the Holy Royal Arch'; the Craft and the Royal Arch are an indivisible unit.

This is reflected in the arms of Grand Lodge which are portrayed on the Grand Lodge Banner and on jewels worn by certain Grand Officers. The dexter side shows the castles, chevron and compasses of the arms used by the premier Grand Lodge: the sinister side shows a man, a lion, an ox and an eagle, the figures shown in the arms of the Grand Lodge of the Antients. These figures are prominent in Royal Arch masonry and, as they are shown on the Grand Lodge Banner, presumably there is no call for a separate Grand Chapter Banner.

It could be argued that if the Banner of Grand Lodge is meant to include Grand Chapter, it should be carried in for Convocations just as it is for meetings of Grand Lodge; however, this does not happen, nor is there any evidence that it has been carried in the past.

Provincial and District Grand Chapters

Very few Provincial or District Grand Chapters have a distinctive banner, possibly because Supreme Grand

Chapter does not have one. There are one or two exceptions, however. Examples of some Provincial Grand Chapter banners are given below.

Bedfordshire

Within an arch showing the initials H Z J between the words 'Holiness to the Lord', a circle enclosing interlaced triangles in which is another triangle, apex uppermost, enclosing a triple tau; above is the seal of the Borough of Bedford, a black eagle displayed, wings inverted and head turned towards the sinister, wearing a gold ducal crown; surmounting the eagle is a gold castle of three tiers.

Buckinghamshire

On a scarlet background is a representation of the sun rising in the east surmounted by a cross of gold inlaid with blue, the purpose of which is to remind companions of those virtues which should be as expansive and all-embracing as the blue vault of heaven. In the lower dexter corner is a shield showing the personal and family coat of arms of Sir Ralph Verney, *Bt, KBE, DL*, who at the time the banner was dedicated was Grand Superintendent of the Province. In the upper dexter quarter is the Volume of the Sacred Law open at the beginning of *Genesis*, and resting on a cushion bearing the inscription 'In Domino confido', proclaiming a belief in God and the importance of His word. In the upper sinister corner are the interlaced triangles of the Royal Arch, a reminder of part of the inscription thereon which may be translated as 'A worshipper of God, a citizen of the world'. In the lower sinister corner is a representation of the Buckinghamshire swan. The whole is surrounded by a tessellated border in the predominant colours of the Royal Arch. At the head of the stave supporting the banner is a triple tau.

Derbyshire

Within a golden circle and on a silver background, a golden triangle, apex uppermost, upon which rest a golden triple tau, which in turn is surmounted by a Derbyshire rose and an Imperial crown.

The Derbyshire rose is taken from the arms of Derbyshire County Council. In a private letter to the author, the Education Officer (Archives) writes:

> From the creation of the County Council in 1889, the Council used the old County badge of a rose with an imperial crown above it, for its seal. The imperially crowned rose is a royal device for use by the crown and those who received the crown's permission to use it. It was claimed in the eighteenth century that Edward IV had granted the badge to Derbyshire and Charles II permitted it to use his own device of a crowned rose.
>
> No-one in fact knows when and why Derbyshire began to use the rose or when and why the imperial crown was added. It is a red and white rose and is possibly the Tudor Rose, a cross between the red and white roses of Lancashire and Yorkshire. I was not aware that it was known as the 'Derbyshire Rose' [*] but this is simply due to its use by the County. [*] Described as such in a letter from the Province to the author.] When the County Council needed a new seal in the 1930s, the Heralds could not trace a royal grant of the right to use the crowned rose. Instead, a rose of the same type was used, together with three stags' heads for the new arms of the County. The arms are described as 'Or, a rose gules surmounted by another argent, both barbed and seeded proper; on a chief sable, three stags' heads caboshed of the third.

Devonshire

Within a red and blue indented Royal Arch floorcloth; in the lower half, the sceptres of the three Principals of a chapter set out in the form of a triangle, apex uppermost, enclosing an open copy of the Volume of the Sacred Law; on the dexter side, a circle enclosing interlaced triangles, and on the sinister side, a circle enclosing a triangle in which is the triple tau; in the upper half, on a stylized background of a sea represented by blue and white wavy lines, and a blue sky with sunbeams, an ancient sailing ship; superimposed are concentric circles showing the name of the Province and the words 'Holy Royal Arch' on a red background. The upper half is taken from the County arms.

Isle of Man

Resting on concentric circles showing the name of the Province, a triangle, apex uppermost, on which is superimposed a circle containing interlaced triangles showing a viking ship, the Isle of Man emblem, i.e. three legs unjessed, the square and compasses and a sword, point uppermost.

Jersey

The arms of Grand Lodge with an escutcheon in the centre showing the arms of Jersey; above the shield and between an outstretched wing of each of the supporting cherubs, a triple tau within a triangle resting on a circle. This banner was dedicated at the celebration of the Province in 1988.

Monmouthshire

Concentric circles with a red background showing the name of the Province; within, on a blue background, interlaced golden triangle enclosing a triangle with a triple tau; the triad Concord, Truth and Peace is shown on the triangle with the base uppermost, and the triad Wisdom, Strength and Beauty on the triangle with its apex uppermost. The words 'Deo regi fratribus honor fidelitas benevolentia' appear around the triangles. Although the words are the same as those on the reverse of the Royal Arch breast jewel, the placing is different.

Northamptonshire and Huntingdonshire

Superimposed on interlaced triangles, two shields; that on the dexter side showing a white rose on a red background, representing the County of Northampton; that on the sinister side, the arms of Huntingdonshire County Council, namely, on a background of blue and white lines indicating the River Ouse and water-courses of the fen area, a green lozenge, the green representing the grazing nature, and the lozenge the natural geographical shape, of the County; across the centre of the lozenge is a battlemented bar which indicates Huntingdon, in particular the fortress commanding the passing of the River Ouse, a fact of great importance in the early history of the town. Above the battlemented bar are three golden wheatsheaves and below a cornucopia, signifying the farming industry in the area. In a scroll above the interlaced triangles are the words 'Provincial Grand Chapter' and in a scroll below, the words 'of Northants & Hunts.'

Nottinghamshire

The armorial bearings of the then Grand Superintendent of the Province, E. Comp. Sir Henry Bromley, *Bt, DL, JP*, who presented the banner on 10 October, 1884; his motto 'Pensex Forte' (Think much) is also shown as are various Royal Arch emblems

Shropshire

Within concentric circles with a red background showing the words 'Provincial Grand Chapter, Shropshire', a blue triangle, apex uppermost, on which is superimposed a shield bearing the arms of Shropshire County Council, namely erminois, three piles (isosceles triangles), two issuant from the chief (the top part of the shield, making the base of the triangles uppermost) and one in base (the lower part of the shield, the triangle having its base uppermost), each charged with a leopard's face; the motto 'Floreat Salopia' is shown in a scroll beneath; as a crest, a wyvern emerging from a whelk shell; according to E. Comp. Harold Templeton, who at the time the following note was made was Grand Superintendent in and over the Province, the crest was 'taken from the armorial bearings of the Venables of Kinderton, one of eight Barons appointed by the Norman Earls of Chester to rule over Cheshire'. Rowland George Venables was the Grand Superintendent 1913–20.

Warwickshire

Concentric circles showing 'Provincial Grand Chapter' on a blue background, enclosing a triangle, apex uppermost on which is superimposed a circle enclosing interlaced triangles in the centre of which is another triangle; a triple tau within a circle is shown below. Above, in a scroll with a white background, the word 'WARWICKSHIRE'.

Wiltshire

A circle showing four green and four white wavy lines on which is superimposed a bustard. The wavy lines are meant to represent the chalk of the Plains and the green the Downland of the Valleys; the bustard is a large running bird that was very common on the Plains of Wiltshire until it was shot out of existence in the early 1930s. Above the circle are interlaced triangles, and below the circle, a triple tau.

Grand Standard Bearers

Despite the fact that Grand Chapter does not have a distinctive banner, it nevertheless appoints Grand Standard Bearers; their usual duty today is to assist the Grand Director of Ceremonies in some ceremonial procedures.

When the Grand Master presides in Grand Lodge, his personal standard is carried in the procession by a Grand Standard Bearer; the same is true of the Pro Grand Master when he presides. One might expect similar action to be taken when either of them presides over Grand Chapter but this is not so.

In some Provinces things are different; both the Provincial Grand Banner (where one exists) and the personal standard of the presiding officer (if he has one) are carried in by Provincial Grand Standard Bearers.

It is a moot point whether the Excellent Grand and Royal Chapter had its own banner; what we do know though, is that the first Grand Standard Bearer was appointed by them in 1779; his name was Cornelius Vanderstopp. The Grand Lodge of the Antients did not appoint Standard Bearers.

The question might well be asked what standard or banner did Companion Vanderstopp carry? Five possibilities come to mind.

First, one of the twelve ensigns of the tribes of Israel; but if so, which one and why? There being no acceptable answer to these questions, it is unlikely that such a banner was carried by the Grand Standard Bearer.

Secondly, a banner showing the emblems on each of the Four Principal Banners, a man, a lion, an ox and an eagle. It is possible that the Grand Standard Bearer of the new Grand Chapter carried such a banner, but this is considered unlikely as such a design was used by the Grand Lodge of the Antients on their Arms. Those individuals responsible for the formation of the Grand Chapter owed allegiance to the premier Grand Lodge which, generally speaking, was on anything but good terms with their rivals.

Thirdly, one of the banners occasionally seen behind the Sojourners in the west and known as the Sojourner's banner. The design on this is the same as that on the banner of Judah, the banner entrusted to the candidate as 'one of the sojourners'. However, Sojourners' banners are not generally used in chapters; there is no evidence of their use in early Royal Arch masonry.

Fourth, it could have been the personal standard of the First Grand Principal at the time the office of Grand Standard Bearer was introduced, namely 1779; records show that this was Captain George Smith, who later found himself in trouble with Grand Lodge and was subsequently expelled from the Society.

The fifth and most likely is the fore-runner of the present-day triple tau, the letter T over the letter H. This device was to be shown on the badge of the Royal Arch mason, as can be seen from the following quotation from the Charter of Compact, the instrument which in 1766 set up the Grand Chapter.

> THIRDLY That every Companion shall wear according to ancient Custom an Apron indented with Crimson, and the Badge TH properly displayed thereon. And also the indented Ribbon or Sash of this Order.

The letters T and H stood for Templum Hierosolymae, (the temple of Jerusalem); this is evidenced by a letter written by Thomas Dunckerley on 27 January, 1792;

> I wish you would amend the TH on the Patent, under my name. It is the signature of our Order, *Templum Hierosolyma Eques*. For the Royal Arch it is TH *Templum Hierosolyma*.

Later the tail of the T dropped on to the crossbar of the H, thereby forming what we now call the triple tau. By about the 1820s the triple tau was in general use and the older device was no longer used.

PART 6:

OUR SISTER CONSTITUTIONS

The Grand Lodge of Ireland

THE author gratefully acknowledges the kindly help he has received from RW Bro, Keith Cochrane *RD., DL*, of the Grand Lodge of Ireland for information given in this section.

Lodge numbers and precedence

It cannot be stated for certain when the Grand Lodge of Ireland began to number their lodges. According to Parkinson *(History of the Grand Lodge of Ireland*, Vol II, p. 271) their first known List of Lodges is found in Smith's *Pocket Companion* (Dublin, 1735); it is headed *A LIST of the warranted* Lodges *in the Kingdom of* Ireland, *as they are Registered in the* Grand Lodge *Book*'. They are numbered 1 to 37; there is some doubt, however, about its accuracy.

The 1751 edition of the *Pocket Companion* also gives a 'List of warranted Lodges in Ireland', but these are not numbered.

Regarding precedence, Spratt's *Constitutions* contained the following clause which is almost identicai to that found in Anderson's 1723 *Constitutions;*

> If any lodge within the bills of mortality shall cease to meet regularly during twelve months successive, its name and place shall be erazed out of (or discontinued in) the Grand Lodge Book; and if they petition to be again inserted and own'd as a Regular Lodge, it must loose *[sic]* its former place and rank of precedency, and submit to a new constitution.

This was slightly amended in a later edition but the position regarding precedence remained unchanged.

An interesting footnote to Law XXV of *Ahiman Rezon* (the Irish *Constitutions*) of 1817 shows the help the Grand Lodge was prepared to give to those lodges that had fallen upon hard times because of lack of members. It reads:

> It is recommended that in cases where Lodges are so reduced in Members and Circumstances as to be unable to keep up the regularity thereof [paying Grand Lodge dues], that the Warrants of such Lodges be returned to the Grand Secretary, in order to prevent their being suspended or cancelled, and the Members thereof subjected to the disqualifications of Regulation XVIII.

Quoting Parkinson (*op cit*):

> The effect of this provision was that, when a Lodge was unable to pay its dues or keep up regular meetings, it could send back its Warrant to Grand Lodge for safe keeping, on the understanding that if at any time thereafter the surviving members could collect enough support to make a fresh start they could then apply to have the Warrant back, apparently without expense. The advantages to Grand Lodge were that the Warrant while in official keeping could not be used for making clandestine Masons, nor fall into non-Masonic hands; the advantages to the Lodge itself were that the Members were not liable for Grand Lodge dues while the Warrant was thus lying dormant and yet they would not lose precedence if at any future time they grew strong enough to revive the Lodge and carry on the old traditions under the same number.

It was not unknown for Irish lodges to purchase lower-numbered warrants that had previously been used by a lodge no longer on the Roll of Grand Lodge. This was expressly forbidden in 1776 but the practice continued after that date.

This, together with the misdemeanours of Alexander Seton, a Deputy Grand Secretary who had unlawfully issued dormant warrants to new lodges, caused many problems in the rightful precedence of lodges. Parkinson summarizes the position as follows (op cit. p. 26):

Not the least part of the legacy of trouble left to the Grand Lodge by Seton's misbehaviour was to be found in the revived warrants he had issued. Grand Lodge, for the sake of harmony, had legalized many of his issues of vacant numbers, and thus not unseldom it happened that quite new lodges found themselves ranking senior to much older lodges with higher numbers in the same district.

It was obvious something would have to be done to remove this undoubted grievance and satisfy lodges which were jealous of their rights of precedence.

Despite the work done by the Committee set up by Grand Lodge to deal with this matter, the situation remained unsatisfactory; quoting Parkinson again (op cit. p. 28):

From 1817, then, the system of numbering warrants in Ireland, so far as our being able to form any idea of a lodge's seniority from the particular number, has been confusion worse confounded. In the course of the nineteenth century some unlucky numbers were re-issued half-a-dozen times to different parts of the world. Today we get the paradox that a lodge whose number runs into the seventh hundred or higher, is, *prima facie*, probably older than one whose number is less than three figures.

The 'today' referred to in the quotation just given must be taken to mean the middle 1950s since Bro. Parkinson's book was published in 1957.

The present position is that every lodge must have a number and the precedence of a lodge (apart from the Grand Master's, see below) depends upon the number of its warrant (Law 99, *Law and Constitutions of the Grand Lodge of Ireland*). Assuming warrants when issued are numbered consecutively, this would appear to be comparable with the position in the United Grand Lodge of England, where the *Book of Constitutions* (also No. 99) begins:

Lodges shall rank in precedence in the order of their numbers as registered in the books of the Grand Lodge.

The numbers registered take into account the various changes that were made up to the last change in 1863; they are entered consecutively.

The age of a lodge depends upon the date of its constitution; it is from that date that the lodge is lawfully permitted to work. This latter point is referred to in the Ceremony of Constitution as laid down in the *Laws* (p. 112, 1989 edition) where the Presiding Officer proclaims;

By virtue of the authority entrusted to me I place in proper position for the use of Lodge, No. , the Three Great Lights, without which no Work can be lawfully transacted in the Lodge.

The *Irish Freemasons' Calendar and Directory* includes a numerical list of lodges showing the date of the constitution of the lodge. This prompts some queries. One would have expected the confusion of the nineteenth century to have been cleared by the last decades of the twentieth century; but it is difficult to understand why a lodge constituted in 1947 (and the date of the warrant must have been before then) should be given a number lower than a lodge constituted in 1813, over one hundred years earlier! Yet such seems to be the case; and there are many other anomalies of a like nature, as evidenced by the following random excerpts from the Calendar. These examples would seem to indicate that Bro. Parkinson's comment above is still valid.

843 (1971)	854 (1797)	859 (1966)	877 (1800)	881 (1800)
890 (1985)	891 (1812)	914 (1988)	935 (1803)	972 (1988)
978 (1816)	979 (1957)	994 (1877)	1000 (1812)	1008 (1813)
1009 (1813)	1012 (1947)	1014 (1950)	1016 (1956)	

It would be interesting to know the reason for the continuation of these apparent anomalies, but as the main subject of this book is the United Grand Lodge of England, with just a brief glance at its sister constitutions, the matter must remain one for future examination.

Another query refers to the missing numbers in the Numerical List of Lodges on the Register of the Grand Lodge. The last page of the list in the 1991 edition of the *Calendar* starts with lodge number 978 and finishes with lodge number 1016; twenty-seven of the intervening numbers are missing. Have they ceased to function?

The numbers of lodges that have ceased to function are not now used again; if a dormant lodge is revived it can continue to use its original number and does not lose precedence, but the period of dormancy does not count in reckoning continuous service.

The only lodge in Ireland to use roman numerals is the Lodge of Research, No. CC (i.e. 200).

The Grand Master's Lodge, Ireland

The Grand Lodge of Ireland, like England, has a lodge with a name but no number; it is the Grand Master's Lodge, and is placed at the head of the roll of their lodges. The following information is taken from *History of the Grand Lodge of Free and Accepted Masons of Ireland*, Vol. 1, pp. 230–1 (Leper and Crossle, Dublin Lodge of Research, No. CC).

Wednesday 3rd of January 1749 [1750 N.S.] Grand Lodge in due Form. The Deputy Grand Master *Putland* acquainted the Grand Lodge that our late Right Worshipful Grand Master Sir *Marmaduke Wyvill* Bart, together with the Right Worshipful and Right Honourable the Lord Kingsborough our present Grand Master, the Deputy Grand Master and Grand Wardens, and many other Gentlemen of Distinction, have formed themselves into a regular Lodge to consult the Good of the Craft, and as far as in their Power lies, promote the Welfare of the Fraternity in general.

The Grand Lodge having a thorough Sense of their tender and affectionate Inclinations, immediately came to the following Resolution and Order.

Resolved,

That the Secretary do return the respectful and grateful Thanks of this Grand Lodge to the Noble and Right Worshipful Gentlemen and Brethren, who have so zealously considered, and generously offered their Assistance to the Promotion and Honour of the Craft.

Ordered

That a Registry be opened in the Front of the Grand Register Book for the said Lodge, and that the same shall henceforth be distinguished and known by the Denomination of the GRAND MASTER'S LODGE; and that all, or any of the Members thereof, who does at any Time think proper to visit the Grand Lodge, shall take place of every other Lodge on the Registry, or Roll Books of this Kingdom; and that each and every of them shall be as fully intitulled *[sic]* to all and every of the Privileges and Freedoms thereof as any other Member or Members that this Grand Lodge is composed of.

The authors of the book continue:

The Lodge thus formed has ever since enjoyed special privileges and honour. For many years, in fact up to 1856, when the Duke of Leinster, Grand Master, advised the surrender of the privilege, the Lodge had the right of recommending to Grand Lodge who the new Grand Officers should be, and these recommendations were usually acted upon, though not invariably. Up to the year 1837 also, every Master Mason raised in the Grand Master's Lodge had a seat and vote in Grand Lodge *ipso facto*. This privilege was then voluntarily surrendered as regards all Master Masons registered after the 9th day of June 1837, but the members of the Lodge, of or above the rank of Master Mason, are still, as always, entitled to wear Grand Officers' clothing and to receive salutes as such.

Lux Diei Lodge. The *Irish Freemasons' Calendar and Directory* records that Lux Diei Lodge was constituted on 3 March 1988 to cater for brethren who find it difficult to attend evening meetings; the lodge is open to any subscribing master mason. The lodge is included in the Alphabetical List of Titles of Lodges, but there is no number against its name.

The Grand Secretary of the Grand Lodge of Ireland was kind enough to explain the reason for this; it is not in fact a warranted lodge but rather a 'Constituted' Lodge along the same lines as the Grand Lodge of Instruction. There is no actual membership as such – all master masons in good standing are entitled to attend and are members whilst present; the three senior offices are held by the Chairman of the Metropolitan Board and the two most senior present or past Grand Officers in the Metropolitan area, but each year acting officers are elected to fill the chairs unless the ex-officio officers are there.

There are no initiations, but the By-Laws permit the passing and raising of candidates of other lodges when requested to do so; otherwise the meetings are of general interest.

Names of lodges

The information regarding names of Irish lodges is neatly summed up in the following Decision of the Board of General Purposes which is printed in *The Grand Lodge of Ireland; Laws and Instructions*.

LODGE TITLES. In the early days of Irish Masonry, lodges were distinguished by the number of the warrant alone. Afterwards however, following the practice of other jurisdictions in which the lodges are identified by the name rather than by the number, either a territorial or symbolic title was occasionally added. In connection with a Memorial for a new warrant the Board expressed the opinion – which was subsequently confirmed by Grand Lodge – that it is undesirable to name a lodge after living individuals.

The last few words represent a change of thought; during the middle of the last century some lodges were named after living individuals. The list of lodges given in the next few pages under the heading 'Personalities' shows that lodges have been given names of individuals in recent times, but it is not known whether any of them were living at the time the lodge name was adopted, by the lodge.

As indicated above, it is not mandatory for a lodge to be known by a name or title, and there are quite a few lodges in this category, though it seems odd that the application form for a new lodge includes the words '. . . to be named . . . lodge . . .'. The 1971 Calendar lists shows about 100 lodges without names or titles; this represents about ten per cent of the number of lodges on the Roll of the Grand Lodge.

Subject to approval by the appropriate authority a lodge may change its name; but such incidents are rare.

A glance at the Irish calendar (or Year Book) indicates that the majority of names of present-day lodges can be classified under the heading 'Place names'; there is not the same variety of names as used by lodges under the English constitution. A few other classifications are listed below. As might be expected there are many lodges bearing the name of a saint, some of which are used by more than one lodge, though in the list below 'duplicates' have been avoided. It is not surprising to find that St Patrick is the most commonly used in this section; the name St John is hardly used at all.

Architectural

No.	NAME	Const	*Meeting Place*
34	CORINTHIAN	1890	Belfast
168	IONIC	1890	Ballymacarrett
378	DORIC	1904	Belfast
410	GOTHIC	1914	Dublin
474	COPESTONE	1919	Crawfordsburn

Biblical

No.	NAME	Const	*Meeting Place*
97	HIRAM'S	1812	Belfast
234	BEZALEEL	1877	Kinsale
503	MOUNT LEBANON	1921	Ballyroney
594	MOUNT CARMEL	1924	Sydenham
713	MOUNT ZION TEMPERANCE	1947	Sydenham
820	KING DAVID	1961	Belfast

Nature

No.	NAME	Const	*Meeting Place*
7	ACACIA	1859	Belfast
101	THE SHAMROCK	1739	N. Huston
326	OAK	1903	Ballinderry
467	OLIVE	1919	Doagh
710	PRIMROSE	1946	Germiston South Africa
715	CORNFIELD	1947	Sydenham
741	EAGLE	1949	Ballymacarrett

Personalities

No.	NAME	Const	*Meeting Place*
61	LESLIE J. THOMPSON	1891	Johannesburg S. Africa
83	FRANCIS CROSSLE	1907	Newry
247	EDWARD H. CROGHAN	1898	Johannesburg S. Africa
253	J. CREED MEREDITH	1898	Belfast
258	GEORGE ANDREWS	1898	Belfast
283	J.D. WILLIAMSON	1909	Ballymacarrett
318	JAMES CHAMBERS	1911	Belfast
346	J. HERON LEPPER	1913	Carrickfergus

No.	Name	Const	Meeting Place
376	James A. Doran	1904	Ballymacarrett
395	Chetwode Crawley	1905	Dublin
445	J.H. Gault	1918	Belfast
449	J McCandless Memorial	1919	Ballymacarrett
497	John B. Crozier	1920	Holywood
512	Andrew Henderson	1921	Newtonabbey
584	Hugh Wallace	1924	Portadown
626	David Irwin Memorial	1928	Clogher
653	Francis Watters	1935	Cape Town South Africa
745	Dick King	1950	Rossburgh South Africa
813	Frank A. Lowe	1959	Harare Zimbabwe.

Royalty

No.	Name	Const	Meeting Place
25	Duke of York	1853	Dublin
222	Prince of Wales	1870	Bray
294	Queen Victoria	1900	Belfast

Saints

No.	Name	Const	Meeting Place
8	St Patrick's	1808	Cork
26	St Jude's	1923	Rosetta
129	St Finbar's	1908	Rossburgh
142	St Paul's	1856	Newcastle
163	St Brendon's	1747	Birr
166	St George's	1908	Belfast
186	St James'	1811	Mealough
209	St Fin Barre's	1918	Cork
469	St Andrew	1919	Belfast
494	St Cecilia	1772	Dublin
637	St Columba Temperance	1930	Carnmorley
640	St Columb's	1785	Londonderry
641	St Helen's	1931	Rosetta
675	St John's	1787	Donaghadee
676	St Donard's	1787	Ballymacarrett
719	St Alban's	1860	Limavady
798	St Peter's	1957	Belfast
903	St David	1959	Hong Kong
1014	St Nicholas	1950	Carrickfergus

Lodge seals

A seal is an impression of a device on wax or other material attached to a document as evidence of authenticity. The device used is often something easily recognizable as belonging to the person or organization giving the authority; quite often the arms, or the crest above the arms of an armigerous individual or organization is used.

Law No. 161 of the *Constitutions and Laws* reads:

Each Lodge shall have a Seal wherewith to verify the Lodge transactions. The device shall consist of a Hand and Trowel, together with the number and name of the Lodge, and the name of the place where held.

The seal is used to verify minutes and authenticate communications to Grand Lodge. There is evidence in the 1815 *Book of Constitutions* of the United Grand Lodge of England that their lodges also had to have a seal, but this requirement has long since disappeared.

The device of the Hand and Trowel used by Irish lodges comes about because those items were shown in the crest of the arms used by the Grand Lodge of the Antients with whom the Grand Lodge of Ireland formed an alliance in 1762.

Badges

The description of the apron worn by master masons includes the words: 'the number or Badge of the Lodge, . . . may be embroidered in silver . . . in such a manner as shall have been approved by the Board of General Purposes, or from such other authority as Grand Lodge may from time to time prescribe.

Such badges may be used by the members of the lodge as the central part of a jewel worn by the founders or past masters of the lodge. The badge was often shown on the lodge summons and the notepaper used by the lodge treasurer and secretary, but it is understood that with ever increasing costs of printing this practice is dropping quite considerably.

Banners

Unlike the practice in the United Grand Lodge of England, the phrase regarding brethren being 'ranged under their respective banners' is not used in Ireland when Grand Lodge (or a Provincial or District Grand Lodge) is opened.

There are some lodges that display a banner whilst they are working. Some early banners (or bannerets as some were called) were designed like the tracing boards used in lodges in England. A photograph of two such bannerets can be seen in *History of the Grand Lodge of Free and Accepted Masons in Ireland* (op. cit., Vol. 1, facing p. 408).

In 1839 Grand Lodge ruled that, for the future, public processions of freemasons were no longer to be held, and many a lodge had its warrant suspended when it ignored this ruling; as parades stopped, so the use of a banner fell away, resulting in fewer lodges adopting one.

Grand Lodge has its own banner which may be described as a shield showing a lion, an ox, a man and an eagle. It is in fact the same design and colours as the sinister side of the arms of the United Grand Lodge of England. The same supporters and crest are also used, but the Hebrew words meaning 'Holiness to the Lord' appear on a scroll below the shield rather than as in England above the crest; furthermore, the harp, the national emblem of Ireland, is superimposed on the wording in the centre of the scroll.

The use of the sinister side of the arms of the United Grand Lodge of England reflect the fact that they were the arms used by the Grand Lodge of the Antients; the premier Grand Lodge used arms showing three castles, and a chevron with compasses thereon. As stated earlier, the Grand Lodge of Ireland entered into an alliance with the Antients; they did not recognize the premier Grand Lodge as the legitimate governing masonic body in England.

When the Grand Lodge is opened the banner is carried in procession by the Grand Lodge Standard Bearer, an officer appointed annually by Grand Lodge. If the Grand Master is armigerous and has his own personal standard, he may personally appoint an officer to carry his banner in procession; the brother so distinguished is known by the title Grand Master's Standard Bearer. If he is not armigerous, or is but does not have a personal banner, there can be no appointment as there is nothing to carry! The jewels worn by these brethren reflect their position; that of the Grand Lodge Standard Bearer shows the arms of Grand Lodge; that of the Grand Master's Standard Bearer show the arms of the Grand Master.

The preceding comments also apply *mutatis mutandis* to both Provincial and District Grand Lodges.

The Supreme Grand Royal Arch Chapter of Ireland

The following is an extract from the *Laws and Constitutions of the Grand Lodge of Ireland*:

3. Pure Ancient Masonry consists of the following Degrees and no others, viz. – The Entered Apprentice, the Fellow Craft, the Master Mason and the Installed Master, but the Degrees of Royal Arch and the Mark Master Mason shall also be recognised so long as the Supreme Grand Royal Arch Chapter of Ireland shall work only those two Degrees in the form in which they are worked at the passing of this Law.

There is therefore a distinct connection between the Grand Lodge of Ireland (established 1725) and the Supreme Grand Royal Arch Chapter of Ireland (established 1829), but it is not as close as the connection between the Craft and the Royal Arch in England.

For example, in Ireland the administrative offices are in the same building; the same individual acts as Grand Secretary in the craft and the Grand Registrar in the Royal Arch (the office known in England and Scotland as the

Grand Scribe E); but, unlike England, there is no requirement for certain other Grand officers in the craft to hold similar appointments in the Grand Chapter.

Other important differences which may be briefly summarized are as follows:

1. The Royal Arch legend is different from that used in England and in Scotland; it deals with the repair rather than the rebuilding of King Solomon's Temple.
2. The four Principal Banners and the ensigns of the twelve tribes of Israel found in English and Scottish chapters are not used in Ireland.
3. The degree of Mark Mason and the ceremony generally known as Passing the Veils are a pre-requisite of the Royal Arch ceremony (this also applies to Scotland).

However, none of these items is relevant to the subject matter of this book.

Other differences include:

So far as identification is concerned, in Ireland a chapter does not have to be attached to a lodge, though many are; this means that the chapter may well have its own individual number. From the information given in the *Calendar* it would seem that the chapter bears the name of the town in which it meets. The use of an identifying badge or banner follows the same lines as the use of such items in a lodge.

2. The precedence of a chapter dates from the date shown on its warrant, unlike in England where the precedence of a chapter depends on that of the lodge to which it is attached, irrespective of the date the chapter was constituted.

The Grand Lodge of Scotland

The author gratefully acknowledges the help he has received from Bro. David Currie in preparing the following notes, particularly in relation to the minutes of the Erection meeting of the Grand Lodge of Scotland and the section headed 'No. O', both of which are reproduced almost entirely in his words.

Lodge numbers and precedence

It is not known for certainty when the enumeration of lodges began in Scotland. The earliest reference to lodge precedence is said to be found in the first of the Regulations concerning the procedure of the Masters and Wardens of the 'Four Lodges' during the preliminary discussions which led to the formation of the Grand Lodge of Scotland. The 'Four Lodges' were:

Canongate Kilwinning
Lodge of Edinburgh (Mary's Chapel)
Kilwinning Scots Arms (now extinct)
Leith Kilwinning (now extinct)

The Regulation dated 15 October 1736 read as follows:

> That the masters and wardens of the four lodges in and about Edinburgh meet in some convenient place and that there be no precedence insisted upon by either of them, but that they take place according as they enter the room.

Bro. David Currie, who worked for some years in the Library of the Grand Lodge of Scotland, in a personal note to the author, wrote;

> The minutes of the Erection meeting of Grand Lodge of 30 November 1736 show that thirty-three lodges were represented. *There is no reference whatsoever in the minute to any system or rule being used to decide the order in which the lodges (with their representatives) were listed.*

Bro. David Murray Lyon, one of the leading Scottish masonic historians and Grand Secretary towards the end of the nineteenth century, in his *History of the Lodge of Edinburgh (Mary's Chapel),* No. 1 (p. 187, Tercentenary edition, The Gresham Publishing Company, London, 1900) wrote '... each lodge was placed on the roll in the order in which it entered the hall'. He then lists the thirty-three lodges. In my opinion he was in error. At least one of the thirty-three lodges was not present, but was represented under a proxy arrangement by the equivalent Office-bearers of another lodge. Some system appears to have been used to ensure that the older lodges appeared at the upper end of the list, but there is not one iota of evidence to show how this was effected. The minute shows the lodges with numbers, but expert examination has shown that the figures were added at a later date.

On St. Andrew's Day 1737 Grand Lodge passed a Resolution;

> ... that all Lodges holding of the Grand Lodge should be enrolled according to their seniority, which should be determined from the authentic documents which they produced, those producing none to be put at the end of the Roll.

This resulted in the following order of lodges at the upper end of the Roll.

Lodge of Edinburgh, St Mary's Chapel, No. 1.
Kilwinning
Canongate Kilwinning No. 2.

It will be noted that Kilwinning appeared in the second position, *without a number*. The earliest document this lodge was able to produce to prove seniority was dated 20 December 1642, despite various legends that the lodge was in existence before that date. The Lodge of Edinburgh (Mary's Chapel) produced evidence of its seniority dating from 1599, some forty-three years earlier than that of Lodge of Kilwinning. They were accordingly placed first on the Roll and Kilwinning was placed second.

There was no serious objection to this for some years. However, a formal complaint was lodged by Kilwinning in 1743; Grand Lodge refuted the complaint, pointing out that as no records had been produced, there was no proof that the lodge making the complaint was the same lodge as the original. Kilwinning considered this was adding insult to injury, and decided to secede from Grand Lodge.

Mother Kilwinning

Following an approach by Grand Lodge, Kilwinning returned to the fold in 1807; her return being conditional on two major factors;
a) she would head the Roll under the title 'Mother Kilwinning'; (contrary to general opinion she was not given the number 0);
b) her master would, by virtue of that Office, be Provincial Grand Master of Ayrshire.

Item b) above led to problems as the years went by. The following extract from an article printed in *The Masonic Square* September 1983, gives the up-to-date picture; it was written by Bro. George Draffen of Newington who died in 1986. He had been a Past Depute Grand Master of the Grand Lodge of Scotland, a Past Junior Grand Deacon, United Grand Lodge of England and master of Quatuor Coronati Lodge No. 2076 in 1979.

> In Scotland the appointment of the Provincial and District Grand Masters lies with Grand Lodge. Appointments are made upon recommendations submitted to a Grand Committee who make a recommendation to Grand Lodge as to the actual appointment. It will be at once seen that the lodges in the Province of Ayrshire – there are 44 of them – could in no way suggest to Grand Lodge the name of a brother to be appointed their Provincial Grand Master. Over the years there had been a certain amount of resentment that one lodge in the Province should be in a position to make an appointment which, in other Provinces lay, through Grand Committee and Grand Lodge, with the lodges in the Province.
> Several attempts were made to solve the problem. Finally it was agreed, at the Quarterly Communication of Grand Lodge held on 5 May 1983, that Clause V in the Agreement of 1807 be modified by a complete deletion of the clause and the substitution for it of the following new clause:
> 'That there be erected and constituted the Provincial Grand Lodge of Kilwinning to have jurisdiction over Lodge Mother Kilwinning and any future lodges erected within the Parish of Kilwinning.
> That Mother Kilwinning at its Annual Meeting in November will nominate a suitable brother for the Office of Provincial Grand Master [i.e. for the Province of Kilwinning] for submission to Grand Lodge as in the case of all Provincial and District Grand Masters.
> That Mother Kilwinning for all time coming shall have the honour to nominate annually a suitable brother for the Officer of Grand Biblebearer whom Grand Lodge shall elect.
> That the numbering of any new Lodge within the Parish of Kilwinning shall be prefaced with 0, such as 01 and 02 etc.
> That Dispensation be granted to all Past Depute Masters of Lodge Mother Kilwinning to receive the benefit of the Ceremony for the Installation of a Master.'

The final sub-paragraph may require a little explanation. The Master of Mother Kilwinning was, as we have seen, also the Provincial Grand Master for Ayrshire. It was quite impossible for him to preside at every meeting of Mother Kilwinning and the presiding Officer was normally a Depute Master appointed by the Master at the Installation Meeting of the Lodge. The Depute Master, however, did not have the secrets of the Chair conferred upon him and he could not attend meetings of the Installing Board in other lodges. The Depute Master of Mother Kilwinning was not also the Deputy Provincial Grand Master of the Province of Ayrshire.

No. 0

A comprehensive search and examination of Grand Lodge records has shown no evidence of No. 0 being allotted to Mother Kilwinning.

Modern opinion is that the clerical staff of Grand Lodge, when writing lists of lodges for internal use, were in the habit of using lodge numbers, as opposed to lodge names, and that they developed the habit of showing Mother Kilwinning as No. 0. The official stationery of the lodge showed only the title until a few years ago, when No. 0 was added. It is quite certain that this number was never allocated by Grand Lodge.

It is understood that when spoken the number of this lodge is rendered as 'Number Nothing' rather than 'Number Nought'.

'bis' and 'ter' lodges

Three other lodges should be mentioned; the details which follow have been taken from various issues of the Grand Lodge of Scotland Year Books, the relevant year being shown at the end of each section.

The Lodge of Melrose St. John No. 1^2. The Lodge of Melrose consistently refused to surrender her independence by uniting with Grand Lodge, although the subject of the union had been discussed several times, first in 1787 when a committee was appointed to make application for a Charter. The committee never acted, as it was decided at a meeting held three months later that, from enquiries made, the Lodge would be better remaining independent.

The next was 1812, when an overture was made by Grand Lodge for union, and the lodge was visited and the books inspected by Alexander Deuchar, then RWM of the Lodge of Edinburgh, who declared himself satisfied that, with the exception of his own lodge, no other lodge in Scotland would produce documents of equal antiquity.

It was not however until 1891 that the lodge ultimately cast in her lot with the Grand Lodge, her antiquity being properly recognised and the third place on the Grand Lodge Roll assigned to her, the number 1^2. The ratification of the Union was formally signed by representatives of the Grand Lodge and the Melrose Lodge on 25 February 1891; thus ended the separate existence of this ancient lodge (Year Book 1955).

The Lodge of Aberdeen No. 1ter. The Charter granted to this lodge by the Grand Lodge of Scotland was dated 30 November 1743; it acknowledged the lodge as a regular lodge 'under the title and denomination of the Lodge of Aberdeen in all time coming'.

At some time the lodge appeared as No. 34 on the Roll, but in 1891 Grand Lodge recognized the lodge as having been in existence 'before 1670' and advanced its position on the Roll to No. 1ter ('ter' being the abbreviation for the Latin word meaning 'thrice') (Year Book 1956).

The Lodge of Glasgow St. John No. 3bis. This lodge, though in existence when the Grand Lodge of Scotland was formed, continued its separate existence, but in May 1849 a suggestion was made for a 'Cordial Union with the Grand Lodge of Scotland'. Many arguments took place regarding precedency but finally it was agreed that the lodge should take the number 3bis, 'bis' being the Latin word for 'twice' (Year Book 1959).

Lodge Caledonian No. 447^2. This number came about as a result of an administration error; two lodges were given the same number.

There is one other lodge on the Roll that has been similarly inserted; it is Lodge Kirkwall, Kilwinning No. 38bis.

Names of lodges

Unlike England, lodges in Scotland would appear to have been known by a distinctive name (as opposed to a lodge meeting at a given place) before being known by a number. This is implied by the following extract from the Preface found in *Scottish Masonic Records* by Bro. George Draffen.

> It is not until we come to the fourth minute book – for the third is lost – that we find lodges referred to by their numbers as well as by their names.

Present-day practice

Every daughter lodge in Scotland with the solitary exception of Mother Kilwinning, must bear a number; it must also bear a title or name which, with the consent of the Grand Committee, it may subsequently change. A daughter lodge is the equivalent of a private lodge in the English constitution.

So far as the use of a name is concerned, there was an exception for a brief period; from 1735-7 there existed a Scottish lodge in Rome which operated without a title, but it operated outwith the Roll, of Grand Lodge. It is now referred to as 'The Jacobite Lodge at Rome.'

If a lodge becomes dormant it may, subject to certain requirements, be reponed (or resuscitated) by Grand Lodge. If that happens the lodge continues to use both the number and name it had before it became dormant. Unlike the position in the United Grand Lodge of England, the lodge may still claim continuous service and its centenary will date from the date shown on its original warrant.

Kilwinning lodges

The names of these early lodges were nearly all place names, and one such name, Kilwinning, is repeated many times. Kilwinning is a small town in Ayrshire, Scotland, about twenty-five miles south-west of Glasgow and sixty west of Edinburgh. The lodge at Kilwinning claims to have a very long history.

In general the use of the name Kilwinning by so many lodges is for one of the following reasons; they were lodges chartered by what is now known as Mother Kilwinning; they were lodges using the ritual developed by Mother Kilwinning, or out of respect and veneration for Mother Kilwinning.

Examples of lodges bearing this name are given in the following list; the town in which the lodge meets, where not obviously apparent, is shown in parenthesis. The date shown in the last column is the date the lodge was instituted or chartered, or the earliest record of the lodge where this is older than the charter issued by the Grand Lodge of Scotland. The list does not include all lodges with the name Kilwinning.

Lodge No.	Name of lodge	Date.
2	Canongate Kilwinning	1677
4	Glasgow Kilwinning	1688
6	Old Kilwinning St John	1678
7	Hamilton Kilwinning	1695
10	Dalkeith Kilwinning	1724
12	Greenock Kilwinning	1728
13	Torpichen Kilwinning	1729
15	Montrose Kilwinning	1736
22	St John Kilwinning (Kilmarnock)	1734
24	Peebles Kilwinning	1716
28	St John Kilwinning (Kirkintilloch)	1735
38*bis*	Kirkwall Kilwinning	1740
51	Loudon Kilwinning	1747
53	Dumfries Kilwinning	1750
57	St John Kilwinning	Before 1600
63	St Michael Kilwinning	1755
68	Doric Kilwinning	1757
90	Forfar Kilwinning	1762
107	Eskdale Kilwinning	1767
135	Tarbolton Kilwinning St James	1771
157	St John Kilwinning (Beith)	1784
173	St John Kilwinning (Largs)	1789
182	Incorporated Kilwinning (Montrose)	1792
194	Sanquhar Kilwinning	1778
208	Stranraer Kilwinning	1768
217	Cumberland Kilwinning (Port Glasgow)	1746
370	Renfrew Country Kilwinning	1755
433	St Thomas Kilwinning (Dalmellington)	1864

Other names

The latest Roll of Lodges indicates that the name adopted by a lodge is more often than not the name of a place. There are other categories, such as saints, well-known personalities and virtues but there is nothing like the variety of categories of names one finds in English lodges. Some examples of the three categories just mentioned are given below; the names are in alphabetical order, the lodge number follows the name. The name is listed only once, but some names are used by more than one lodge, particularly the name of St John.

Saints

Name	*No.*	Name	*No.*	Name	*No.*
Adrian	185	Aethan's	1227	Andrew	25
Anthony	154	Ayle	95		
Baldred	313	Barchan	156	Barnabas	230
Bride	118	Bryde	579		
Christopher	1453	Clair	349	Clement	202
Colm	1022	Columba	729	Conal	1193
Congan	922	Conval	1359	Cuthbert	41
Cyre	121				

Name	No.	Name	No.	Name	No.
David	36	Devenic	1277	Donan	933
Drostane	789	Duthus	82		
Ebbe	70	Enoch	1282		
Fergus	466	Fillans	815	Fothad's	1059
George	190	Gilbert	790		
James	123	John	16	Johnstone	242
Kearan	1155	Kenneth	1441	Kentigern	429
Kessac	269	Kilda	881		
Laurence	136	Leonard	580	Lucia	1336
Luke	132				
Machar	54	Magdalene	100	Margaret	548
Mark's at Glasgow	102	Marnock	109	Martin	1217
Mary	31	Matthew	549	Maurs	1398
Medans	1335	Michael	38	Mirrins	129
Modan	985	Molios	774	Mungo	27
Munn	496				
Nathalan	259	Nicholas	93	Ninian	66
Olaf	1188				
Patrick	1309	Paul	204	Peter	120
Regulus	77	Ronan's	856		
Serf	327	Servanus	771	Skae	1252
Stephen	746				
Ternan	443	Thomas	40		
Vigean	101	Vincent	553		
Winnick	205				

Personalities

Name	No.	Name	No.
Robbie Burns	860	Sir George Cathcart	617
Earl Haig	1260	David Livingstone	1162
Harry Laver	1403	Macdonald of Sleat	1379
Sir Charles Napier	1064	Lord Newlands	1074
David Ogilvie	1371	Captain Spiers	791
Sir Walter Scott	859	Alan Wilson	851
Sir William Wallace	868		

Virtues

Name	No.	Name	No.
Benevolence	1411	Charity	783
Concord	1341	Good Will	961
Hope	1156	Harmony	1110
Hope and Sincerity	634	Peace and Harmony	834
Perseverance	1370	Temperance and Benevolence	1233
Unity	1109	Universal Brotherhood	1281
Universal Peace	1208		

The Lodge of Holyrood House (St Luke) No 44

Generally speaking lodges bearing a place-name met there at one time, but this does not apply in at least one case. According to Bro. R.S. Lindsay (*A History of the Mason Lodge of Holyrood House (St Luke's) No. 44*; pp. 58–9, T. and A. Constable Ltd at the University Press, Edinburgh, 1935)

> From the fact that the name of the Lodge is Holyroodhouse Lodge, it might be supposed that the title was adopted because the earliest meetings were held in the Palace of Holyroodhouse; but the supposition is unfortunately more flattering than the facts will allow.

In fact a masonic meeting was held at Holyroodhouse, but not under the auspices of Holyroodhouse Lodge. The occasion was on 24 June 1858; Bro. Lindsay gives the detail in the book just quoted.

> The foundation stone [of Freemasons' Hall, Edinburgh] was laid by the Grand Master, Lord Glenlyon, on 24th June, and it was estimated that special trains brought into Edinburgh that day some 4000–5000 brethren and their friends from the country. Grand Lodge was opened at noon in the Great Gallery of the Palace of Holyroodhouse before some 700 brethren in full regalia, . . .

During its history this lodge has been called 'Holyroodhouse' and 'St Luke'. It now carries both titles in one; 'The Lodge of Holyroodhouse, (St Luke)'.

Sashes and badges

Apart from the following item, the *Constitutions and Laws* of the Grand Lodge of Scotland make no specific mention of the name of a Daughter lodge. The extract is taken from the Third Schedule, which deals with regalia, and in this particular instance, sashes, which are a traditional part of Scottish masonic regalia, though they are not worn in all lodges.

> *Masters, Past Masters, Office-Brearers and Master Masons.* – If [sashes are] worn, of the colour adopted by the lodge . . . embroidered or otherwise distinctly marked thereon the name and number, or the badge. of the lodge . . .

Many lodges show masonic ranks on sashes worn by Officer-bearers, for example 'Lodge . . . No. . . . RWM.'

A daughter lodge may adopt a badge, but it must not use any insignia of the Grand Lodge; nor must it adopt a coat of arms which would bring it into conflict with the Lord Lyon's office; permission to used a badge is not required from Grand Lodge, nor does the badge have to be approved by the Grand Master

The colours adopted by a lodge

Lodges are generally identified by a number, a name, a badge and sometimes by a banner. In Scotland, however, a daughter lodge has yet another means of identification; it may adopt a colour to decorate in the approved manner, aprons and sashes.

The basic colour of the apron is white. The approved manner of decorating the apron is laid down in the *Constitutions and Laws*, In general terms the decoration, that is to say the colour adopted by the lodge, applies to the rosettes on the apron of the fellow-of-craft (as he is known in Scotland) and the master mason; to the levels of the aprons worn by masters and past masters. The master masons and past masters may also have a coloured edging to their aprons, but it must not exceed two inches in width.

Lodges in Scotland have always been allowed to choose their own basic colours and, despite the fact that Thistle-green is the colour used by the Grand Lodge and Provincial Grand Lodges and should not otherwise be used, it is in fact also worn by some daughter lodges.

The first mention of green as the Grand Lodge colour occurs on 15 October, 1736 in Regulation No. 7 of the Grand Lodge.

> That the first elected Grand Master and Grand Wardens shall each of them furnish a proper jewel for their respective offices, which are to belong to the said Lodge, and are to be delivered to their successors in office, and always to be worn at a green ribbon.

Bro. Draffen, in his book *Scottish Masonic Records* gives charts showing the colour adopted by lodges; extracts are shown below. It will be noted that many have changed the colour on more than one occasion.

Lodge No.	Colour adopted
Mother Kilwinning	Green, later changed to green and gold.
1[1]	Light blue later changed to light blue and silver.
2	Crimson, later changed to dark crimson.
5	Crimson, then white and pink; to crimson lake and later crimson lake and gold.

Lodge No.	Colour adopted
7	Crimson, then crimson and blue; to blue and then dark blue.
9	Dark blue, white edge; then green; later white and dark blue, then blue and finally green and gold.
11	Purple, then purple and gold.
14	Dark blue, then Navy apron and green sash.
15	Red with blue edge, then maroon and blue.
22	Scarlet and gold, then crimson and gold, finally cardinal red and gold.
37	Green, then emerald green.
39	Stewart tartan, then blue.
62	Dark blue with white edge; then blue and white, finally green and gold
67	Blue, then Forbes tartan.
83	Blue, then light blue and finally light blue and silver.
90	Sky blue, yellow edge, then sky blue.
93	Green, then green and gold, finally shamrock green.
105	Royal blue, gold edge; then blue and orange; blue and gold and finally dark blue.
195	Tartan, black and blue edge; then Caledonian tartan, then blue.
238	42nd tartan, later 42nd tartan and gold.
251	Sky blue, then green.

Banners

The heraldic description of the Grand Lodge banner is based on the former Coat of Arms:

Parted per pale Azure and Vert, in the dexter a saltire Argent, and in the sinister, on a chevron Or between three towers proper, a pair of compasses extended chevronwise Sable: Above the shield is placed a helmet befitting its degree with Mantling Vert doubled Or and on a Wreath of its Liveries is set for Crest a tower as in the Arms, and in an Escroil over the same this Motto In the Lord is All Our Trust.

A simple description of the shield would read: on the right-hand side (left-hand as one looks at it) a silver cross on a blue background; on the left-hand side (right-hand as one looks at it) on a golden inverted V between three towers a pair of compasses, extended, black.

The Lord Lyon has recently granted the addition of supporters to the shield: these take the form of two men dressed in period costume and wearing a master mason's apron, one of whom holds a square, the other a level; the men stand on a chequered cloth individually on both sides of the shield.

The jewel worn by the Grand Standard Bearers shows two banners in saltire, one of which bears the Arms of Grand Lodge, the other the figure of St Andrew, the patron saint of Scotland.

Supreme Grand Chapter of Royal Arch Freemasons of Scotland

Unlike England and Ireland the Supreme Grand Chapter of Royal Arch Freemasons of Scotland is a completely autonomous organization. It maintains a cordial relationship with the Grand Lodge of Scotland; it operates from a different building from that occupied by Grand Lodge; it has its own *Constitution and Laws*; comparable posts are not held by the same individual; each individual chapter has its own name and number and is not attached to a Craft lodge. Further it controls a number of other masonic degrees that are not controlled by either England or (with a couple of exceptions) Ireland in their respective jurisdictions.

Before being exalted, the candidate for Royal Arch masonry in Scotland must have taken the three Craft degrees and the Mark degree, which since 19 December 1860, may be worked in either a lodge or a chapter; he must also have taken the degree of Excellent Master (Passing the Veils); this is an integral part of the ceremony of exaltation.

There is no minimum eligibility period before joining the Royal Arch; this means that provided the candidate is properly qualified he can be raised one day and exalted the next. Another difference is that a companion may be elected to the Third Principal's chair without having been master of a Craft lodge.

A chapter may become dormant because it has failed to meet or to make the necessary returns to Supreme Grand Chapter for three years; or it may voluntarily return its charter to Supreme Grand Chapter. Subject to specific requirements a dormant chapter may apply to be reponed (or resuscitated); if this is approved, the chapter may be restored to its former place on the Roll of Supreme Grand Chapter, bearing the same precedency, number and name it had before it became dormant.

Numbers and precedence of chapters

The Supreme Grand Chapter of Royal Arch Freemasons of Scotland was Erected on 28 August 1817. Prior to that date there were chapters working in Scotland. Comp. G.S. Draffen, in his booklet *The Triple Tau* (Published with the authority of the Supreme Grand Royal Arch Chapter of Scotland; 1955) records:

At that date [28 August 1817] the various chapters in the country could be conveniently divided into five groups;

1) those chapters which held charters from the Supreme Grand and Royal Arch Chapter of England;
2) those chapters which for a long period of years had held no connection with Craft lodges;
3) those chapters which were at work under charters issued by the Royal Grand Conclave of Scotland;
4) those chapters which were at work under an Irish charter, and
5) those chapters which had very recently begun to confer the Royal Arch Degree without benefit of any charter or Time Immemorial tradition.

The new-founded body [the Supreme Grand Chapter] was made up almost entirely from classes 1) and 2).

Companion Draffen gives two appendices in his booklet; the first is headed 'List of Chapters Chartered in Scotland by The Supreme Grand and Royal Arch Chapter of England'; this shows nine chapters, one of which, Land of Cakes, is still at work, using the same name and appearing as number 15 on the Roll of the Grand Chapter of Scotland.

The other appendix is a consolidated list of all Scottish Royal Arch Chapters up to number 456. An interesting feature of this list is that there are six chapters which show two numbers. According to Companion Draffen, in 1895 a Grand Chapter known as the Early Grand Royal Arch Chapter was absorbed by the Supreme Grand Royal Arch Chapter of Scotland. Some of the chapters belonging to the Early Grand Chapter were dormant; three stated that they preferred to unite with other chapters. The remainder were allowed to add their old Early Grand numbers as appendices to their new numbers; for example.

No. 249 Moira Union, Kilmarnock,	E.G. 2
No. 250 Ayr, Ayr,	E.G. 3
No. 251 Loudon, Newmilns,	E.G. 6
No. 252 Stewarton, Stewarton,	E.G. 7
No. 253 Hurlford, Hurlford,	E.G. 17

Five of the dormant chapters were later reponed, but they were not allowed to keep their old Early Grand numbers.

The *History of The Edinburgh Royal Arch Chapter, No. 1* (William A. Davis FSAA; H. & J. Pilland & Wilson, Edinburgh, 1911) gives the story of how that Chapter became No. 1 on the Roll of Supreme Grand Chapter. The chapter was founded in January 1779 and was one of the chapters which brought the new Grand Chapter into being.

On 16 August 1818 a General Meeting was called:

for the purpose of submitting to their consideration the generous conduct of seven Royal Arch Chapters who had resigned in favour of them their rights to precedency on the Roll of Supreme Grand Chapter of Scotland, in consequence of the active part this Chapter has taken in the Establishment of that Sublime Body – a line of conduct evincing the most noble feelings for the welfare of the Order, their attachment to the Edinburgh Chapter, and their disinterestedness towards themselves. A distinguished honour has thus been conferred on the Edinburgh Chapter, which we dared not anticipate, and in a manner worthy of these Chapters who had so long acted in the pure principles of Royal Arch Masonry.

The seven chapters are noted below; the present number and date the chapter was chartered is also given.

Present No. 2	Stirling Rock Chapter	(Chartered 1743)
Present No. 3	Enoch Chapter Montrose	(Chartered 1765)
Present No. 4	Operative Chapter Banf	(Chartered 1766)
Present No. 5	Linlithgow Chapter	(Chartered 1768)
Present No. 6	Union Chapter Dundee	(Chartered 1773)
Present No. 7	Noah Chapter Brechin	(Chartered 1774)
Present No. 8	Haran Chapter Lawrence Kirk	(Chartered 1774)

Every chapter must have a charter showing the date it was granted; this date governs the precedency of the chapter. It must also bear a number and name. With regard to the latter, the *Laws and Constitutions* state that the name of a proposed new chapter 'shall not be that of any living person'.

Names of chapters

Generally speaking the names adopted by most chapters are names of places; there is not the same variety of categories adopted by lodges and chapters in England, although there are a few saints, virtues, biblical names and names of personalities. Some examples of these are given below. As in the case of the lodges, the names are given in alphabetical order and the number of the chapter follows the name, which is given only once, although some names are used by more than one chapter.

Saints

Name	*No.*	Name	*No.*	Name	*No.*	Name	*No.*	Name	*No.*
Andrew	110	Anthony	149						
Baldred	283	Barnabas	348	Blane	163	Brandane	498	Bryde	390
Clement	221	Columba	481	Congan	473				
David	164								
George	385	Giles	432						
James	495	Johnstoun	134						
Kiaran	158								
Laurence	328								
Machar	37	Machute	471	Martin	565	Mary	370		
Michael	31	Modan's	719						
Nicholas	155	Ninian	382						
Olaf	878								
Peter	30								
Ringan	300	Rollox	144						
Ternan	521	Thomas	168	Islay	320				
Vincent	457								

Virtues

Name	*No.*	Name	*No.*	Name	*No.*
Amity	133	Bon Accord	193	Charity	760
Concord	153	Faith and Charity	72	Friendship	160
		Harmony	220		
Honor, Concord and Fidelity	305			Morality	700
Peace and Harmony	173	Peace Universal	192	Perseverance	71
Progress	516	Sincerity	779	Temperance	219
Unity	353				

Biblical Names

Name	*No.*	Name	*No.*	Name	*No.*	Name	*No.*	Name	*No.*
Elijah	12	Enoch	3	Noah	7	Josiah	10	Solomon	38

Personalities

NAME	*No.*	NAME	*No.*	NAME	*No.*
PRESIDENT BRAND	241	ROBERT BRUCE	243	ROBERT BURNS	143
ALBERT JOSEPHSON	586	DAVID LIVINGSTONE	576	JOSEPH LUKINS	653
SIR CHARLES NAPIER	433	BARON OF RENFREW	114	SIR WALTER SCOTT	579
ADMIRAL VERNON	380	ALAN WILSON	566		

Appendix A

List of lodges mentioned in earliest Grand Lodge minute dated 25 November, 1723

The Goose and Grid Iron in S[t] Pauls Church Yard.
The Queens head in Knaves Acre.
The Queen's head Turnstile Holborn.
The Cheshire Cheese in Arundell Street.
The Horne Tavern at Westminster.
Kings head in Ivy Lane.
The Griffin in Newgate Street.
The Three Cranes in the Poultry.
The Three Compasses in Silver Street.
The ffountaine Tavern in the Strand.
The Rose and Crown in King Street Westm[r],
The Greyhound in ffleet Street.
The Crown Tavern at Cripplegate.
The Rummers at Charing Cross.
The Half Moon in the Strand.
The Coffee house at S[t] Johns Gate Clerken Well.
The Castle Tavern in Drury Lane.
The Duke of Bedfordshead in Southton Street Covent Garden.
The Castle Tavern S[t] Giles's.
The Cardigan head at Charing Cross.
The Swan Tavern ffish Street Hill.
The Bullhead in Southwark.
The Anchor in Dutchy Lane.
The Baptist head Chancery Lane.
The Sunn in Clare Markett.
The Half moon Cheapside.
The Crown behind the Roy[ll] Exchange.
The Swan at Ludgate Street.
The Prince of Denmarkshead in Cavendish Street.
Bens Coffee house in New Bond Street.
The Ship in Bartholomew Lane.
The Kings Arms in St. Pauls Churchyard.
The Queens Head in Great Queen Street.
The Crown at St. Johns Wapping.
The George at Charing Cross.
The Ship behind the Royall Exchange.
The Dolphin in Tower Street.
The Duke of Chandois's Arms at Edgworth.
The Crown at Acton.
The Busiebody at Charing Cross.

Dicks Coffeehouse near the New Church in the Strand.
The Ship without Temple Barr.
The Naggshead in Princes Street.
The Ship off ffish Street Hill.
The Bell Tavern Westminster.
The Crown and Anchor near St Clements Church.
The Blew Boar in ffleet Street.
The Old Devill at Temple Barr.
Toms Coffeehouse Clare Street near Clare Markett.
The Red Lyon in Tottenham Court Road.
The Blew Posts in Holborne.
The Red Lyon in Richmond in Surry.

Appendix B

Revised Engraved List of Lodges, 1729

A list of Regular Lodges *according to their* Seniority & Constitution.

The list shows the name by which the lodge was known; this is followed by the current number and name of the lodge or the date of its erasure.

The Goose and Gridiron;	No. 2 Lodge of Antiquity.
Rose and Rummer, Holbourn;	Crossed out in 1736
Horn, Westminster;	No. 4 Royal Somerset House and Inverness
King's Head in Ivy Lane;	No. 6 Lodge of Friendship
Three Cranes in the Poultry;	Erased 25 March 1745
Tom's Coffee House, Clare Street;	No. 8 British Lodge
The Crown behind the Royal Exchange;	No. 10 Westminster and Keystone
Duke of Chandois Arms, Edgworth;	Erased April, 1744
One Tun in Noble Street;	No. 16 Royal Alpha
The Lion, Brewer Street;	No. 14 Tuscan Lodge
Queen's Head, Knaves Acre;	No. 12 Lodge of Fortitude and Old Cumberland
Three Tuns, Swithin's Alley;	No. 18 Old Dundee Lodge
The Anchor, Dutchy Lane;	No. 20 Royal Kent Lodge of Antiquity
Queen's Head, Great Queen Street;	Erased March, 1830
Bull's Head, Southwark;	Erased 24 April, 1776
Red Lion, Tottenham Court Road;	Erased November, 1745
Buffalo and Garter, Bloomsbury;	Erased November, 1745
Paul's Head, Ludgate Street;	Erased March, 1745
Green Dragon, Snow Hill;	No. 21 Lodge of Emulation
The Dolphin, Tower Street;	Erased March, 1745
Nag's Head, Drury Lane;	Erased April, 1782
Ship, Fish Street Hill;	Lapsed in 1803
Half Moon, Cheapside;	No. 23 Globe Lodge
Bedford's Head, Covent Garden;	Erased April, 1775
Mitre, Greenwich;	Erased February, 1800
King's Arms, Strand;	Erased November, 1745
Crown and Sceptres, St Martin's Lane;	Erased March 1745
Queen's Head, Bath;	Erased in 1736
Nag's Head, Bristol;	Erased in 1736
Maid's Head, Norwich;	Erased February, 1809
Swan, Chichester;	Erased in 1769
Pied Bull, Chester;	Erased in 1755
Castle and Falcon, Chester;	Erased in 1739
Nag's Head, Carmarthen;	Erased 1754
East India Arms, Gosport;	Erased in 1838
Angel, Congleton, Cheshire;	Erased November, 1754
Cross Keys, Henrietta Street;	Erased April, 1746
Swan, Tottenham High Cross;	No. 26 Castle Lodge of Harmony
Swan and Rummer, Finch Lane;	Erased 1838

Rummer, Paternoster Row;	Erased March, 1830
King's Arms, Westminster;	Erased 1737
King Henry VIII's Head, Seven Dials;	Erased June, 1742
Rose at Marylebone;	No. 28 Old King's Arms
Swan, Grafton Street, Soho;	Erased April, 1744
Magpie, without Bishopsgate;	Erased 1737
Mount's Coffee House;	Erased December, 1748
Three Crowns, Stoke Newington;	Erased April, 1743
King's Head, Salford;	Erased November, 1754
Castle & Leg, Holborn;	No. 29 St. Alban's Lodge
French Arms, Madrid;	Erased 1768
Green Lettice, Holborn;	Lapsed 1729
Wool Pack, Warwick;	Erased November, 1754
Bishopsgate Coffee House;	Surrended warrant November, 1743
Rose and Crown, Greek Street;	Erased November, 1745.

Appendix C

A List of Lodges Illustrating Anomalies in Precedence

A list of forty-four lodges bearing a number higher than No. 3 (constituted 1754) and therefore with a lower precedence, but all of which were constituted before No. 3.

No.	*Constituted.*	*No.*	*Constituted*
4	T.I.	5	1730
6	1721	8	1722
10	1722	12	T.I.
14	1722	16	1722
18	1723	20	1723
21	1723	23	1723
26	1725	28	1725
29	1728	33	1730
37	1732	39	1732
41	1733	42	1733
43	1733	45	1733
46	1735	48	1735
51	1735	52	1736
55	1736	56	1736
58	1737	59	1739
60	1738	61	1738
64	1739	66	1739
67	1740	69	1742
71	1747	75	1751
77	1751	78	1752
82	1753	83	1753
85	1753	86	1753

Appendix D

Numbers (1863 enumeration) allocated to lodges (up to current number 100).

Abbreviations: Const. = Constituted, TI = Time Immemorial, PGL = Premier Grand Lodge, GLA = Grand Lodge of the Antients, UGL = United Grand Lodge of England.

Date	*Present*		*PGL number*							*GLA*	*UGL numbers*	
Const.	*number*	*Current name*	*1729*	*1740*	*1755*	*1770*	*1780*	*1781*	*1792*	*number*	*1814*	*1832*
1735		The Grand Stewards'	117	115	70	60	47	47				
(In 1792 this Lodge was placed, without a number, at the top of the list where it remains to this day.)												
1756	1	Grand Master's								1	1	1
T.I.	2	Lodge of Antiquity	1	1	1	1	1	1	1		2	2
1754	3	Lodge of Fidelity								2	3	3
T.I.	4	Royal Somerset House & Inverness	3	2	2	2	2	2	2		4	4
1756		St George's								3	5	5
1730		Corner Stone	63	56	34	31	28	28	26		40	37
	5	St Georges & Corner Stone (following amalgamation of above two lodges in 1843)										5
1721	6	Lodge of Friendship	4	4	3	3	3	3	3		6	6
1751	7	Royal York Lodge of Perseverance								4	7	7
1722	8	British	6	5	4	4	4	4	4		8	8
1762	9	Albion								5	9	9
1722	10	Westminster and Keystone	7	6	5	5	5	5	5		10	10
1754	11	Enoch								6	11	11
T.I.	12	Lodge of Fortitude & Old Cumberland	11	10	6	6	6	6	6		12	12
1761	13	Union Waterloo								7	13	13
1722	14	Tuscan	10	9	7	7	7	7	7		14	14
1752	15	Kent								8	15	15
1722	16	Royal Alpha	9	8	8	8	8	8	8		16	16
1923	18	Old Dundee	12	11	9	9	9	9	9		18	18
1769	19	Royal Athelstan								10	19	19
1723	20	Royal Kent Lodge of Antiquity	13	12	10	10	10	10	10		20	20
1723	21	Lodge of Emulation	19	18	13	13	12	12	12		22	21
1757	22	Neptune								13	23	22
1723	23	Globe	23	22	16	16	15	15	14		25	23
1766	24	Newcastle-upon-Tyne								15	26	24
1810	25	Robert Burns								16	27	25
1725	26	Castle Lodge of Harmony	38	34	22	21	19	19	18		29	27
1811	27	Egyptian								21	33	29

APPENDIX D

Date Const.	*Present number*	*Current name*	*PGL number 1729*	*1740*	*1755*	*1770*	*1780*	*1781*	*1792*	*GLA number*	*UGL numbers 1814*	*1832*
1725	28	Old King's Arms	43	38	25	24	22	22	21		34	30
1728	29	St Alban's	49	43	26	25	23	23	22		35	32
1753	30	United Mariners								23	36	33
1776	31	United Industrious								24	34	31
1755	32	St George's Lodge of Harmony								25	38	35
1730	33	Britannic	75	62	37	33	29	29	27		42	38
1754	34	Mount Moriah								31	47	40
1761	35	Medina	(See note below)		57	39	33	33	31		48	41

Lodge claims to be original No. 111, constituted 17 February 1733 (London) it became No. 57 in the 1755 enumeration. According to Lane's *Masonic Records 1717–1894* it lapsed about 1761 and a new lodge (later named Medina) was constituted that year; it seems to have acquired the warrant of No. 111, now No. 57 (Cowes, Isle of Wight). A Warrant of Confirmation was issued on 24 April 1824 and their Centenary Warrant is dated 1 October, 1862.

Date Const.	*Present number*	*Current name*	*PGL number 1729*	*1740*	*1755*	*1770*	*1780*	*1781*	*1792*	*GLA number*	*UGL numbers 1814*	*1832*
1808	36	Glamorgan								33	50	43
1732	37	Anchor and Hope	105	93	55	46	36	36	33		51	44
1812	38	Lodge of Union								35	52	45
1732	39	St John the Baptist*	97	86	239	48	38	38	35		53	46

*This lodge was erased in 1754; resorted in 1759 as No. 239 and reinstated to old position in 1770.

Date Const.	*Present number*	*Current name*	*PGL number 1729*	*1740*	*1755*	*1770*	*1780*	*1781*	*1792*	*GLA number*	*UGL numbers 1814*	*1832*
1813	40	Derwent								36	54	47
1733	41	Royal Cumberland	113	101	59	49	39	39	36		55	48
1733	42	Lodge of Relief	118	103	61	51	40	40	37		57	50
1733	43	St Paul's	125	109	64	53	41	41	38		58	51
1803	44	Lodge of Friendship								39	59	52
1733	45	Strong Man	110	98	68	57	44	44	41		61	53
1735	46	Old Union	130	114	69	59	46	46	43		62	54
1763	47	Newstead								44	63	55
1735	48	Lodge of Industry	132	117	72	61	48	48	44		64	56
1810	49	Gihon								46	65	57
1803	50	Knights of Malta								47	66	58
1735	51	Angel	141	126	76	64	51	51	47		67	59
1736	52	Union	146	131	80	66	52	52	48		68	60
1812	53	Royal Sussex								49	69	61
1813	54	Lodge of Hope								50	70	62
1736	55	Constitutional	150	135	84	70	54	54	50		71	63
1736	56	Howard Lodge of Brotherly Love	151	136	85	71	55	55	51		72	64
1775	57	Humber								53	73	65
1737	58	Lodge of Felicity	162	147	90	74	58	58	54		75	66
1739	59	Royal Naval	179	166	100	77	61	61	57		79	70
1738	60	Lodge of Peace and Harmony	172	158	96	80	64	64	60		82	72
1738	61	Probity	176	162	97	81	65	65	61		84	73
1811	62	Social								62	85	75
1757	63	St Mary's								63	86	76
1739	64	Lodge of Fortitude		165	99	83	67	67	63		87	77
1810	65	Lodge of Prosperity								68	91	78
1739	66	Grenadiers	189	178	110	89	73	73	68		92	79
1740	67	Lodge Star in the East		185	117	93	77	77	70		93	80
1807	68	Royal Clarence								72	95	81
1742	69	Lodge of Unity		190	122	96	79	79	72		96	82
1759	70	St John's								74	98	83
1747	71	Lodge of Unity		198	132	103	83	83	76		99	84
1810	72	Royal Jubilee								77	100	85
1760	73	Mount Lebanon								81	104	87
1811	74	Athol								83	105	88

Date Const.	*Present number*	*Current name*	*PGL number 1729*	*1740*	*1755*	*1770*	*1780*	*1781*	*1792*	*GLA number*	*UGL numbers 1814*	*1832*
1751	75	Lodge of Love and Honour		209	146	116	94	95	87		110	89
1761	76	Lodge of Economy								88	111	90
1751	77	Lodge of Freedom		211	148	118	96	97	89		113	91
1752	78	Imperial George		219	154	122	99	100	92		115	92
1813	79	Pythagorean								93	116	93
1805	80	St John's								94	118	95
1812	81	Doric								96	120	96
1753	82	Foundation		226	162	127	104	105	96		121	97
1753	83	United Lodge of Prudence		227	163	128	105	106	97		122	98
1806	84	Doyle's Lodge of Friendship								98	123	99
1753	85	Faithful		232	169	134	108	109	99		124	100
1754	86	Lodge of Loyalty		235	172	136	110	111	101		126	101
1810	87	Vitruvian								104	128	103
1754	88	Scientific			182	143	115	116	106		131	105
1754	89	Lodge of Unanimity		256	194	154	122	123	111		136	106
1763	90	St John's								113	138	107
1755	91	Lodge of Regularity		259	198	162	129	130	117		142	108
1755	92	Moira		263	200	164	130	131	118		143	109
1755	93	Social		206	168	134	135	120			145	110
1755	94	Phoenix		207	169	135	136	121			146	111
1802	95	Eastern Star								128	151	112
1756	96	Burlington		217	176	142	143	128			152	113
1757	97	Palatine		218	177	143	144	129			153	114
1805	98	St Martin's								130	154	115
1757	99	Shakespear		221	179	145	146	131			156	116
1757	100	Lodge of Friendship		223	182	147	148	133			159	117

Appendix E

Examples of Chapters constituted before 1813 and still extant

(* denotes chapter chartered by the Grand and Royal Arch Chapter of Jerusalem)

Note: Chapters numbered 43, 253 and 283 show a constitution date after 1813; this is because the continuity of the Grand and Royal Arch Chapter has still to be confirmed; the date shown is the date the chapter attached to the lodge. The list shows firstly the present number, name and constitution date of the chapter then the present name and constitution date of the lodge.

* 2 Chapter of St James; 1788	–	Lodge of Antiquity; T.I.
3 Chapter of Fidelity; 1786	–	Lodge of Fidelity; 1754
5 St George's Chapter; 1785	–	St George's and Corner Stone Lodge; 1730
7 Royal York Chapter of Perseverance; 1801	–	Royal York Lodge of Perseverance 1751
* 8 British Chapter; 1812	–	British Lodge; 1722
* 12 United Chapter of Prudence; 1808	–	Lodge of Fortitude and Old Cumberland; T.I.
13 Union Waterloo Chapter; 1788	–	Union Waterloo Lodge; 1761
19 Mount Sinai Chapter; 1811	–	Royal Athelstan Lodge; 1769
* 21 Cyrus Chapter; 1811	–	Lodge of Emulation; 1723
22 Mount Sion Chapter; 1809	–	Neptune Lodge; 1757
32 Jerusalem Chapter; 1792	–	St George's Lodge of Harmony; 1755
37 Concord Chapter; 1786	–	Anchor and Hope Lodge; 1732
40 Chapter of Emulation; 1813	–	Derwent Lodge; 1813
* 41 Royal Cumberland Chapter; 1782	–	Royal Cumberland Lodge; 1733
* 42 Chapter of Unanimity; 1769	–	Lodge of Relief; 1733
* 43 Chapter of Fortitude; 1821	–	St Paul's Lodge; 1733
* 51 Patriotic Chapter; 1807	–	Angel Lodge; 1735
* 52 Royal George Chapter; 1788	–	Union Lodge; 1736
57 Humber Chapter; 1811	–	Humber Lodge; 1775
* 60 Chapter of Hope; 1786 (Previously Chapter of St George No. 140)	–	Lodge of Peace and Harmony; 1738
* 61 Chapter of Sincerity; 1790	–	Lodge of Probity; 1738
68 Royal Clarence Chapter; 1790	–	Royal Clarence Lodge; 1807
70 St John's Chapter; 1795	–	St John's Lodge; 1759
* 75 Volubian Chapter; 1810	–	Lodge of Love and Honour; 1751
76 Chapter of Economy; 1803	–	Lodge of Economy; 1761
77 Hermes Chapter; 1798	–	Lodge of Freedom; 1751
* 92 Moira Chapter; 1813	–	Moira Lodge; 1755
* 97 Chapter of Strict Benevolence; 1797	–	Palatine Lodge; 1757
*111 Chapter of Vigilance; 1788	–	Restoration Lodge; 1761
*116 Cana Chapter; 1769	–	Royal Lancashire Lodge; 1760
*120 Palladian Chapter; 1791	–	Palladian Lodge; 1762
*124 Chapter of Concord; 1787	–	Marquis of Granby Lodge; 1763
*126 Chapter of the Nativity; 1769	–	Lodge of Silent Temple; 1762
128 Prince Edwin's Chapter; 1806	–	Prince Edwin's Lodge; 1803
130 Royal Gloucester Chapter; 1783	–	Royal Gloucester Lodge; 1772
*137 Chapter of Amity; 1780	–	Lodge of Amity; 1765

*139 Chapter of Paradise; 1798	–	Britannia Lodge; 1761
143 Mount Moriah Chapter; 1783	–	Middlesex Lodge; 1775
*150 School of Plato Chapter; 1811	–	Lodge of Perfect Unanimity; 1786
151 Albany Chapter; 1808	–	Albany Lodge; 1801
*170 All Souls Chapter; 1807	–	All Souls Lodge 1767
177 Domatic Chapter; 1793	–	Domatic Lodge; 1786
*187 Chapter of Charity; 1769	–	Royal Sussex Lodge of Hospitality; 1769
189 Chapter of Sincerity; 1789	–	Lodge of Sincerity; 1769
*202 Chapter of Friendship; 1788	–	Lodge of Friendship; 1771
204 Caledonian Chapter; 1797	–	Caledonian Lodge; 1802
213 Chapter of Perseverance; 1796	–	Lodge of Perseverance; 1795
221 St John's Chapter; 1800	–	St John's Lodge; 1797
223 Chapter of Concord; 1800	–	Lodge of Charity; 1797
225 St Luke's Chapter; 1804	–	St Luke's Lodge; 1785
*237 Virtue and Hope Chapter; 1812	–	Indefatigable Lodge; 1777
242 Magdalen Chapter; 1803	–	St George's Lodge; 1780
*250 Minerva Chapter; 1783	–	Minerva Lodge; 1783
*251 Chapter of Loyalty and Virtue; 1811	–	Loyal Lodge; 1783
*253 Chapter of Justice; 1822	–	Tyrian Lodge; 1785
*255 Chapter of Iris; 1807	–	Lodge of Harmony; 1785
*257 Chapter of Friendship; 1769	–	Phoenix Lodge; 1786
*265 Chapter of Judea; 1791	–	Royal Yorkshire Lodge; 1788
*275 Chapter of Perseverance; 1792	–	Lodge of Harmony; 1789
*279 Chapter of Fortitude; 1796	–	St John's Lodge; 1790
*283 Wisdom Chapter; 1820	–	Lodge of Amity; 1791
*287 Chapter of Stone of Friendship Ezel; 1793	–	Lodge of Unanimity; 1792
*289 Chapter of Fidelity; 1793	–	Lodge of Fidelity; 1792
*290 Chapter of Prosperity; 1795	–	Huddersfield Lodge; 1793
*294 Constitutional Chapter; 1794	–	Constitutional Lodge; 1793
295 Chapter of Love and Friendship; 1797	–	Combermere Lodge of Union; 1793
*298 Chapter of Unity; 1807	–	Lodge of Harmony; 1793
300 Chapter of Perseverance; 1807	–	Lodge of Minerva; 1793
*302 Chapter of Charity; 1798	–	Lodge of Hope; 1794
*307 Chapter of Good Intent; 1811	–	Lodge of Prince Frederick; 1809
*308 Chapter of Affability; 1807	–	Lodge of Prince George; 1796
*312 Britannia Chapter; 1783	–	Lion Lodge; 1797
*314 Holy Royal Architect Chapter; 1803	–	Lodge of Peace and Unity; 1797
*320 Chapter of Integrity; 1807	–	Lodge of Loyalty; 1798
*322 Hope Chapter; 1807	–	Lodge of Peace; 1806
*323 Chapter of Charity; 1807	–	Lodge of Concord; 1806
*327 Chapter of St John; 1809	–	Wigton St John's Lodge; 1809

Appendix F

Examples of chapters constituted after 1813 having a name different from that of the lodge

Examples of chapters constituted after 1813 which, from the date of constitution, have borne a name different to that of the lodge to which they are attached; the names and constitution dates of both lodge and chapter are shown.

1477 Mold Chapter; 1927	–	Sir Watkin Lodge; 1873
1478 Thynne Chapter; 1921	–	Longleat Lodge; 1874
1490 Prudence Chapter; 1899	–	Lodge Pioneer; 1874
1536 Cornwallis Chapter; 1916	–	United Military Lodge; 1875
1549 Stanmore Chapter; 1880	–	Abercorn Lodge; 1875
1555 Victoria Jubilee Chapter; 1887	–	Royal Prince of Wales Lodge; 1875
1593 Trafalgar Chapter; 1879	–	Royal Naval College and United Service Lodge; 1875
1661 Alexander Chapter; 1881	–	Newton Lodge; 1876
1674 Clwyd Chapter; 1921	–	Caradoc Lodge; 1877
1697 Fraternity Chapter; 1932	–	Lodge of Hospitality; 1877
1739 St Alkmund's Chapter; 1913	–	Carnarvon Lodge; 1878
1750 Adair Chapter; 1887	–	Coleridge Lodge; 1878
1752 Atholl Chapter; 1921	–	Ogmore Lodge; 1878
1967 Macartney Chapter; 1912	–	Beacon Court Lodge; 1882
(Macartney was the name of the first MEZ of the chapter)		
1983 St Edmund's Chapter; 1899	–	Martyn Lodge; 1882
2170 Hercules Chapter; 1895	–	St George Lodge; 1886
2233 Public Schools Chapter; 1909	–	Old Westminsters' Lodge; 1887
2475 Beach Chapter; 1899	–	Border Lodge; 1893
2533 Gildenburg Chapter; 1921	–	Fitzwilliam Lodge; 1894
2536 London Stone Chapter; 1901	–	Staines Lodge; 1894
2571 Addison Potter Chapter; 1898	–	Holmes Lodge; 1895
2656 Campbell Chapter; 1898	–	Adam's Peak Lodge; 1897
2682 William Harvey Chapter; 1903	–	Sancta Maria Lodge; 1897
2795 Corona Chapter; 1911*	–	Commercial Travellers Lodge; 1899
2862 Ruhuna Chapter; 1946	–	Grant Lodge; 1901
2885 Carthusian Chapter; 1905	–	Charterhouse Deo Dante Dedi Lodge; 1901
Name of lodge when constituted was Deo Dante Dedi; Charterhouse added in 1907.		
3221 Wessex Chapter; 1922	–	London Dorset Lodge; 1907
3261 Broadsmith Chapter; 1908	–	Randle Holme Lodge; 1907
4935 Wigornia Chapter; 1958	–	Lodge of Bon Accord; 1927
5560 Silver Jubilee Chapter; 1935	–	Lodge of Unity; 1902
5840 Caesaria Chapter; 1943	–	Sarnia-Ruduna Lodge; 1941
6648 Essex Schools Chapter; 1966	–	Old Chigwellian Lodge; 1948
6755 Highstone Chapter; 1946	–	Border Stone Lodge; 1948

* *(No longer working)*

Bibliography

It is not considered necessary to include a bibliography in a book such as this. Much of the information has come from lodge and chapter histories that can be found in the Library at Freemasons' Hall, Great Queen Street, London, WC2B 5AZ, some of which have been kindly given to me by the secretary of the lodge or scribe E of the chapter.

In the main, details of any special books quoted have been given in the text; by and large, however, the books consulted by me are easily available and may be found on the shelves of any public library.

INDEX

Current lodges and chapters mentioned (in numerical order)

# indicates lodge recently removed from list. Italics = chapters. Illustrations in italics and underlined.

INDEX

INDEX

INDEX

INDEX

SERENDIPITY

INDEX

INDEX

Scotland (Lodges)

INDEX

Current lodges and chapters mentioned (in alphabetical order)

# indicates lodge recently removed from list. Italics = chapters. Illustrations in italics and underlined.

INDEX

INDEX

INDEX

Ireland

INDEX